Y0-EHC-777

VOLUME 499   SEPTEMBER 1988

THE ANNALS

of The American Academy *of* Political
and Social Science

RICHARD D. LAMBERT, *Editor*
ALAN W. HESTON, *Associate Editor*

CONGRESS AND THE PRESIDENCY: INVITATION TO STRUGGLE

Special Editor of this Volume

ROGER H. DAVIDSON

University of Maryland
College Park

Ⓢ SAGE PUBLICATIONS *NEWBURY PARK BEVERLY HILLS LONDON NEW DELHI*

THE ANNALS

© 1988 *by* The American Academy *of* Political *and* Social Science

ERICA GINSBURG, *Assistant Editor*

Editorial Office: 3937 Chestnut Street, Philadelphia, Pennsylvania 19104.

For information about membership* (individuals only) and subscriptions (institutions), address:

SAGE PUBLICATIONS, INC.

2111 West Hillcrest Drive   275 South Beverly Drive
Newbury Park, CA 91320   Beverly Hills, CA 90212

From India and South Asia,
write to:

SAGE PUBLICATIONS INDIA Pvt. Ltd.
P.O. Box 4215
New Delhi 110 048
INDIA

From the UK, Europe, the Middle
East and Africa, write to:

SAGE PUBLICATIONS LTD
28 Banner Street
London EC1Y 8QE
ENGLAND

SAGE Production Editors: JANET BROWN and ASTRID VIRDING
*Please note that members of The Academy receive THE ANNALS with their membership.

Library of Congress Catalog Card Number 87-063006
International Standard Serial Number ISSN 0002-7162
International Standard Book Number ISBN 0-8039-3106-9 (Vol. 499, 1988 paper)
International Standard Book Number ISBN 0-8039-3105-0 (Vol. 499, 1988 cloth)
Manufactured in the United States of America. First printing, September 1988.

The articles appearing in THE ANNALS are indexed in *Book Review Index; Public Affairs Information Service Bulletin; Social Sciences Index; Monthly Periodical Index; Current Contents; Behavioral, Social, Management Sciences;* and *Combined Retrospective Index Sets.* They are also abstracted and indexed in *ABC Pol Sci, Historical Abstracts, Human Resources Abstracts, Social Sciences Citation Index, United States Political Science Documents, Social Work Research & Abstracts, Peace Research Reviews, Sage Urban Studies Abstracts, International Political Science Abstracts, America: History and Life,* and/or *Family Resources Database.*

Information about membership rates, institutional subscriptions, and back issue prices may be found on the facing page.

Advertising. Current rates and specifications may be obtained by writing to THE ANNALS Advertising and Promotion Manager at the Newbury Park office (address above).

Claims. Claims for undelivered copies must be made no later than three months following month of publication. The publisher will supply missing copies when losses have been sustained in transit and when the reserve stock will permit.

Change of Address. Six weeks' advance notice must be given when notifying of change of address to insure proper identification. Please specify name of journal. Send change of address to: THE ANNALS, c/o Sage Publications, Inc., 2111 West Hillcrest Drive, Newbury Park, CA 91320.

Origin and Purpose. The Academy was organized December 14, 1889, to promote the progress of political and social science, especially through publications and meetings. The Academy does not take sides in controverted questions, but seeks to gather and present reliable information to assist the public in forming an intelligent and accurate judgment.

Meetings. The Academy holds an annual meeting in the spring extending over two days.

Publications. THE ANNALS is the bimonthly publication of The Academy. Each issue contains articles on some prominent social or political problem, written at the invitation of the editors. Also, monographs are published from time to time, numbers of which are distributed to pertinent professional organizations. These volumes constitute important reference works on the topics with which they deal, and they are extensively cited by authorities throughout the United States and abroad. The papers presented at the meetings of The Academy are included in THE ANNALS.

Membership. Each member of The Academy receives THE ANNALS and may attend the meetings of The Academy. Membership is open only to individuals. Annual dues: $30.00 for the regular paperbound edition (clothbound, $45.00). Add $9.00 per year for membership outside the U.S.A. Members may also purchase single issues of THE ANNALS for $7.95 each (clothbound, $12.00).

Subscriptions. THE ANNALS (ISSN 0002-7162) is published six times annually—in January, March, May, July, September, and November. Institutions may subscribe to THE ANNALS at the annual rate: $66.00 (clothbound, $84.00). Add $9.00 per year for subscriptions outside the U.S.A. Institutional rates for single issues: $12.00 each (clothbound, $17.00).

Second class postage paid at Philadelphia, Pennsylvania, and at additional mailing offices.

Single issues of THE ANNALS may be obtained by individuals who are not members of The Academy for $8.95 each (clothbound, $17.00). Single issues of THE ANNALS have proven to be excellent supplementary texts for classroom use. Direct inquiries regarding adoptions to THE ANNALS c/o Sage Publications (address below).

All correspondence concerning membership in The Academy, dues renewals, inquiries about membership status, and/or purchase of single issues of THE ANNALS should be sent to THE ANNALS c/o Sage Publications, Inc., 2111 West Hillcrest Drive, Newbury Park, CA 91320. *Please note that orders under $25 must be prepaid.* Sage affiliates in London and India will assist institutional subscribers abroad with regard to orders, claims, and inquiries for both subscriptions and single issues.

THE ANNALS

of The American Academy *of* Political *and* Social Science

RICHARD D. LAMBERT, *Editor*
ALAN W. HESTON, *Associate Editor*

——————————— FORTHCOMING ———————————

WHITHER THE AMERICAN EMPIRE:
EXPANSION OR CONTRACTION?
Special Editor: Marvin E. Wolfgang
Volume 500   November 1988

THE GHETTO UNDERCLASS:
SOCIAL SCIENCE PERSPECTIVES
Special Editor: William Julius Wilson
Volume 501   January 1989

UNIVERSITIES AND THE MILITARY
Special Editor: David A. Wilson
Volume 502   March 1989

See page 3 for information on Academy membership and
purchase of single volumes of **The Annals.**

CONTENTS

BOOK DEPARTMENT CONTENTS

SOCIOLOGY

ECONOMICS

ANNALS, *AAPSS*, **499**, September 1988

"Invitation to Struggle":
An Overview of
Legislative-Executive Relations

By ROGER H. DAVIDSON

ABSTRACT: The U.S. Constitution's central structural dilemma is the relationship between Congress and the president. The document itself provides little guidance for the day-to-day conduct of these relations. Although we commonly call the system "separation of powers," it is really an arrangement of separate institutions sharing functions. A basic spirit of accommodation no doubt smooths policymaking, but the system's built-in counterweights are useful in encouraging this accommodation and forcing all the players to seek consensus. Divided government, in which the White House and one or both houses of Congress are controlled by opposing parties, has become more common in recent years. Although demanding skilled leadership in both branches, this situation need not preclude decisive and coherent policymaking. The most serious imbalance, not fully anticipated by the Founders, consists of the so-called war powers: a huge military establishment, unknown prior to World War II, gives the president a sizable advantage in making decisions about taking the nation to war. In such circumstances, how can we preserve the Founders' premise that such decisions are best left in the hands of representative assemblies?

Roger H. Davidson is professor of government and politics at the University of Maryland, College Park. He has served as professional staff member in Congress and as senior specialist in American government and public administration at the Congressional Research Service. He has been consultant to the White House and several national study commissions and was elected to the National Academy of Public Administration. Dr. Davidson is author or coauthor of more than 100 articles or books on Congress and national policymaking.

THE architect of the capital city, Major Pierre L'Enfant, followed political theory and practical advice when he placed the president and Congress on opposite sides of the new city of Washington. The Congress would occupy a single large building on the top of Jenkins' Hill, the highest promontory. On a plain a mile or so away would be the executive mansion, surrounded by executive branch agencies. A broad avenue would serve for ceremonial exchanges of communications between the two, but a bridge linking them was not built until the third decade of the nineteenth century. Symbolically, the Capitol faced eastward and the executive mansion northward, their backs turned on each other.[1]

The relationship of executive and legislative branches lies at the heart of the successes—and failures—of the U.S. government. When delegates gathered in Philadelphia in the summer of 1787 to draft the Constitution, this problem was very much on their minds and pervaded much of their deliberation.

HISTORICAL LEGISLATIVE-EXECUTIVE STRUGGLES

On the other side of the Atlantic, after all, the leading problem of political theory and practice had for some eight centuries been the relationship between the Crown and Parliament. Out of prolonged struggles, some of them bloody, a strong and independent Parliament emerged that rivaled and eventually eclipsed the power of the Crown. By the time the American colonies were established in the seventeenth century, Parliament was in the process of wresting taxing and lawmaking power from the

Crown, turning itself into a sovereign body.[2] From these clashes, moreover, emanated a remarkable body of political and philosophical writings, including works by Thomas Hobbes, James Harrington, and John Locke. Educated people in the New World, regarding themselves inheritors of English rights and customs, learned and discussed these events and writings as if they were their own.

Executive-legislative struggles occurred as well in the colonies. Colonial assemblies, originally created on the initiative of London authorities in order to promote political stability, grew in power and legitimacy. Members of these legislatures were closely bound to their constituents and buoyed by a lively political culture marked by widespread citizen participation. The assemblies themselves had broad powers, including taxing, spending, regulating land, and providing for public facilities. In contrast, the governors, appointed by officials in London, were posted for brief spans of time in a distant land. They lacked a sizable local aristocracy to buttress their rule, as well as the kind of patronage used by the Crown to manage Parliament. Royal vetoes from London could nullify legislative acts, but these were sparse and often too late to deter the colonials.

Separated from their home government and dependent on colonial assemblies for revenues and even for their own salaries, the governors increasingly took the course of least resistance and sought to reach accords with the locals. By the time the revolutionary period began, legislatures politically dominated

1. James S. Young, *The Washington Community, 1800-1828* (New York: Columbia University Press, 1966) (pp. 75-76).

2. Charles A. Beard and John P. Lewis, "Representative Government in Evolution," *American Political Science Review*, 26:223-40 (Apr. 1932).

most of the colonies. Equally important, colonial legislators formed the core of the opposition to the restrictive colonial policies instituted by the Crown in the 1760s, communicating with one another first through committees of correspondence and then, after 1774, through the Continental Congress.

Once independence was proclaimed and the English governors headed for home, therefore, the new nation naturally relied upon legislative institutions for guidance. It was a time when "everything [was] drawn within the legislative vortex," as Edmund Randolph put it during the Virginia ratification debate.[3]

Strictly speaking, no national executive existed between 1776 and 1789, the years of the Revolutionary War and the Articles of Confederation. Although the Continental Congress struggled on its own to conduct the war and manage diplomatic relations, the results were often haphazard. After the Articles were adopted in 1781, the government's frailty proved the folly of relying on the legislature alone to direct the nation's affairs. The government's inability to take decisive action in order to regulate interstate commerce, stabilize the currency, retire the Revolutionary War debts, or even keep the peace alarmed thoroughly all but the most radical leaders. The stage was set for what some have called a counterrevolution, but that description goes too far; rather, it was more of a postrevolutionary adjustment, a move toward a powerful central government with clearly delineated legislative, executive, and judicial powers.

THE PRESIDENT'S LEGISLATIVE POWERS

"The legislative is not only the supreme power," wrote John Locke, "but is sacred and unalterable in the hands where the community have placed it."[4] Following history and philosophical principle, the writers of the Constitution devoted article I to the legislative branch. Congress is granted a breathtaking array of powers. Indeed, article I, section 8, which enumerates Congress's powers, embraces the bulk of governmental authority as the Founders understood it.

The historic power of the purse—control over taxing and spending—was unambiguously awarded to Congress. Sweeping powers over the nation's economic life were also granted. Congress may coin money, incur debts, regulate interstate and foreign commerce, undertake public works and improvement projects, provide for a militia, and call it forth to repel invasions or suppress rebellions. Congress also plays an active part in foreign relations; it can declare war, ratify treaties, raise and support armies and navies, and make rules governing the military forces. Finally, Congress is granted the power "to make laws which shall be necessary and proper for carrying into execution the foregoing powers," the famous elastic clause.

Yet these powers are bounded and checked. Even though article I, section 1, purports to vest Congress with "all legislative powers herein granted," this assertion is not fully borne out by the Constitution's other provisions. Presidents are awarded crucial legislative powers by article II. They can convene one or both houses of Congress in

3. Quoted in Charles C. Thach, Jr., *The Creation of the Presidency, 1775-1789: A Study in Constitutional History* (Baltimore, MD: Johns Hopkins University Press, 1969), p. 31.

4. John Locke, *Two Tracts on Government*, ed. Philip Abrams (New York: Cambridge University Press, 1967), p. 374.

special session. Although they cannot personally introduce legislation, they "shall from time to time give to the Congress information on the state of the Union, and recommend to their consideration such measures as [they] shall judge necessary and expedient." In other words, presidents can shape the legislative agenda, even if they cannot assure that their proposals will be taken seriously, much less enacted. As James P. Pfiffner points out in his article in this issue of *The Annals*, presidents since Franklin D. Roosevelt have taken a much more active agenda-setting role than their nineteenth-century predecessors. Presidents may vary widely in legislative success, but all are now expected to submit a legislative program.

Presidents also have the power to veto congressional enactments. Once a bill or resolution has passed both houses of Congress and has been presented to the president, the president must sign or return it within 10 days, excluding Sundays. A two-thirds vote is required in each house to overrule a president's veto.

The veto power makes the president a major player in legislative politics. Of approximately 2500 vetoes from George Washington through Ronald Reagan, less than 4 percent were overridden by Congress. In his article in this *Annals* issue, Richard A. Watson analyzes all vetoes cast by modern presidents, from Franklin D. Roosevelt through Jimmy Carter. Although vetoes are rarely overridden, Watson notes that many of the vetoed bills eventually resurface in a different form.

Perhaps more important is the threat of a veto. Working on legislation, Capitol Hill protagonists are constantly looking over their shoulders to ascertain whether the president is likely to sign the bill or not.

Presidents are rarely without allies on Capitol Hill. Buttressing these allies and broadening support is a constant challenge to presidents and their legislative liaison aides.

Popular literature suggests that skillful presidents can make Congress dance to their tune, while inept chief executives are powerless in coaxing their programs into law. Political scientists have found, however, that presidential success and failure are more apt to be dictated by other factors. In their *Annals* article, Jon R. Bond, Richard Fleisher, and Michael Northrup measure presidential success against such variables as the party affiliation of members of Congress, members' political ideology, and presidential popularity. By and large, legislators' partisan and ideological commitments exert the strongest effect on presidential support. The president's popularity with the public has some effect, but not a major one.

In order to maximize influence over Congress, modern presidents appeal to the general public over the heads of the legislators. White House staffs devote enormous amounts of time to gaining media attention for presidents and stimulating popular support. It is widely assumed that media coverage tends to enhance power and that presidents are more successful than Congress at exploiting the media. Stephanie Greco Larson challenges this conventional wisdom in her *Annals* article, arguing that the hard evidence is far from unequivocal. No doubt presidents and their advisers will be hard to convince on this score. In any event, the public nature of the presidency will be a fixture in legislative-executive struggles for the foreseeable future.

CONGRESS'S
ADMINISTRATIVE CLOUT

When the drafters of the Constitution turned from the legislature to the executive, they had few historical examples to guide them. They were in no mood to install a monarchy, yet they conceded that one of the worst flaws of the Articles was the absence of a strong, independent executive. "Energy in the Executive is a leading character in the definition of good government," asserted Alexander Hamilton in *Federalist* number 70.[5] So the Founders ventured into the uncharted territory of article II. It is not surprising that the language of this portion of the Constitution is often vague and general, in stark contrast to the specificity of article I.

The executive article begins with the so-called vesting clause: "Executive power shall be vested in a president." There is also the take-care clause, instructing the president to "take care that the laws be faithfully executed." The president heads the executive branch and nominates ambassadors, judges, and other "officers of the United States." Moreover, the president is commander in chief of the armed forces and has the power to make treaties with foreign powers, subject to ratification by two-thirds of the Senate.

As in the president's treaty-making role, presidential power is not exercised in isolation. While the president wields executive power, it is Congress that perforce defines much of what that power is. The basic design of the executive branch, including cabinet departments and other agencies, is contained in laws passed by Congress and signed

5. Alexander Hamilton, *Federalist* no. 70, in *The Federalist*, ed. Edward Mead Earle (New York: Modern Library, n.d.), p. 454.

by the president. These laws define the mandates of the agencies and sometimes even spell out an agency's management structure. Separate laws define federal personnel policy, pay scales, and ethical requirements.

The power of the purse also limits administrative discretion. "No money shall be drawn from the Treasury, but in consequence of appropriations made by law," states article I, section 9. From the very beginning, Congress has given clear directions about how it wishes the executive branch to spend the money it appropriates. While appropriations bills typically award agencies lump sums to carry out their duties, more detailed directions are usually contained in other legislative pronouncements—authorization bills, committee reports, or even informal guidance from Capitol Hill panels with which an agency must deal year after year. Hence administrative discretion is often strictly bounded.

Even in diplomacy and national defense, the Constitution divides powers between the president and Congress. Because these were traditional royal prerogatives, they have normally resisted legislative encroachment. Even champions of legislative rights and balanced constitutions, like Locke and Montesquieu, held that executives should possess broad authority to deal with foreign powers and cope with crises. The Constitution thus grants the president the tools to conduct negotiations with foreign powers and names the president commander in chief of the armed forces.

Yet even here the Founders preferred to blend functions. The Senate must approve ambassadors, envoys, and other major presidential appointees. Treaties a president makes must be ratified by the Senate. If funds are required to meet treaty obligations, the House is involved, with its special claims over the appropriations process.

The power of the purse also regulates the flow of funds to the armed forces. In the hearing room of the House Armed Services Committee, a brass plaque, placed opposite the witness table, sets forth excerpts from article I, section 8: "The Congress shall have power . . . to raise and support armies . . . [and] to provide and maintain a navy."

Finally, only Congress, which represents the people, can declare war. An early draft of the Constitution gave Congress the power to "make war." On second thought, the drafters changed this to "declare war."

SEPARATE INSTITUTIONS, SHARED POWERS

The resulting constitutional system is popularly known as separation of powers. A simplified view holds that these powers are discrete and unblendable, like bottles of inert chemicals on a shelf. A prominent exponent of this view was former Chief Justice Warren Burger, who expressed it in several important Supreme Court decisions. In *Immigration and Naturalization Service* v. *Chadha* he wrote:

The Constitution sought to divide the delegated powers of the new Federal Government into three defined categories, Legislative, Executive, and Judicial, to assure, as nearly as possible, that each branch of government would confine itself to its assigned responsibility. The hydraulic pressure inherent within each of the separate Branches to exceed the outer limits of its power, even to accomplish desirable objectives, must be resisted.[6]

The Supreme Court seemed to accept this view in other cases as well. For

example, in its celebrated 1986 decision in *Bowsher* v. *Synar*, striking down the original version of the Gramm-Rudman-Hollings budget law, the Court, again speaking through Burger, implied that once an act was passed by Congress and signed by the president, the legislative branch had no further role to play in it.

In practice, however, the constitutional system is one not of separated powers but of separate institutions sharing powers. Madison observed that the Constitution created not a system of separate institutions performing separate functions but one of separate institutions sharing functions, so that "these departments be so far connected and blended as to give to each a constitutional control over the others."[7] Madison was certainly worried about one institution's encroaching upon the others, especially aggression by the legislature, but he disdained "parchment barriers" against such encroachment. Rather than inveighing against any and all interbranch collaboration, he held that the powers of one should not be "directly or completely administered by either of the other departments" and that none should wield "an overruling influence" over the others.[8] In other words, interbranch relations were matters of compromise and accommodation, not of absolute prohibition.

Whatever the theory of the matter, history seems to bear out Madison's practical approach to interbranch relationships. The ink was hardly dry on the Constitution before politicians in the new nation proceeded to blur the boundaries of the three branches. Secretary of the Treasury Alexander Hamilton aggressively sought mastery over Congress, as

6. *Immigration and Naturalization Service* v. *Chadha*, 462 U.S. 919, 952 (1983).

7. James Madison, *Federalist* no. 48, in *The Federalist*, ed. Earle, p. 321.
8. Ibid.

did his archenemy, Thomas Jefferson, when he became president a decade later. Lines of demarcation between the three branches were repeatedly trespassed.

Throughout history, accommodation among the branches has proved essential to make the framers' intricate mechanism work effectively. As Justice Joseph Story once wrote, the framers sought to "prove that rigid adherence to [separation of powers] in all cases would be subversive of the efficiency of government and result in the destruction of the public liberties."[9] Justice Robert Jackson noted in 1952 that "while the Constitution diffuses power the better to secure liberty, it also contemplates that practice will integrate the dispersed powers into a workable government."[10]

The post-Burger Supreme Court seems to have retreated from the rigid, simplistic interpretation of separation of powers and to have assumed a complex, Madisonian view. In the 1988 case of *Morrison* v. *Olson*, the Court held by a 7-1 margin that the independent counsel law was consistent with the Constitution. Established by the 1978 Ethics in Government Act, independent counsels can be appointed by the Justice Department to investigate charges of wrongdoing within the executive branch.

The Court's opinion, rendered by Chief Justice William Rehnquist, who clerked for Justice Roberts, set forth a flexible, multifaceted set of conditions for separation of powers. First, the law in question did not involve "an attempt by Congress to increase its own powers at the expense of the executive branch." Nor did it represent "any judicial usurpa-

tion of properly executive functions." Third, the act did not "impermissibly undermine" executive branch powers. Finally, it did not disrupt the proper balance between the branches by "preventing the executive branch from accomplishing its constitutional assigned functions."

These tests add up to something very different than a hermetically sealed separation of powers. Although Chief Justice Rehnquist attempted to separate the independent counsel case from such earlier holdings as *Chadha* and *Bowsher*, the approach was strikingly different. Rehnquist contended that "we have never held that the Constitution requires that the three branches of Government 'operate with absolute independence.'" Surely the Founders would have understood this pragmatic approach to separation of powers.

FROM ISOLATION TO SYMBIOSIS

Legislative-executive relations display a distinct although uneven trend toward greater formal structure. The Constitution itself gives little guidance about how these relations are to be conducted, leaving these details to the workings of history. "Of legal authority for presidential leadership of Congress," wrote James S. Young, "the Constitution was nearly as bare as Mother Hubbard's cupboard."[11] Symbolic of the tentative quality of interbranch relations in the early nineteenth century was the perilous causeway that linked Capitol Hill with the White House in the city of Washington's early years.

If Congress and the executive worked at arm's length during most of the

9. Joseph Story, *Commentaries on the Constitution of the United States,* 5th ed. (Boston: Little, Brown, 1905), 1:396.

10. *Youngstown Sheet and Tube Co.* v. *Sawyer,* 343 U.S. 579, 635 (1952).

11. Young, *Washington Community,* p. 158.

nineteenth century, the exceptions were found in the three strongest presidencies of the period: those of Thomas Jefferson, Andrew Jackson, and Abraham Lincoln. These three took an active part in the legislative process. Jefferson, the acknowledged leader of the Democratic-Republican Party, worked with floor lieutenants to enact legislation drafted in the executive branch. Jefferson's mastery flowed from his personal ties with lawmakers and his central role in the party network. A generation later, Jackson drew his influence from something approaching a popular mandate. Lacking a coherent legislative faction but commanding vast public adulation, Jackson used patronage and the veto to bend the legislative process to his aims. Lincoln, facing civil strife, used emergency powers as a bludgeon to force congressional action. Throughout the Civil War, he proposed and lobbied for legislation and threatened the veto to win approval for his policies.

These three presidents used available resources to gain a measure of control over Congress—Jefferson used his party; Jackson, his popularity; Lincoln, his emergency powers. These powers were personal and time-bound, however; they were not passed on to successors. In fact, quite the opposite happened: as soon as these strong presidents left the scene, reaction set in and legislators recaptured their powers.

After Lincoln's assassination in 1865, a period of legislative ascendancy ensued that lasted for more than a generation. Woodrow Wilson asserted in 1885 that "the business of the president, occasionally great, is usually not much above the routine. Most of the time it is mere administration, mere obedience of directions from the masters of policy, the

standing committees [of Congress]."[12]

The modern legislative role of the president, while drawing on certain precedents from earlier strong executives, is primarily an invention of the present century. Theodore Roosevelt (president during the years 1901-9), Woodrow Wilson (1913-21), and Franklin D. Roosevelt (1933-45) all brought extensive legislative agendas to Capitol Hill. It was Wilson who inaugurated the practice of delivering his State of the Union address in person, to maximize public attention and media coverage.

The legislative presidency became a permanent fixture after World War II. Only then could it be said that the role was institutionalized, performed not because of some unique combination of personality and circumstance but because everyone—including Congress, the press, and the public—expected it.

The other side of this relationship is Congress's increasingly detailed, and even systematic, attention to implementation of laws. Legislators' scrutiny, or oversight, of administration dates from the earliest days, from the 1792 investigation into General Arthur St. Clair's humiliating military defeat at the hands of Miami and Shawnee Indians. American history has been punctuated by legislative investigations, often highly publicized, into major public concerns. While implied rather than explicit in the Constitution, legislative investigations have been upheld by the Supreme Court insofar as they are reasonably related to the lawmaking function.[13] Harry S Truman, who made his national reputation

12. Woodrow Wilson, *Congressional Government* (Baltimore MD: Johns Hopkins University Press, 1981), p. 170.

13. *McGrain* v. *Daugherty*, 273 U.S. 180 (1927).

chairing a committee investigating procurement and supplies during World War II, told his fellow senators in 1944 that "the manner in which the power [of investigation] is exercised will largely determine the position and prestige of the Congress in the future."[14]

After World War II, Congress moved to make its investigatory work more systematic. The Legislative Reorganization Act of 1946 directed committees to exercise "continual watchfulness" over the executive agencies and programs for which they were responsible; subsequent enactments extended that directive. To be sure, highly publicized investigations continued, from the notorious McCarthy-era witch hunts to the Watergate and Iran-contra inquiries. More and more, however, committees' schedules were filled with routine oversight hearings into the activities of executive agencies and the fate of legislative enactments.

Contemporary patterns of legislative oversight are reviewed in this volume by Frederick M. Kaiser. Oversight of the executive, including the presidency itself, has increased over the past two decades. It is no longer confined to sporadic investigations or even to periodic oversight hearings. It permeates a wide range of activities on the part of members and their staffs.

Commentators have long accepted as gospel the thesis that lawmakers shun oversight because it offers little political payoff, especially when compared to sponsoring new legislation or claiming credit for constituency work. Kaiser gives us grounds for questioning this piece of received wisdom. Especially in

an era of fiscal shortfalls, oversight may be a more attractive means of advertising and credit claiming than sponsorship of new legislation. Congress has, moreover, provided new resources for individual and committee overseers.

PATTERNS OF INTERBRANCH CONTROL

Even in the modern age of activist presidents, power shifts between Congress and the president are a recurring feature of American politics. The balance of power is delicately poised and constantly open to change. It is certainly affected by partisan control of the two chambers and by issues, circumstances, and personalities.

Of all the factors affecting interbranch relationships, partisan control would seem the most obvious. Even with their well-known looseness and lack of ideological rigor, American political parties ought to provide a measure of policy coherence and the interbranch coalitions that would lead to presidential success. When the White House and both chambers of Congress are controlled by a single party, we ought to experience an approximation of party government: cooperative leadership from both branches in which the party's major priorities can be transferred into a reasonably coherent set of enactments.

Eras of true legislative harmony, while few and far between in this country, have almost always occurred when a single party controlled both ends of Pennsylvania Avenue. Most notable in this century were Wilson's first term with his New Freedom legislative agenda (1913-17), Franklin D. Roosevelt's Depression-era New Deal (1933-36), and the early days of Lyndon B.

14. Quoted in Arthur M. Schlesinger, Jr., and Roger Bruns, *Congress Investigates: A Documentary History, 1792-1974* (New York: Chelsea House, 1983), p. x.

Johnson's Great Society (1963-65). All were periods of frantic lawmaking, which produced landmark legislation and innovative government programs.

Such party-government periods as these are not without their problems. The pace of lawmaking is sometimes so rapid that political institutions cannot absorb the new programs. Succeeding developments may retrench or even reverse ill-considered or ineffective programs. One generation's achievements can turn into another's stumbling blocks.

Few eras produce such outpourings of legislation, even when the same party remains in control of both policymaking branches. Wilson's determined effort at party government continued until 1917, when the advent of World War I diverted attention to wartime mobilization; the last two years of his administration found Congress in Republican hands and his postwar peace plan in ruins. Roosevelt's Hundred Days of 1933 was probably the most remarkable period of legislative productivity in the nation's history. After 1936, however, Roosevelt extracted very little domestic legislation from Capitol Hill, which was dominated by the conservative coalition of southern Democrats and Republicans. In the wake of John F. Kennedy's assassination in 1963, Johnson rolled over the conservative alliance to push through a broadranging so-called second New Deal in education, civil rights, health, transportation, and a host of other areas. Yet the legislative juggernaut soon lost momentum, a casualty of overinflated expectations and rising conflict over the Vietnam war.

A recent period of party control that fell far short of party government occurred during Jimmy Carter's administration (1977-81). Although Democrats commanded huge majorities in both houses,

relations between Carter and Capitol Hill leaders started badly and never really took off. The ineptness of Carter and his staff in dealing with congressional leaders is usually blamed for the lack of legislative productivity. Actually, support for Carter's initiatives on Capitol Hill was quite respectable. But important, new governmental programs lost their appeal in the wake of a sluggish economy and rising skepticism about the efficacy of earlier enactments.[15]

More commonplace has become government that is divided between the two parties. Of the 21 Congresses between 1947 and 1989, 12 have been all or partly in the hands of the party opposed to the president. This includes two years of the Truman presidency, all but two years of Eisenhower's, and all of Nixon's, Ford's, and Reagan's.

Occasionally, divided government can produce brief interludes of interbranch harmony. Ronald Reagan's first year, 1981, was such a time. Working with a GOP-controlled Senate and a bloc of southern boll weevil swing votes in the House, Reagan and his advisers succeeded in enacting a highly focused yet far-reaching economic package of tax cuts, domestic-spending cuts, and greatly increased military spending. Reagan's reputation as the great communicator dates from that period.

It was not long, however, before the opposition Democrats found their voice and, aided by an economic depression, brought many of the Reagan initiatives to a standstill. The remainder of Reagan's tenure was marked by something resembling pitched warfare between the two branches.

15. Charles O. Jones, *The Trusteeship Presidency: Jimmy Carter and the United States Congress* (Baton Rouge: Louisiana State University Press, 1988).

Divided government, in name or in spirit, is likely to be with us for some time. Party labels are worn lightly these days by elected officials as well as by voters, who divide their loyalties as freely as they split their ballots. Politicians at all levels are tempted to fashion their own candidacies, bypassing partisan appeals and relying on personal factors or campaign technology. Some analysts foresee a split-level partisan alignment, in which the Republicans lock in the presidency while the Democrats own control of the House of Representatives and perhaps the Senate.[16]

Stalemate is a constant danger of divided government. Sometimes the two branches wage battle over policies and prerogatives; at other times, a quiet distance is more the order of the day. Constitutional reformers lament what Lloyd Cutler termed "the structural inability of our government to propose, legislate, and administer a balanced program for governing."[17] The remedy is seen to be injection of parliamentary forms.

To join the executive and legislative branches, reformers are intrigued with the idea of juggling the political calendar to encourage candidates to run as a team ticket for office. They have expended much time figuring out how to make terms for the president, Senate, and House of Representatives parallel, or nearly so. The idea is to induce voters to think of candidates together, and to prevent the so-called midterm election phenomenon, in which the president's party tends to lose ground in congressional elections two years after the president's election.

For their part, voters seem unimpressed with the team-ticket notion. Massive ticket splitting has marked recent elections. Moreover, voters seem to like divided government: public opinion surveys indicate that people condone and even prefer having divided government so that the two branches can check each other.[18]

Nor does the government's fragmented structure preclude vigorous, purposeful action under the right circumstances. At the very moment that critics like Cutler were lamenting the leadership crisis of the weak presidencies of Ford and Carter, Reagan demonstrated with his 1981 economic package the kind of leadership they advocated.

Reforms designed to promote majoritarian government, moreover, do not fit the nation's pluralistic political culture. The absence of a unified elite and the presence of a cacophony of groups and interests render virtually impossible the kind of broad-gauged consensus that would have to underlie such a regime, making a fragmented, open decision-making system virtually inevitable. No doubt the presence of vigorous opposition has checked many unwise initiatives on the part of the executive or legislative branches. Subsequent experience uncovered many excesses in Johnson's Great Society programs, crafted during a period of majoritarian government; the folly of Reaganomics, alas, will haunt our nation for many years. Indeed, the problem is often not the absence of unity but the lack of concerted and coherent opposition.

16. See Thomas E. Mann, "The Permanent Minority Party in American Politics," *Brookings Review*, 6:33-38 (Winter 1988).

17. Lloyd Cutler, "To Form a Government," in *Reforming American Government: The Bicentennial Papers of the Committee on the Constitutional System*, ed. Donald L. Robinson (Boulder, CO: Westview Press, 1985), p. 11.

18. Roger H. Davidson, David M. Kovenock, and Michael K. O'Leary, *Congress in Crisis* (Belmont, CA: Wadsworth, 1966), pp. 62-63.

SOME CASES IN POINT

Legislative-executive relationships are not always win-or-lose contests. If one branch is up, the other is not necessarily down. Internal power fluctuations—within the executive branch or within the two legislative chambers—complicate the ebb and flow of power. The articles in this volume serve to illustrate the variety and complexity of legislative-executive relations.

The controversial budget politics of the last two decades have produced at least two major statutory innovations: the Congressional Budget and Impoundment Control Act of 1974 and the 1985 Deficit Reduction Act, known by the names of its principal authors, Gramm-Rudman-Hollings. These enactments are discussed in this volume by James A. Thurber and Darrell M. West, respectively. Their analyses demonstrate the difficulty of declaring winners and losers in such interbranch clashes. Enacted in the face of executive pressures to shift legislative spending priorities, the two acts had mixed results. Although they gave presidents leverage to induce certain spending cuts, they also added to Congress's informational resources and even bolstered legislative budgetary priorities. It is incontestable that these innovations have made budgeting both more open and more complicated.

Major tax alterations also illustrate the interplay of president and Congress. In his *Annals* article, James M. Verdier examines three decades of major tax-code revisions in light of partisan politics, economic conditions, public opinion, and policy expertise. Presidents take the lead in pushing tax reform onto the public agenda, but once there, tax reform falls victim to the particularism of Congress.

The complexity of interbranch relations, albeit in a different form, is illustrated in Margaret Jane Wyszomirski's account of the National Endowment for the Arts' 23-year history. Presidential initiative and congressional support both attended the agency's birth during the Johnson administration. This stimulated the rise of an arts constituency and an attendant triangular alliance of agency leaders, congressional supporters, and arts interest groups. As this subgovernment matured, it moved away from dependence upon presidential leadership.

THE WAR-POWERS DILEMMA

The greatest source of imbalance in legislative-executive relations centers on the so-called war powers: decisions committing U.S. troops in potentially hostile situations abroad. The Founders were maddeningly inconclusive in providing guidance on this problem. The president, of course, is commander in chief, but Congress raises and equips armies and navies and is the sole agency empowered to declare war.

Is it prudent to leave questions of war and peace in the hands of a legislative body, with all its compromises and imperfections? The Founders here made a bold choice that is not always easy to live with. Military or foreign policy advocates, harboring their own intense views of the national interest, all too often look with horror on the seemingly messy and inconsistent deliberations of Congress.

In the recent Iran-contra affair, we saw the disdain with which zealots like Lieutenant Colonel Oliver L. North and Vice Admiral John M. Poindexter viewed the workings of the national legislature. Yet no one ever claimed that dedication to open, democratic processes was easy;

it requires patience and a commitment to cooperation that not a few dedicated people find beyond them. Yet, as Louis Fisher argues in his *Annals* article, the Constitution dictates shared foreign policy and gives little support to the notion of a superior influence by one branch or the other.

The Founders' failure to resolve the question of the war powers was of little consequence as long as the standing military forces were small and weak. This was the case up to World War II: wars brought on frantic expansion of the military, with rapid demobilization once hostilities ended. As Christopher J. Deering details in the present volume, however, this pattern changed dramatically after World War II, with the advent of a huge permanent military establishment. Contemporary commanders in chief, regardless of their policy preferences, are far stronger than their predecessors in taking initiative and

setting the terms of debate. The 1973 War Powers Resolution, designed to put Congress back in the picture, has not been successful.

The war-powers debate may turn out to be the major destabilizing factor in the 200-year ebb and flow of presidential and congressional power. Here the Constitution is literally an "invitation to struggle," and it is left to the ingenuity and goodwill of legislative and executive leaders to resolve the problem.

Our constitutional system demands mutual trust and accommodation on the part of leaders of the two political branches. Neither the president nor Congress is monolithic; neither dominates all facets of policy. Their relationship yields temporary winners and losers but is unlikely to produce parties that are victorious or vanquished for the long term. Those who are Madisonians at heart wish to keep it that way.

ANNALS, *AAPSS*, **499**, September 1988

The President's Legislative Agenda

By JAMES P. PFIFFNER

ABSTRACT: The president has come to be known as our chief legislator within the past fifty years, with Franklin Roosevelt and his successors taking a much more active role in the legislative process than nineteenth-century presidents took. Despite elaborate efforts and a fully developed congressional liaison capacity in the White House, however, only three presidents have been markedly successful with Congress: Franklin Roosevelt, Lyndon Johnson, and Ronald Reagan. This article examines some of the lessons that have been learned about presidential effectiveness with Congress. Even the most successful presidents, however, have not been able to sustain their legislative effectiveness throughout their terms, and this article analyzes the frustrations of divided government and proposals for constitutional reform to alleviate the problem. The article concludes that whether one approves of these reform proposals depends how one conceives of the problem.

James P. Pfiffner is professor of government and politics at George Mason University. He is the author of The Strategic Presidency: Hitting the Ground Running *(1988) and* The President, the Budget, and Congress: Impoundment and the 1974 Budget Act *(1979) and editor of* The President and Economic Policy *(1986). He has taught at the University of California, Riverside, and California State University, Fullerton, and has worked in the Director's Office of the U.S. Office of Personnel Management.*

WHILE it is a commonplace in the last decades of the twentieth century that the president is our chief legislator, it was not always thus. In the nineteenth century, Congress dominated the policymaking process. President Taft was the first modern president to send a draft of a legislative proposal to Congress, and that was seen as a bit presumptuous. Woodrow Wilson was the first president in 100 years to go to the Capitol to present a message in person.

Major changes came during the legendary 100 days, when the newly inaugurated Franklin Roosevelt initiated a spate of legislation designed to bring the country out of the Great Depression. Bills were drafted in the White House, sometimes with and sometimes without congressional participation, and sent to Capitol Hill for passage. Only one major bill was drafted by Congress, and no bill was altered in any fundamental way from Roosevelt's intentions.

Roosevelt's huge victories were an exception, and it was not until the Truman administration that the president became more systematic about legislative leadership, taking such measures as sending an annual legislative message to Congress and assigning two full-time specialists to be in liaison with Congress.[1]

President Eisenhower was the first to establish an Office of Congressional Liaison, though primarily as a buffer for demands for patronage and pork barrel from the Hill. Eisenhower did not intend to push an extensive legislative agenda actively, but when he neglected to send an annual legislative agenda to Congress, there was an outcry from the Hill, and he resumed the practice initiated by Truman. Because of his ambitious legislative program, John F. Kennedy made Larry O'Brien, one of his more powerful and trusted aides, director of his Office of Legislative Liaison. O'Brien stayed on to head Lyndon Johnson's legislative efforts during one of the most productive legislative sessions in American history.[2]

The 1960s saw the emergence of a full-blown presidential apparatus to deal with Congress, though the fortunes of presidents since then have fluctuated considerably. In the 1960s, the active presidency was championed by liberals who saw Franklin Roosevelt as a role model, solving large-scale national problems by pushing legislative programs through Congress.

The war in Vietnam ended the liberals' fascination with a strong presidency. Johnson's penchant for secrecy and his continuation of the war after public and congressional opinion began to turn against it began a period characterized by Arthur Schlesinger, Jr., as "the imperial presidency."[3] Just as the war brought out the worst side of Johnson, as he circled the wagons around his flagging presidency, it also soured the first term of Richard Nixon, as he strove futilely to bring an honorable end to the war. The secrecy, paranoia, and hostility toward Congress and the press that began in his first term planted the seeds of the Watergate scandals that would finally bring his presidency down.

President Ford faced a Democratic Congress that was reasserting itself after the resignation of President Nixon. It countered presidential vetoes with legislative vetoes and asserted its own budget priorities with its newly formulated bud-

1. See James L. Sundquist, *The Decline and Resurgence of Congress* (Washington, DC: Brookings Institution, 1981), chap. 6.

2. See Nigel Bowles, *The White House and Capitol Hill* (Oxford: Clarendon Press, 1987).
3. Arthur Schlesinger, Jr., *The Imperial Presidency* (Boston: Houghton Mifflin, 1973).

get process.[4] Jimmy Carter came to office with a Democratic majority in Congress rivaling that of Lyndon Johnson, but in a time of greatly changed political expectations. Carter's fiscal conservatism was not matched in Congress, and a series of blunders early in his administration soured relations with Congress. At the end of the Carter presidency, there were proposals to amend the Constitution in order to enable the president "to form a government" and there was talk of the "no-win presidency."

President Reagan's impressive legislative victories during his first year in office demonstrated that a determined and popular president could, even with control of only one house, have his way with Congress. In 1981, there were comparisons of his victories with those of FDR and LBJ, but the bloom was soon off the rose. The last six years of the Reagan presidency have been marked by stalemate with Congress over the fiscal problems that were created by the legislative victories of his first year in office. Reagan's legislative support score declined steadily from 80 percent in his first year to less than 50 percent in 1987.[5] His second term has been dominated by the Iran-contra scandal, which seemed to display many of the elements of Schlesinger's imperial presidency.

FACTORS IN PRESIDENTIAL SUCCESS

What can explain the widely varying rates of success of presidents with Con-

4. For an analysis of the reassertion of congressional prerogatives, see Thomas Cronin, "A Resurgent Congress and the Imperial Presidency," *Political Science Quarterly*, 95(2):209 (Summer 1980).

5. The legislative support scores are calculated by Congressional Quarterly. *Congressional Quarterly Weekly Report*, 16 Jan. 1988, p. 93.

gress over the past three decades? Franklin Roosevelt, Lyndon Johnson, and Ronald Reagan were spectacularly successful—but only at the beginning of their presidencies. They were not able to sustain their earlier levels of success. Presidents Kennedy, Nixon, Ford, and Carter each had legislative victories, but their administrations are not considered models of legislative effectiveness, and each was frustrated in his dealings with Congress.

One possible explanation of differing legislative success is the legislative skill and political judgment of different presidents. Another is the partisan balance in Congress: some presidents have more members of their party in House and Senate seats and thus might expect more support in Congress for their agenda. Another explanation is the nature of the times: the international situation, the state of the economy, public opinion, and the existing policy agenda of pressing issues that must be dealt with.

Certainly, partisan support in Congress can be crucial to a president's legislative success. Both Roosevelt and Johnson had significant partisan majorities in both houses of Congress to help them pass their proposals. Reagan's success, however, was achieved even though his party controlled only the Senate, with the House dominated by the Democratic Party. Jimmy Carter had substantial Democratic majorities in both houses but was not able to mobilize congressional support the way Johnson had done. So while partisan support in Congress can be crucial, it is not determinative.

Another explanation of presidential success is the nature of the policy agenda when the president is elected. While some scholars have emphasized how some presidents seemingly have been able to shape and direct the congressional agenda, others have emphasized how presidents are constrained by agendas already in place when they are elected. Charles O. Jones has argued that presidents are constrained by the broad issues facing the nation that are reflected in public opinion.[6]

Jones argues that presidents are constrained by existing policy agendas when they come to office and that their legislative success is affected by whether they and members of Congress can agree on the specific policy alternatives necessary to deal with existing problems. Jones emphasizes that both Johnson and Reagan faced existing policy agendas when they came to office but were legislatively successful because they were able to mobilize congressional majorities around those agendas. Jones also argues that no president can dominate the policy agenda throughout a term.

In trying to understand why some presidents are more successful than others in their dealings with Congress, many analysts examine the various strategies and tactics used by the White House to get its way with Congress. On the surface, this seems to be a natural place to start. Stories of Lyndon Johnson's arm twisting and cajolery are fascinating, and those tactics are assumed to be the reason for his impressive successes with Congress. Other scholars see these legislative skills as surface factors that do not fundamentally affect a president's chances for legislative success.

The most systematic attack on the thesis that a president's legislative skills make a large difference in success on the Hill has been made by George Edwards.

In a series of empirical studies of votes in Congress over the past several decades, Edwards has come to the conclusion that "there is no systematic relationship between presidential legislative skills and congressional support for the White House. . . . Moreover, [presidents] are *not* more likely to win close votes, on which skills might play the crucial role in obtaining the last few votes needed to pass a program."[7]

Edwards argues that legislators are influenced by a number of factors in deciding how to vote on a particular piece of legislation. Among these factors are ideology, personal policy preferences, and constituency pressures. He argues that presidential appeals are unlikely to overcome these strong pulls on a legislator. The partisan makeup of Congress has much more influence than pressures from the president. Thus Lyndon Johnson's successes had much more to do with Democratic dominance of the Eighty-Ninth Congress than with his legendary legislative skills.

Of course, a new president will do better with Congress if he wins his election to office by a landslide, runs ahead of members of Congress in their own states and districts, has large partisan majorities in both houses of Congress, and maintains high popular approval with the public. Few presidents are blessed with such circumstances, however. In the mid-twentieth century, many presidents have been faced with a divided government, close elections, a decrease in popularity over their terms, and loss of seats in midterm elections.

Edwards's conclusions do not mean,

6. See Charles O. Jones, "Presidents and Agendas: Who Defines What for Whom?" in *The Managerial Presidency*, ed. James P. Pfiffner (Chicago: Dorsey Press, forthcoming).

7. George C. Edwards, "Reforming the 'President': The Individual as Leader," *PS*, 20(3):623 (Summer 1987). See also idem, *At the Margins* (New Haven, CT: Yale University Press, forthcoming).

however, that presidential skills can be ignored. First of all, the aggregate data on voting that he uses in his analysis cannot capture all of the ways in which legislators might be affected by presidential actions,[8] and some forms of congressional support for the president cannot be measured by roll-call votes.[9] Second, members of Congress believe that presidential skills make a difference. They feel the heat from presidential pressure, especially from presidents of their own party. They react hostilely when they think they have been slighted by the White House.

Third, the absence of presidential skills can hurt a president. It is likely that President Carter would have done better if his White House staff had not made some mistakes early in his administration that seemed to alienate many members of his own party in Congress. There is, of course, no way to prove this. Edwards would argue that no member of Congress would vote against his own interests and against the president out of spite. On the other hand, President Carter's head of legislative liaison, Frank Moore, felt that "a lot of times you can get a guy's vote just by having done a lot of little things. And a lot of times they'll vote against you, just out of damn spite."[10]

TACTICS AND STRATEGY

If one were advising a new president about how to behave toward Congress

so as to maximize the chances of legislative success, what could be recommended based on the experience of recent presidents? This section will consider the advantages of getting off to a quick start, various carrots and sticks that recent presidents have used in dealing with Congress, and the rifle and shotgun strategies of presenting agendas to Congress. The final section will deal with the broader issue of whether changes in the Constitution would alleviate the frustrations of divided government.

A quick start

If a president wants to do well with Congress, a fast start is helpful; early victories can set the tone for the administration and take advantage of the mandate from the voters. The most important reason for moving quickly is what Paul Light calls the policy cycle of decreasing influence. He argues that presidents begin their terms in office with a maximum of political capital that must be exploited quickly before it is dissipated. At an administration's beginning, presidential popularity is likely to be at a peak; Congress is more likely to be sympathetic to presidential appeals for support than after tough policy decisions have been made. In addition, after the first year, members will be focusing on the midterm elections, and the president's party can almost always expect to lose seats in both houses of Congress in those elections.[11]

Moving quickly means introducing legislation early in the term. Light found that, between 1960 and 1980, of the items introduced between January and March of the first year, 72 percent were

8. See Barbara Kellerman, *The Political Presidency: Practice of Leadership* (New York: Oxford University Press, 1984), p. 49.
9. See, for example, Cary Covington, "'Staying Private': Gaining Congressional Support for Unpublicized Presidential Preferences on Roll Call Votes," *Journal of Politics*, 1987, pp. 737-55.
10. Robert Shogun, *Promises to Keep* (New York: Thomas Y. Crowell, 1977), p. 209.

11. Paul Light, *The President's Agenda* (Baltimore, MD: Johns Hopkins University Press, 1982), p. 36.

eventually enacted. During the next three months, the rate dropped to 39 percent, and from July to September, it fell to 25 percent.[12] Lyndon Johnson put it this way:

I keep hitting hard because I know this honeymoon won't last. Every day I lose a little more political capital. That's why we have to keep at it, never letting up. One day soon, I don't know when, the critics and the snipers will move in and we will be at stalemate. We have to get all we can, now, before the roof comes down.[13]

The irony is that the cycle of decreasing influence is mirrored by a cycle of increasing competence. That is, presidents learn from early mistakes and become more effective in their relations with Congress. Unfortunately, the hangover from early mistakes can overshadow increasing competence.

Early mistakes can hurt a president's reputation on the Hill out of proportion to their initial significance. Stories of the Carter White House's unreturned phone calls and reported insensitivity toward Congress came back to dog Carter later in his administration long after the initial problems had been remedied. Speaker of the House Thomas P. "Tip" O'Neill, Democrat of Massachusetts, was miffed when his family received poor seats for an inaugural gala at the Kennedy Center. He blamed the slight on Carter's aide Hamilton Jordan. "As far as Jordan was concerned, a House Speaker was something you bought on sale at Radio Shack."[14]

Another, more substantive, blunder of the early Carter administration,

viewed with perfect hindsight, was the water projects fiasco. In early 1977, President Carter decided that, in line with his fiscal conservatism, he would eliminate a number of water projects from the 1978 budget. The projects were chosen as examples of congressional pork barrel whose benefits did not outweigh their costs, but from the congressional perspective they were the lifeblood of service to one's district.

Bert Lance, Carter's director of the Office of Management and Budget, said the intention was to show Congress who was in charge, but it turned out to be a disaster. "We alienated a large portion of the Congress: those who had projects and those who had hopes of having projects: 100 percent alienation. It was not a good decision in my judgment, but the president felt very strongly about it."[15] Members of Congress were irate, in part because some were not consulted about the decision but primarily because they saw the projects as crucial to their own political interests. In the end, Carter lost when the Senate attached the water projects as a rider to an economic stimulus bill wanted by the administration.

According to Stuart Eizenstat, "I don't think Carter's image ever recovered from some of those early mistakes."[16]

Carrots and sticks

In order to move quickly, it is important to organize the congressional liaison operation early, before the inauguration. Immediately after the election, campaign debts will come due, and the new administration will be flooded by requests and demands from the Hill,

12. Ibid., p. 45.

13. Jack Valenti, *A Very Personal President* (New York: Norton, 1975), p. 144.

14. Tip O'Neill, *Man of the House* (New York: Random House, 1987), p. 311.

15. Interview with Bert Lance, Calhoun, GA, 21 June 1983.

16. Interview with Stuart Eizenstat, Washington, DC, 14 July 1983.

primarily for patronage. The function of the Office of Congressional Relations is to help bridge this gap between the two branches of government in policy cooperation that cannot be bridged by the weak party system in the United States.[17]

If the Office of Congressional Relations is to be effective, it must use professionals in dealing with Congress; this is not the time or place for on-the-job training. President Carter was hurt by appointing Frank Moore to head congressional liaison. Moore had worked for Carter in Georgia in dealing with the legislature there, but he had no experience on Capitol Hill. According to Tip O'Neill, Moore "didn't know beans about Congress."[18] In contrast, President Reagan's first head of congressional liaison was Max Friedersdorf, an experienced hand on the Hill who was respected as a professional on both sides of the aisle. His approach to his job was that one has to "know all of their individual idiosyncrasies and know how they think and act. You have to know when Tip O'Neill needs a cigar."[19]

One of the traditional ways of winning friends and influencing votes in Congress is patronage—making political appointments in the executive branch at the behest of members of Congress. There can be no doubt that the pressure to make these appointments is high. Both Carter and Reagan faced thousands of requests from the Hill early in their administrations. "The House and Senate Republicans just start cramming people down your throat," complained Pendleton James, who headed presidential

personnel for President Reagan.[20]

The mileage to be gotten out of patronage is not great, however, and it is concentrated at the beginning of an administration. The president receives only a little credit when he makes an appointment, and he receives much grief when he fails to make an appointment. President Taft's dictum still holds: "Every time I make an appointment I create nine enemies and one ingrate." Most often the job of the president's congressional liaison in dealing with patronage is one of damage limitation.[21] Almost every president is criticized by his own political party when, early in his administration, not enough jobs for the party faithful are forthcoming.[22]

Similarly, using programs or construction projects in congressional districts to win votes in Congress is often overrated. In the first place, an administration does not have carte blanche in placing projects. White House pressure can be helpful at times, but most laws governing projects contain quite specific criteria, which are conscientiously applied by bureaucrats. Even when the White House can influence the outcome, it is not always wise to do so. "I never swapped a vote for a project," recalled Johnson aide Henry Hall Wilson. "That would have been extremely crude, and wouldn't have worked. Once word got around, everybody would have wanted to trade their votes for projects."[23]

17. See Bowles, *White House and Capitol Hill.*

18. O'Neill, *Man of the House*, p. 308.

19. Quoted in Joel Swerdlow, "How to Handle the First 100 Days," *Potomac Magazine, Washington Post*, 9 Jan. 1977, p. 25.

20. *Wall Street Journal*, 31 Aug. 1982.

21. See Bowles, *White House and Capitol Hill*, p. 74. See also Theodore Sorensen, *Kennedy* (New York: Harper & Row, 1965), p. 349.

22. See James P. Pfiffner, "Nine Enemies and One Ingrate: Political Appointments during Presidential Transitions," in *The In-and-Outers*, ed. Calvin Mackenzie (Baltimore, MD: Johns Hopkins University Press, 1987), pp. 60-76.

23. Bowles, *White House and Capitol Hill*, p. 79.

For the most part, therefore, an effective congressional liaison operation is concerned not with specific arm twisting and vote trading but rather with the longer-term strategic task of creating an atmosphere of cooperation between the White House and Congress. Instead of trying to convert votes on specific issues from opposition to support, congressional liaison operatives, according to Cary Covington, concentrate on

the relatively mundane and routine actions of maintaining and mobilizing their existing coalitional base of support . . . the bulk of their time is spent communicating with congressmen, listening to their concerns, keeping them informed of the status of the president's priorities, rewarding the president's supporters, and seeking to create a diffusely sympathetic environment, rather than pressuring recalcitrant or wavering members into adopting the president's position.[24]

Creating a favorable atmosphere for the president in Congress is a long-term undertaking, and negative pressure must be applied very selectively. "It's just not a good idea to tell people to jump out the window on behalf of your bill," according to Larry O'Brien. "You don't go up to a member when a vote is coming up and say 'Hello, congressman, we haven't met in three months, but we've got a problem on a bill now.' You keep in touch with him. . . . In a tough headcount, the important marginal difference is made 9 out of 10 times by the element of human relations."[25]

The human and social factors in presidential relations with Congress are important, according to the professionals.

24. Cary Covington, "Mobilizing Congressional Support for the President: Insights from the 1960s," *Legislative Studies Quarterly*, 12(1):91-92 (Feb. 1987).

25. Bowles, *White House and Capitol Hill*, pp. 65, 73.

The matter of the *Sequoia* serves as an example. Since the 1930s, presidents had used the *Sequoia*, the presidential yacht, as an informal setting for low-key congressional lobbying. Nevertheless, Jimmy Carter decided to sell the yacht to symbolize his administration's austerity. This action did not win praise from O'Neill: "More than any of the other trappings of power, the *Sequoia* provided a unique opportunity for the president to spend a relaxed couple of hours socializing and talking business with small groups of legislators in a serene and friendly environment," Tip O'Neill has observed. "If somebody had only arranged a few evenings on that yacht with the right people, the president [Carter] could have accomplished far more on Capitol Hill than he actually did."[26] The kind of political small talk and storytelling that Lyndon Johnson relished and Ronald Reagan is so adept at was eschewed by Jimmy Carter, however, and that hurt him on the Hill.

The human and social side of courting Congress is also emphasized in the granting of small favors to members of Congress. The Johnson White House, for example, was generous and systematic about giving out personally signed photographs of the president, cuff links with the presidential seal, tours of the White House for constituents, visits to the White House, flights on Air Force One, and trips on the *Sequoia*. These favors were kept track of carefully and were consciously used to political advantage. In a detailed analysis of White House invitations, Cary Covington found that the Kennedy and Johnson administrations carefully used invitations to the White House to reward their strong supporters, regardless of party. The strategy

26. O'Neill, *Man of the House*, p. 315.

was used to assure the support of allies rather than to recruit new supporters.[27]

Other tokens that are highly prized by members of Congress are pens used by the president in signing bills into law. These are mounted in glass cases and framed with inscriptions of the titles of the laws for which they were used. Presidents at times go to some length to have more pens for presentation. They can sign each letter of their names with a different pen and add dates and locations of signing in order to use enough pens. In what must be a record, President Johnson used 72 pens in the signing of the Economic Opportunity Act in 1964. By contrast, President Carter, at the end of his first two years, still refused to use more than two pens to sign a bill.[28]

The lesson to be drawn is that, though vote trading, arm twisting, and the granting of specific favors do go on, the bulk of the presidential courting of Congress is done in a low-key manner and is aimed at rewarding friends and maintaining the president's coalition. The assumption is that if these activities are done well, the tough, marginal votes will be easier to win in the crunch. While Edwards argues that these votes are only marginal, professional politicians insist on their importance.

Presenting the agenda:
The rifle or the shotgun?

President Carter has been criticized for sending too many initiatives to Congress and for failing to set priorities

among them. "Everybody has warned me not to take on too many projects so early in the administration," Carter wrote in his diary, "but it's almost impossible for me to delay something that I see needs to be done."[29] At one point, there were eight major proposals in the House Rules Committee at one time. "We overloaded the circuits and blew a fuse," recalls Frank Moore.[30] The volume of legislation was aggravated by Carter's refusal to rank his many initiatives.

The shotgun strategy seems to have hindered the Carter administration in its first year in office. Carter wrote in his memoirs:

With the advantages of hindsight, it now seems that it would have been advisable to have introduced our legislation in much more careful phases—not in such a rush. We would not have accomplished any more, and perhaps less, but my relations with Congress would have been smoother and the image of undue haste and confusion could have been avoided.[31]

Crowding the legislative calendar in the beginning is not necessarily fatal, however, as demonstrated by Lyndon Johnson.

The question of priorities may instead be a problem of perception. If an administration tries to do many things and fails on a majority of them, the public perception of competence may be lower than if it tries to do only a few things and succeeds.

The Reagan administration very self-consciously chose the rifle strategy. This strategy systematically neglected many goals voiced in the Republican cam-

27. Cary Covington, "'Guess Who's Coming to Dinner': The Distribution of White House Social Invitations and Their Effects on Congressional Support," *American Politics Quarterly*, in press.

28. See Bowles, *White House and Capitol Hill*, pp. 105, 213.

29. Jimmy Carter, *Keeping Faith* (New York: Bantam Books, 1982), p. 65.

30. Telephone interview with Frank Moore, 4 Sept. 1986.

31. Carter, *Keeping Faith*, p. 87.

paign, particularly so-called social issues such as busing, abortion, school prayer, and crime as well as promises to abolish the newly created Departments of Energy and Education. According to Max Friedersdorf, "The president was determined not to clutter up the landscape with extraneous legislation."[32] This drastic limiting of presidential priorities was part of the administration's strategic approach to the presidency. Under this approach, the economy was seen to be the most important issue facing the country, and success on budget priorities—increasing defense spending, cutting social spending, and cutting taxes—was paramount.

This focus in the early Reagan administration's agenda—along with the shrewd tactics of using reconciliation and effective politics in the administration's southern strategy—was an important component in the impressive legislative victories in Reagan's first year. The point here is not necessarily that the rifle is more effective than the shotgun, because Johnson was successful with the shotgun. Rather, the point is that the strategies ought to be consciously chosen and combined with other elements of presidential effectiveness.

THE DEADLOCK OF DEMOCRACY

You have an arrested Government. You have a Government that is not responding to the wishes of the people. You have a Government that is not functioning, a Government whose very energies are stayed and postponed. If you want to release the force of the American people, you have go to get posses-

sion of the Senate and the Presidency as well as the House.[33]

The presidential candidate was arguing that divided government, when the same political party does not control both houses of Congress and the presidency, was preventing the will of the majority from being enacted. He urged the voters to elect a government of a single party, and they did. The candidate was Woodrow Wilson, and the year was 1912. The Wilson presidency and its New Freedom programs marked one of the periods of greatest creativity and cooperation between the president and Congress in the years between Reconstruction and the New Deal.

Later in the twentieth century, an eminent historian made a similar complaint. "Our government lacks unity and teamwork. . . . We oscillate fecklessly between deadlock and a rush of action. . . . We can choose bold and creative national leaders without giving them the means to make their leadership effective."[34] James MacGregor Burns's book, *The Deadlock of Democracy*, published in 1963, argued that periods of creative and productive cooperation between the president and Congress were the exception rather than the rule in American history. He proposed several changes, legislative and constitutional, that would allow our system to have "responsible, committed, effective, and exuberant leadership."[35]

So the frustrations of the separation-of-powers governmental structure are

32. Quoted in Stephen J. Wayne, "Congressional Liaison in the Reagan White House," in *President and Congress: Assessing Reagan's First Year*, ed. Norman Ornstein (Washington, DC: American Enterprise Institute, 1982), p. 56.

33. Wilson, quoted in Lloyd N. Cutler, "The Cost of Divided Government," *New York Times*, 22 Nov. 1987.

34. James MacGregor Burns, *The Deadlock of Democracy* (Englewood Cliffs, NJ: Prentice-Hall, 1967), pp. 324-25.

35. Ibid., p. 340.

not new, but they do seem to be worsening. Lloyd Cutler has pointed out that for the 150 years from John Adams through Franklin Roosevelt we experienced divided government only 25 percent of the time. Later, however, that proportion increased. From Truman through Reagan, the branches were divided 60 percent of the time, and for the past two decades, 80 percent of the time. In the past 20 years, the party winning the presidency failed to hold both houses of Congress in four of five elections. In the whole nineteenth century, this happened only four times.[36] Ticket splitting among voters has also increased: 4 percent of congressional districts split votes between the president and House member in 1900, while 45 percent did so in 1984.

Nevertheless, the system can work quite effectively at times. In 1933 and again in 1965, large Democratic majorities supported presidents bent on major changes. In 1981, Ronald Reagan rode the crest of a wave of public dissatisfaction with the economy. Though the Republicans did not control the House, Reagan was able to capitalize on the Democrats' disarray in forging a coalition in the House to pass virtually all of his legislative priorities in his first year in office.

Even successful chief legislators have not been able to sustain their momentum throughout their terms, however. Roosevelt suffered legislative setbacks after his initial victories. Johnson's ruling coalition dissolved with the Ninetieth Congress and growing opposition to the war in Vietnam. Reagan and Congress have been at loggerheads since 1982.

In normal times, when we are not in a period of major congressional-presi-

dential synergy, laws are still passed and issues are addressed, though not in the systematic way that many would desire. Compromise is the rule, and no one is fully satisfied.

After experiencing the Carter administration's frustration with Congress, Lloyd Cutler, White House counsel to President Carter, wrote an article titled "To Form a Government," in which he argued that the constitutional roadblocks in the system of checks and balances were too great and that it was time for a series of reforms to move us toward a parliamentary system.[37] Scholars began to write about the lack of two-term presidents since Eisenhower and the "no-win presidency."

In 1981, Ronald Reagan did the unexpected: he began his administration with a series of legislative victories that made impressive changes in the national agenda and policy priorities. Brandishing his claimed mandate, he and his able lieutenants, Office of Management and Budget director David Stockman and chief of staff James Baker, moved with dispatch to rewrite President Carter's lame-duck budget. They then shepherded Reagan's economic priorities—deep cuts in taxes and the domestic budget along with increases in defense spending—through the gauntlet of congressional procedures to win virtually all of their major priorities within their first six months in office.[38]

The 1981 experience demonstrated that, despite the reassertion of con-

---

36. Cutler, "Cost of Divided Government."

37. Lloyd Cutler, "To Form a Government," *Foreign Affairs*, 59:127 (Fall 1980).

38. For an analysis of Reagan's 1981 legislative and budget victories, see James P. Pfiffner, "The Reagan Budget Juggernaut: The Fiscal 1982 Budget Campaign," in *The President and Economic Policy*, ed. James P. Pfiffner (Philadelphia: ISHI, 1986).

gressional prerogatives in the 1970s and especially the new procedures of the 1974 Budget Act, presidential leadership was still possible and necessary. Reagan showed that a strong president, even when not elected with a landslide victory, could mobilize public opinion and put together a coalition in a split Congress to enact major changes in the policy agenda.

That impressive initial leadership has not been sustained throughout the Reagan presidency. Immediately after the initial budget victories, consensus broke down over how to deal with the huge deficits generated by the early Reagan economic policies. The rest of the 1980s have been dominated by budgetary deadlock between the president and Congress.

While the lack of budget cooperation during the Reagan presidency is not unusual for divided government, an even more serious breakdown in comity between the branches occurred in the Iran-contra scandal.

During 1985 and 1986, the Reagan administration decided to try to obtain release of U.S. hostages held in Lebanon by giving arms to Iran in exchange for Iran's help in freeing the hostages. While the United States, through secret and devious means, managed to ship a significant amount of arms to Iran, only two hostages were released. When word of the attempted deals leaked out, the administration tried to cover it up but eventually admitted to the effort.

The arms-for-hostages deal was against the official U.S. policy of not dealing with terrorists, and it undercut U.S. relations with those allies whom the United States had importuned not to sell arms to Iran. It also contradicted President Reagan's previous frequent condemnations of giving in to terrorists. While the actions taken may have been

unwise, and while the administration should not have lied to Congress and the public in covering up the relationship with Iran, the decision to attempt a rapprochement with a hostile nation is generally at the discretion of the president.

When the payments from Iran for the U.S. arms were diverted to help the contra rebels in Nicaragua, however, the bounds of comity were clearly overstepped. The aid was given during the time when the Boland amendment prohibited "any direct or indirect" aid to the contras. This violation of the spirit of the Constitution prompted the Iran-contra committee of Congress to state:

In the Iran-Contra Affair, officials viewed the law not as setting boundaries for their actions, but raising impediments to their goals. When the goals and the law collided, the law gave way. The covert program of support for the Contras evaded the Constitution's most significant check on Executive power: the President can spend funds on a program only if he can convince Congress to appropriate the money.[39]

CONCLUSION

Over the years, Americans have been fascinated with proposals for constitutional changes that might relieve the frustrations of divided government and the breakdown of comity. The 1980s were marked by a resurgence of such proposals to deal with unacceptably high budgetary deficits and disagreements between the president and Con-

39. U.S., Congress, Senate, Select Committee on Secret Military Assistance to Iran and the Nicaraguan Opposition, and U.S., Congress, House, Select Committee to Investigate Covert Arms Transactions with Iran, *Report of the Congressional Committees Investigating the Iran-Contra Affair*, 100th Cong., 1st sess., Nov. 1987, S. Rept. 100-216 and H. Rept. 100-433, p. 18.

gress over foreign policy. The perennial favorites of the balanced-budget amendment and the item veto captured the imagination of some.

More fundamental reforms to the separation-of-powers system, however, have been proposed by those who think that the system is inherently biased toward stalemate and that a more expeditious system is necessary for the United States in the twentieth century. Among the reforms that have been proposed are a four-year term for House members and an eight-year term for senators and some device to force voters to vote for a party ticket. In addition, mechanisms have been proposed to allow the president and/or Congress to dissolve the government and require new elections when an impasse has been reached. All of these proposals, among others, are predicated on the need for more party discipline in Congress and the desire to move the United States toward a parliamentary model of government.

Arthur Schlesinger, Jr., who believes the problem is one of personnel—we should elect better presidents—disagrees with those who seek solutions in structural change.[40] He points out the irony that reformers during the Nixon administration thought that a more nearly parliamentary system would give the legislature more power and allow it to fight presidential usurpation more effectively, while during the Carter administration, reformers felt that a more nearly parliamentary system would give the president the power that he needed to command legislative support and lead the country.

In pointing to British experience over the past century, Schlesinger concludes that the British have read their history better and that a parliamentary system leads to dominance by the executive.[41]

Whether one thinks that fundamental constitutional change is necessary to deal with the problems of institutional conflict previously cited depends on how one conceives of the problem. If one believes that the problem is one of a latent majority within the electorate in favor of concerted action but frustrated by the checks and balances of the separation-of-powers system, then one will likely favor fundamental change in our institutions. In this situation, a more nearly parliamentary system would allow the government to act more expeditiously.

If, on the other hand, the inability of Congress and the president to agree on the solution to the deficit problem or on a coherent foreign policy accurately reflects divisions within the electorate, a structural change will not solve the problem of lack of agreement. With a country divided, allowing one side to have its way will lead to further conflict rather than concerted action.

Schlesinger argues that presidential leadership is necessary in situations of crisis. That leadership cannot be conferred, however, by giving the president the authority to act without congressional approval. Presidential leadership must be demonstrated by convincing Congress and the electorate of the wisdom of a particular course of action. If the president is successful in convincing the public that a given course of action is wise, Congress will follow.[42]

40. For the arguments for structural change, see James L. Sundquist, *Constitutional Reform and Effective Government* (Washington, DC: Brookings Institution, 1986); James MacGregor Burns, *The Power to Lead* (New York: Simon & Schuster, 1984).

41. Arthur Schlesinger, Jr., *The Cycles of American History* (Boston: Houghton Mifflin, 1986), pp. 301-4.

42. See Sam Kernell, *Going Public* (Washington, DC: CQ Press, 1987).

Ronald Reagan was convincing in 1981. The Democrats in Congress did not fully support the Reagan economic prescription, but they were convinced that the people, particularly in their home districts, did; and they gave him the votes he needed to enact his program. But Reagan has not provided that kind of leadership in the budgetary arena during the remainder of his administration. He has continued to propose his 1981 program, but members of Congress have felt that the fiscal and political situation of the country has changed and that the same policies are no longer appropriate. Reagan has refused to make the kind of compromises that Republicans in the Senate and within his own administration urged upon him, and deadlock has resulted. Congress alone has not been able to enact budgetary solutions; presidential leadership is necessary but has not been forthcoming.

In foreign policy, President Reagan has felt that the Sandinista government in Nicaragua is a fundamental threat to the United States and that support to the contras is vital to U.S. interests. He has made this argument in Congress and to the public, but neither has agreed.[43] Congress expressed its policy position by passing the Boland amendment, which was signed by the president.

The Reagan administration resorted to secret support for the contras. When it failed to secure support for the policy in Congress, it decided to circumvent the Constitution by resorting to secret aid through nonappropriated funds.

American historical experience has shown that foreign military entanglements that are not supported by Congress cannot be sustained by presidential will. In order to sustain active military commitments, presidents must convince the people and Congress that military action is essential to our national interests. If they refuse to or cannot convince the people or Congress, the policies are doomed to die from lack of support.

Schlesinger sums up the argument against making it easier for a president to commit the United States to military action. "The separation of powers . . . has permitted action when a majority is convinced that the action is right. In short, if the executive has a persuasive remedy, you don't need fundamental constitutional change. If the executive remedy is not persuasive, you don't want fundamental constitutional change."[44]

Without fundamental constitutional change, the kind of presidential-congressional cooperation that marked the early years of the administrations of Franklin Roosevelt, Lyndon Johnson, and Ronald Reagan will recur only in unusual sets of circumstances—landslides, partisan majorities in Congress, and broad public consensus that change is needed. Short of that change, presidents seeking cooperation in Congress will be forced to make their cases convincingly to the Congress. In making their cases, the kinds of legislative skills that a president possesses will continue to play an important role.

43. For a discussion of the series of votes on aid to the contras, see Victor C. Johnson, "Congress and Contra Aid 1986-87," in *Latin America and Caribbean Contemporary Record*, vol. 6, *1986-87*, ed. Abraham F. Lowenthal (New York: Holmes & Meier, forthcoming).

44. Schlesinger, *Cycles of American History*, p. 311.

The President's Veto Power

By RICHARD A. WATSON

ABSTRACT: Drawing upon experiences with legislatively dominated government at the state and national levels in the post-Revolution period, the Founders granted the president the power to veto bills passed by Congress. An analysis of all vetoes cast by modern presidents in office from 1933 to 1981, beginning with Franklin Roosevelt and ending with Jimmy Carter, indicates that Roosevelt used the power most frequently. If, however, one focuses on public bills of national significance and takes into account the number of years each of these presidents served, Gerald Ford was the most significant vetoer of the period. Harry Truman vetoed more major bills than any of the other modern presidents and was also overridden most frequently by Congress on such bills. Most vetoed bills are eventually passed and signed by the president in a different form. The president can also affect legislation by threatening to veto proposed bills: such action may prevent their passage at all or may influence Congress to put them in a form that is acceptable to him.

Richard Watson, professor of political science at the University of Missouri, Columbia, received LL.B. and Ph.D. degrees from the University of Michigan. He has served as a fellow at the Center for Advanced Study in the Behavioral Sciences at Stanford and as a guest scholar at the Brookings Institution. His two most recent books are The Politics of the Presidency *(coauthored with Norman C. Thomas) and* The Presidential Contest, *both published in 1988. He is working on a study of presidential vetoes and national policymaking.*

NOTE: The author would like to acknowledge the financial support of the Earhart Foundation, Project '87, and the University of Missouri-Columbia Research Council.

THE most potent legal weapon available to the president in his perennial battles with Congress is the veto power by which he can prevent at least temporarily, and often permanently, the enactment of measures passed by that legislative body. In his classic *Congressional Government*, Woodrow Wilson characterized the power as, "beyond all comparison," the president's "most formidable weapon"; in exercising the veto, he explained, "the president acts not as the executive, but as a third branch of the legislature."[1]

Today, among all the leaders of the world's major democratic countries, only the American president possesses and actually uses the executive veto power in the process of policymaking.[2] This article traces briefly the establishment and development of the president's veto power and then focuses on the use of that power by modern presidents, beginning with Franklin Roosevelt and ending with Jimmy Carter. It next analyzes congressional responses to these modern vetoes and concludes with an assessment of the impact of the president's veto power on policymaking by the national government.

ESTABLISHMENT OF THE PRESIDENT'S VETO POWER

While the origins of the president's veto power can be traced back to the early Roman Republic and later to England, its more immediate precedents developed here in America at the state level. Most of the governorships in the period following the Revolution were weak offices overshadowed by state legislatures, reflecting the colonists' unfortunate experiences with the arbitrary executive power exercised by King George III and colonial governors sent as emissaries of the Crown. There were, however, two exceptions to that rule. The British occupation of New York required that state to develop a strong governorship free of legislative dominance in order to handle its military and civilian affairs. In Massachusetts, the voters adopted a constitution that included a popularly elected governor, who was eligible to succeed himself. Both states granted the governor substantial powers, including that of vetoing legislation passed by the state legislature.

Experiences with the national government in the post-Revolution period paralleled those of the states. The distaste for executive power was reflected in the Articles of Confederation, which provided for a national legislative body but no executive branch at all. Attempts to administer laws through ad hoc committees, councils, or conventions proved to be unsuccessful. Ultimately, Congress was forced to create departments of diplomacy, war, and finance and to appoint eminent people, such as Robert Livingston, John Jay, and Robert Morris, to head their activities.[3]

Thus experiences at both the state and national levels with weak and nonexistent executives convinced those who gathered for the Constitutional Convention that there should be some type of national executive and that he should

---

1. Woodrow Wilson, *Congressional Government: A Study in American Politics* (Boston: Houghton Mifflin, 1885), p. 52.

2. The monarch of Great Britain still theoretically possesses the power to withhold assent from measures passed by Parliament, but no British monarch has actually utilized that power since 1707.

3. C. C. Thach, Jr., *The Creation of the Presidency, 1775-1789: A Study in Constitutional History* (Baltimore, MD: Johns Hopkins University Press, 1922), chap. 3.

possess the veto power, as did the governors of New York and Massachusetts. The fact that the governors of those two states served effectively without endangering political freedom convinced many of the delegates that a strong chief executive accountable to the people was not to be equated with a tyrannical king or colonial governor.

A number of arguments were made in favor of vesting the veto prerogative in the president, the principal one being that the executive needed such a power to protect itself against encroachment at the hands of Congress. James Madison also stated at the convention that it would help to prevent "popular or factious injustice,"[4] by which he meant rule by the capricious majority or by selfish minorities. It would also be "an additional check against the pursuit of those unwise and unjust measures which constituted so great a portion of our calamities."[5]

While the delegates were in agreement on the desirability of an executive veto, they disagreed on the form the veto should take. One basic issue was whether the executive should exercise the veto in conjunction with the members of the judiciary, as was provided for in the New York Constitution, or alone, as was done under the Massachusetts Constitution. Madison argued that the president would be more firm in his resolve to use the veto if he exercised it jointly with the judges and that having the latter share in the veto power would help to avoid the passage of laws that were unwise in principle or incorrect in form. Elbridge Gerry of Massachusetts countered that "the Executive while standing alone would be more impartial than

when he could be covered by the sanction and seduced by the sophistry of the Judges"[6] and that blending the judicial and executive departments in that way would "bind them together in an offensive and defensive alliance against the Legislature and render the latter unwilling to enter into a contest with them."[7] Ultimately, Gerry's arguments prevailed, and the president alone was granted the power to veto laws passed by Congress.[8]

Another major issue concerning the veto was whether it should be absolute or whether it should be qualified, that is, subject to being overridden by the two houses of Congress. Despite the fact that Alexander Hamilton and James Wilson favored the absolute veto, the delegates ultimately adopted the qualified form of the veto, with a two-thirds veto in both houses required to override the president's veto. They did, however, provide for one variant of the absolute veto. If a bill was presented to the chief executive at the end of a legislative session and he took no action on it, and if Congress had adjourned by the end of the ten-day period he had to consider it, the president was said to have exercised a pocket veto, one that could not be overridden by Congress.

Thus the veto power that emerged from the deliberations of the Constitutional Convention became a potentially important weapon for the president in his struggles with Congress. It remained to be seen, however, how that weapon would actually be utilized by our chief executives.

4. Max Farrand, ed., *The Records of the Federal Convention of 1787* (New Haven, CT: Yale University Press, 1966), 2:587.
5. Ibid., p. 74.
6. Ibid., 1:139.
7. Ibid., 2:78.
8. It should be noted, however, that the Supreme Court does possess a type of veto through the power of judicial review, whereby it can declare congressional laws unconstitutional and thus render them null and void.

DEVELOPMENT OF THE
PRESIDENT'S VETO POWER

Early presidents were not inclined to use the veto power. Three years passed in George Washington's administration before he vetoed an act of Congress, and another four years before he cast his second and final veto. John Adams, Thomas Jefferson, and John Quincy Adams cast no vetoes at all, and James Monroe vetoed only one piece of legislation. The only early president to use the power with any frequency was James Madison, who vetoed seven bills in all. Thus the first six presidential administrations, covering a period of 40 years, from 1789 to 1829, witnessed a total of ten vetoes, and as indicated, seven of those were attributable to Madison alone.

When early presidents did veto legislation, they tended to emphasize constitutional objections. For example, Madison's use of the power on legislation relating to Protestant churches cited the First Amendment language that "Congress shall make no law respecting an establishment of religion."[9] The fact that the president thought a bill was unwise—that is, constituted bad public policy—was not generally considered a sufficient reason for vetoing it.

When Andrew Jackson assumed the presidency in 1829, the use of the veto power changed radically. Jackson vetoed 12 bills in his eight years in office, more than all his predecessors combined. Moreover, he did not hesitate to substitute his judgment on policy matters for that of the Congress. In his famous message vetoing a bill regarding a national bank, Jackson not only cited constitutional grounds for his disapproval but also emphasized concerns of social and economic justice in order to gain the support of the "humble members of society" for his action.[10] Joseph Kallenbach suggests that the veto message "was a powerful appeal to the citizenry of the country for support, a campaign document for the forthcoming presidential election."[11]

Subsequent presidents continued to differ on the extent to which they cast vetoes and their reasons for doing so. Some continued the early tradition: Van Buren vetoed only one bill; Harrison, Taylor, and Fillmore, none at all. John Tyler, however, followed the Jackson precedent by vetoing ten bills, which led his opponents in Congress to introduce a resolution to impeach him for "the high crime and misdemeanor of withholding his assent to laws indispensable to the just operations of government, which involved no constitutional difficulty on his part."[12] The resolution failed.

For the most part, however, what Kallenbach terms Jackson's "tribunative" view of the veto authority ultimately prevailed. Andrew Johnson cast 29 vetoes; Grant, 93; and Grover Cleveland, a total of 584 in his two administrations. Writing at the end of the first century of the nation's existence, Edward Mason summarized the major differences between the veto in 1789 and 1889 as follows: "[In 1789] it was used sparingly and in a cumbrous manner as a weapon of constitutional welfare; today it is used frequently and easily as a means of preventing mistakes in the administration of the business of government."[13]

9. James D. Richardson, *A Compilation of the Messages and Papers of the Presidents, 1789-1897* (Washington, DC: Authority of Congress, 1900), 1:489-90.

10. Ibid., 2:590.

11. Joseph Kallenbach, *The American Chief Executive: The Presidency and the Governorship* (New York: Harper & Row, 1966), p. 354.

12. *Congressional Globe*, 27th Cong., 3d sess., 12:144.

13. Edward Mason, *The Veto Power: Its Origin, Development, and Function in the Govern-*

For the most part, presidents who cast vetoes prevailed in their conflicts with Congress. None of Jackson's 12 vetoes was overridden. It was not until 1845, the day that President Tyler left office, that Congress first overrode an executive veto. Prior to Franklin Roosevelt's ascension to office, only Andrew Johnson, who suffered 15 overrides, lost a significant number of veto battles with the national legislature.[14]

USE OF THE VETO POWER BY MODERN PRESIDENTS

Students of the presidency generally consider Franklin Delano Roosevelt as the first of the modern presidents.[15] With his administration, the national government established the concept of the positive state, whereby it undertook the obligation to provide for the welfare of all the American people. In the process, Roosevelt pushed major domestic programs through the Congress, reorganized the executive branch, became an effective molder of public opinion through the use of his fireside chats and press conferences, and led the nation in a world war that spanned several continents. Thus the present analysis of modern presidential vetoes begins with Roosevelt and ends with Jimmy Carter, the most recent president who has finished his term of office. This 48-year span, from 1933 to 1981, covers eight presidencies, one-fifth of those over our 200-year history.

ment of the United States, 1789-1889 (Boston: Ginn, 1891), p. 140.

14. Next in terms of frequency was Woodrow Wilson, who was overridden on six occasions.

15. See Fred Greenstein, Larry Berman, and Alvin Felzenberg, Evolution of the Modern Presidency: A Bibliographical Survey (Washington, DC: American Enterprise Institute, 1977).

Table 1 shows the incidence of the use of the veto power by each of the presidents who served during this period. Franklin Roosevelt in just over 12 years cast 635 vetoes, exceeding the 584 that Grover Cleveland exercised in his eight years in office. Next in line were Harry Truman and Dwight Eisenhower, whose 250 and 181 vetoes, respectively, rank them as third and fourth among all the persons who have served in the office. In contrast, John F. Kennedy and Lyndon Johnson cast only 21 and 30 vetoes, respectively; of the presidents serving in this century, only Warren Harding, with 6 vetoes, exercised the power on fewer occasions.

In assessing the importance of vetoes cast by presidents, however, it is important to distinguish between those relating to private and public legislation. The former names a particular individual or entity such as a business that is to receive relief from the federal government in the form of a claim based on a financial loss, the payment of a pension, a granting of citizenship, and the like. In contrast, a public bill relates to matters affecting all individuals and businesses, or those belonging to certain categories or classifications. Public bills are more significant because they affect a much broader range of individuals and groups than private bills do.

Table 1 indicates the number of private and public bills vetoed by each of the presidents in the period from 1933 to 1981. It should be noted that during the first five presidencies, that is, from Roosevelt through Johnson, vetoes of private legislation were more numerous than those of public bills. Beginning with the Nixon presidency and continuing through the Carter administration, the opposite situation prevailed: vetoes of public bills far exceeded those of private ones. A

TABLE 1
VETOES CAST BY PRESIDENTS ROOSEVELT THROUGH CARTER, 1933-81

| President | Bills Vetoed | | | Number of | |
	Private	Public	Total	Years Served	Vetoes per Year
Roosevelt	497	138	635	12.37	51.33
Truman	169	81	250	7.63	32.77
Eisenhower	103	78	181	8.00	22.62
Kennedy	12	9	21	2.90	7.24
Johnson	16	14	30	5.10	5.88
Nixon	3	40	43	5.69	7.56
Ford	5	61	66	2.31	28.57
Carter	2	29	31	4.00	7.75
Total	807	450	1,257	48.00	26.19 (average)

SOURCES: *Presidential Vetoes, 1789-1976*, comp. Senate Library (Washington, DC: Government Printing Office, 1978); *Presidential Vetoes, 1977-1984*, comp. Senate Library (Washington, DC: Government Printing Office, 1985).

major reason for this change was the passage in 1966 of a law that greatly facilitated the consideration by the United States Claims Court of private cases referred to it by Congress.[16] As a result, in recent years, Congress has passed far fewer private bills that presidents could veto.[17] In addition, Presidents Nixon and Carter vetoed a smaller percentage—less than 1 percent—of private bills that were passed by Congress than any of the other six presidents.[18]

While the distinction between private and public bills is significant, it should also be noted that not all public legislation is of equal importance. For example, some of it deals with essentially local matters, such as the sale of the Port of Newark Army Supply Base to the city of Newark, or minor national legislation, such as the authorization of the postmaster general to operate motor vehicles seized for violations of customs laws. An analysis of the 450 public bills vetoed between 1933 and 1981 determined that 259 of them involved significant policies of concern to the nation.[19]

Table 2 focuses on the incidence of vetoes of public bills over the period 1933-81, with particular attention to those relating to legislation of national significance. The three most recent presidents not only vetoed more public than

16. The legislation authorized trial commissioners of the Claims Court, rather than the Court itself, to consider and report on congressionally referred cases. *Guide to Congress*, 3d ed. (Washington, DC: CQ Press, 1982), p. 359.

17. For example, in just over five years of the Johnson administration, Congress passed 1088 private bills; in the some five and three-fourths years that President Nixon served, 494 such bills were enacted; and during the four years of the Carter administration, 293 private bills were passed.

18. Franklin Roosevelt vetoed 497 of 3916 private bills, which represents about one in eight of those passed by Congress during his administration. Next in terms of frequency was Harry Truman, whose 169 vetoes of 3453 private bills constitutes about one of every twenty such laws enacted during his presidency.

19. As a check on my subjective judgments on the matter, I compared my list of significant presidential vetoes cast since 1945 against vetoes discussed in *Congressional Quarterly*, which began publication that year. I found in almost all cases that it covered the same vetoes as were on my list. When it did not, I resolved the matter in favor of inclusion of vetoes that appeared on either of the lists.

TABLE 2
VETOES OF PUBLIC BILLS BY PRESIDENTS ROOSEVELT THROUGH CARTER, 1933-81

President	All Public Bills Vetoed		Number of Years Served	Significant Bills Vetoed per Year
	Nonsignificant	Significant		
Roosevelt	78	60	12.37	4.85
Truman	44	37	7.63	4.85
Eisenhower	44	34	8.00	4.25
Kennedy	5	4	2.90	1.38
Johnson	5	9	5.10	1.76
Nixon	2	38	5.69	6.68
Ford	6	55	2.31	23.81
Carter	7	22	4.00	5.50
Total	191	259	48.00	5.40 (average)

SOURCES: *Presidential Vetoes, 1789-1976; Presidential Vetoes, 1977-1984.*

private bills, as previously noted, but a high proportion of the public bills they vetoed were also of national significance. When the length of term is taken into account, all three of them cast more vetoes of significant bills per year than did any of their five predecessors. That statistic also indicates that President Ford was by far the most important vetoer of the 1933-81 period, while Presidents Kennedy and Johnson were the least important vetoers.

One final aspect of presidential vetoes cast during the 1933-81 period should be assessed, namely, which of the eight presidents vetoed the greatest number of major bills, that is, those of most importance to the nation? This judgment is admittedly a very subjective one, but I believe that Harry Truman earns the distinction. Among the 37 nationally significant bills that he vetoed were a number relating to both the domestic economy and internal security. Included in the former category were the Taft-Hartley law regulating labor-management relations and the McCarran bill that sought to convey title to offshore oil resources—mistakenly referred to as "tidelands" oil—owned by the national government to the states. Included in

the latter were the Internal Security Act, also sponsored by Senator McCarran, which required the registration of Communist and other suspect groups with the attorney general and authorized the detention of persons thought likely to commit espionage and sedition, and the McCarran-Walter Act, controlling the immigration and deportation of "subversives" and persons with Communist affiliations. In addition to this historic legislation, President Truman also vetoed the Kerr bill, exempting independent gas producers from regulation by the Federal Power Commission, and three separate tax bills, even though presidents generally defer to Congress on revenue measures. Truman's own assessment after he left office that he "found it necessary to veto more major bills than any other president with the possible exception of Grover Cleveland"[20] would also apply to the veto record of the six presidents who succeeded him in office.

CONGRESSIONAL RESPONSE

When a president casts a regular veto—not pocket veto—he returns the affected bill to the house in which it

20. Harry S. Truman, *Memoirs*, vol. 2, *Years*

originated, the Senate or the House of Representatives. He also issues an official veto message setting forth his reasons for exercising the veto. The chamber involved must then decide what to do about the matter. It may take an immediate vote to sustain or override the veto, or the vote may be postponed to a fixed date. The matter may also be referred to a committee, and if it is not reported back to the entire chamber— which is typically the case—the veto is considered to be unchallenged. A vote to sustain the president's veto or not to challenge it ends the matter. If the chamber decides by a two-thirds vote[21] to override the president's veto, the bill is sent to the second chamber, which has similar options in dealing with it. Only if the second house also votes to override the bill by a two-thirds vote is the veto overridden by the entire Congress; the bill thus becomes law.

The infrequency with which Congress overrode presidential vetoes, noted for the earlier period, continues in the modern era. Of the 1257 vetoes cast between 1933 and 1981, only 42 were actually overridden by both houses of Congress.[22]

---

of Trial and Hope (Garden City, NY: Doubleday, 1956), p. 479.

21. The Supreme Court has held that the two-thirds requirement applies to the override vote itself—providing a quorum is present—not to the membership of the chamber. *Missouri-Pacific Railway Co.* v. *Kansas*, 248 U.S. 276 (1919).

22. In addition to these 42 occasions when Congress actually voted to override presidential vetoes, two other vetoes cast by President Nixon were considered to be overridden because the federal courts ruled that his attempts to use pocket vetoes during short, intra-, and intersession adjournments of Congress were unconstitutional. In so ruling, the courts noted that Congress had made arrangements to have officers receive veto messages while it was in adjournment, and so the Congress had not prevented their return as is contemplated by the Constitution for valid pocket vetoes. Under these circumstances, the two bills became law and are counted officially as being

Thus fewer than 1 in 25 vetoes cast over the 48-year period ended in a clear defeat for the chief executive.

This overall statistic is very misleading, however. Of the 1257 vetoes, 517 were pocket vetoes of private and public bills that Congress had no power to override. Moreover, of the 807 private bills vetoed by Presidents Roosevelt through Carter, only one—by Truman—was overridden. Finally, Congress failed to override any of the 191 nonsignificant public bills referred to in Table 2. A better comparison of the relationship between presidential vetoes and congressional overrides involves only regular vetoes of public bills of national significance. Table 3 contains information on that category of presidential vetoes.

Table 3 indicates that Congress did override Presidents Roosevelt through Carter on many such occasions. As indicated by the final column on the right, 24 percent of presidential vetoes of public bills of national significance were ultimately overridden by Congress. Column 4 shows that Congress attempted to override presidential vetoes 62 percent of the time when it could do so, and 39 percent of those attempts were successful (see column 6).

The table also shows great variation in the way in which Congress responded to vetoes cast by the various presidents. President Truman was ultimately overridden the greatest percentage of the time, 37; however, Congress attempted to override President Nixon the most, on 87 percent of his vetoes. Presidents Truman and Carter share the dubious distinction of being successfully overridden by Congress on the greatest proportion of attempts, namely, 50 percent.

The overrides of President Truman's

---

overridden by Congress even though they actually were not.

TABLE 3
CONGRESSIONAL RESPONSE TO REGULAR VETOES ON
NATIONALLY SIGNIFICANT PUBLIC BILLS, 1933-81

President	Vetoes	Attempts to Override		Successful Overrides		Vetoes Overridden (percentage)
		Number	Percentage	Number	Percentage	
Roosevelt	38	19	50.00	9	47.37	23.68
Truman	30	22	73.33	11	50.00	36.67
Eisenhower	20	10	50.00	2	20.00	10.00
Kennedy	0	0	0	0	0	0
Johnson	4	0	0	0	0	0
Nixon*	24	21	87.50	5	23.81	20.83
Ford	42	28	66.67	12	42.86	28.57
Carter	11	4	36.36	2	50.00	18.18
Total	169	104	61.54 (average)	41	39.42 (average)	24.26 (average)

SOURCES: *Presidential Vetoes, 1789-1976*; *Presidential Vetoes, 1977-1984*.
*This row does not include action on two pocket vetoes that were later declared to be unconstitutional. See fn. 22 of the present article.

vetoes also occurred on the most important bills. Included were three of the four historic pieces of legislation listed in the previous section—the Taft-Hartley bill, the internal security bill, and the McCarran-Walter Act; Congress did not challenge his vetoes of the offshore oil and natural gas bills. Moreover, Congress also overrode one of his vetoes of income-tax legislation. In the period from 1933 to 1981, Congress was not inclined to try to override a president on private or public bills with no significance for national policymaking, but Congress attempted to override the president in about three of five vetoes of bills of national significance and was successful in overriding about one in four such vetoes.

EFFECT OF THE PRESIDENT'S VETO POWER ON SIGNIFICANT LEGISLATION

The exercise of the president's veto power does not end the battle between Congress and the White House over the

affected legislation. As indicated earlier, Congress may override the veto, which has the effect of enacting the bill into law, and the override may be considered a complete victory for the legislative body on that matter. Alternatively, Congress may persist by sending a similar bill back to the president or his successor and, if it is then signed by the chief executive into law, this procedure may be thought of as constituting a partial victory for Congress.

The president may also prevail in the battle. Congress's taking no further action on the matter may be considered a complete victory for the chief executive. Moreover, the president or a successor may sign into law a bill that is closer to the president's view on the matter than to Congress's.[23] This result constitutes a partial victory for the president.

23. In veto messages, presidents frequently indicate the specific provisions they object to in the legislation involved and may also suggest what they would like to see substituted in their place. They may also express their views in press conferences and other public forums.

TABLE 4
OUTCOME OF PRESIDENTIAL VETOES OF
NATIONALLY SIGNIFICANT PUBLIC BILLS, 1945-81

President	Vetoes	Victory for Congress			Victory for President			Compromise between President and Congress
		Complete	Partial	Total number	Complete	Partial	Total number	
Truman	37	11	9	20	5	7	12	5
Eisenhower	34	2	7	9	6	8	14	11
Kennedy	4	0	1	1	1	0	1	2
Johnson	9	0	0	0	2	2	4	5
Nixon	38	7	5	12	3	2	5	21
Ford	55	12	8	20	9	9	18	17
Carter	22	2	2	4	3	7	10	8
Total	199	34*	32	66	29	35	64	69†

SOURCES: *Presidential Vetoes, 1789-1976*; *Presidential Vetoes, 1977-1984*.
*Includes two pocket vetoes that were held to be unconstitutional.
†Includes two vetoes of bills that involved legalities and hence were not considered to have resulted in a victory for either Congress or the president.

Finally, the battle may end in what is essentially a compromise. This occurs when subsequent legislation is passed that contains provisions favored by both the president and Congress and it is not possible to say the view of one prevailed over the other.

To determine the outcome of vetoes of nationally significant legislation, each of the affected bills was traced in the same and subsequent sessions of Congress[24] through the use of *Congressional Quarterly*. Because that journal did not begin publication until 1945, the analysis begins with that year and ends in 1981. It therefore covers seven administrations, beginning with that of President Truman and ending with that of President Carter. Table 4 contains the essential information on the 199 vetoes of nationally significant public bills cast during that period.

24. Bills were followed five years beyond the one in which the veto occurred, under the assumption that if follow-up efforts on affected legislation were to be made, they would occur during that period of time.

The table indicates that a veto of a nationally significant bill does not generally end the matter. On only 29 bills— those classified in Table 4 as complete presidential vetoes—or about 1 in 7 bills of the total of 199, did no further action take place. The eventual outcomes of conflicts between the president and Congress in the period 1945-81 were fairly evenly divided. Congress won complete or partial victories on 66 bills, the president on 64, and 69 ended in a compromise that favored neither branch. Table 4 also shows that Presidents Eisenhower, Johnson, and Carter tended to win in their battles with Congress over vetoed bills and that Truman and Nixon tended to lose while Kennedy and Ford split fairly evenly in their conflicts with the national legislature.

One final observation is in order with respect to the effect of the president's veto power on legislation. It should not be judged simply on the basis of how often it is actually exercised. Simply by threatening to veto a proposed measure, the president can often deter Congress from passing it. Such a threat can also influence Congress to put a measure in a form that is acceptable to him. President Eisenhower successfully utilized the threat of a veto to affect social programs proposed by the Democratic Congress. This tactic worked because Democratic congressional leaders—Lyndon Johnson, as majority leader of the Senate, and Sam Rayburn, Speaker of the House—wished to avoid conflict with the popular chief executive and were willing to accept half a loaf rather than risk a presidential veto that they calculated could not be overridden.

ANNALS, *AAPSS*, **499**, September 1988

Public Opinion and Presidential Support

By JON R. BOND,
RICHARD FLEISHER, and
MICHAEL NORTHRUP

ABSTRACT: Previous research identifies three variables that might bridge the inevitable conflict between the president and Congress: political party, political ideology, and presidential popularity. While the literature provides unambiguous evidence that party and ideology affect presidential support in Congress, the evidence that public approval affects support is mixed. The study reported in this article seeks to clarify the relationship using a research design that corrects some of the limitations of previous work. The analysis reveals that variables within Congress—party and ideology—have the strongest effect on presidential support. Although presidential popularity exerts statistically significant effects, the substantive effects are marginal. Public approval has slightly stronger effects on foreign-policy issues than on economic issues, and the effects are generally stronger on members of the president's party than on members of the opposition. The marginal effects do not increase in strength as we refine the measure of popularity to approach the relevant public for members of Congress.

Jon R. Bond is professor of political science at Texas A&M University. He has published articles on presidential-congressional relations, congressional elections, and judicial behavior.

Richard Fleisher is associate professor of political science at Fordham University. He has published articles on realignment, party voting in Congress, partisan and presidential-congressional relations.

Michael Northrup graduated from Texas A&M University with a B.A. in political science. He is currently working as a briefing attorney for the Texas Supreme Court.

A basic principle of democracy is that governmental institutions should be responsive to popular preferences. The American system of separately elected executive and legislative branches makes politicians in these institutions responsive to different sets of popular preferences. This arrangement inevitably leads to conflict between the president and Congress.

Previous research has identified several variables that might mitigate the inevitable conflict between the president and Congress and might serve as sources of support for the president's policy preferences. Of these variables, presidential popularity with the public is the most intriguing because it focuses on responsiveness to popular preferences. The evidence that public approval affects support in Congress, however, is mixed. The inconclusive findings may result in part from limitations in the data and research designs. This article seeks to clarify the relationship between presidential popularity and support from members of Congress using data and a research design that correct some of those limitations. Before describing our approach, however, we should review the theory, findings, and limitations of previous research.

LITERATURE AND THEORY

The scholarly literature identifies three variables that might cause members of Congress to support the president: political party, political ideology, and presidential popularity.[1] Party and ideol-

ogy operate from within Congress; public approval is a force external to Congress.

Political party

Research on presidential-congressional relations consistently reveals that members of the president's party support his positions more than do members of the opposition.[2] The president's partisans are predisposed to support his policy preferences for several reasons. First, because members of the same political party must satisfy similar electoral coalitions, they share many policy preferences. While the strength of presidential coattails has decreased recently, V. O. Key's observation remains valid: "When a president goes into office a substantial number of legislators of his party stand committed to the broad policy orientation of the president."[3]

Second, because members of the president's party who seek reelection must

---

1. This list, of course, is not exhaustive. Although other factors such as the president's leadership and the complexity of the policy agenda are no doubt important, we have no way to measure them reliably. Moreover, their effects are likely to be at the margins, in specific cases with particular individuals, rather than general, systematic effects across a representative sample of cases. Because we are seeking to develop general explanations, focusing on party, ideology, and public approval is appropriate.

2. George C. Edwards, *Presidential Influence in Congress* (San Francisco: Freeman, 1980); Jon R. Bond and Richard Fleisher, "The Limits of Presidential Popularity as a Source of Influence in the House," *Legislative Studies Quarterly*, 5:69-78 (Feb. 1980); idem, "Presidential Popularity and Congressional Voting: A Re-examination of Public Opinion as a Source of Influence in Congress," *Western Political Quarterly*, 37:291-306 (June 1984); Paul C. Light, *The President's Agenda: Domestic Policy Choice from Kennedy to Carter* (Baltimore, MD: Johns Hopkins University Press, 1982).

3. V. O. Key, *Politics, Parties and Pressure Groups*, 5th ed. (New York: Thomas Y. Crowell, 1964), p. 658. On the decline of presidential coattails, see John A. Ferejohn and Randall L. Calvert, "Presidential Coattails in Historical Perspective," *American Journal of Political Science*, 28:127-46 (Feb. 1984).

run on his record as well as on their own, they have an incentive to help him succeed. Kingdon found that Republican representatives "often referred to their stake in the administration's success" as a reason for supporting Nixon's policy positions.[4] Research on congressional elections reveals that the president's performance affects the electoral fate of his party, at least indirectly.[5]

Third, members of the same party share a psychological attachment to a common political symbol.[6] They are, in a sense, members of the same political family. American parties, of course, are diverse, so disagreements between the president and members of his party are inevitable, but, as Neustadt observes, "bargaining 'within the family' has a rather different quality than bargaining with members of the rival clan."[7]

Finally, the president has political resources to aid reelection of loyal party members.[8] The effects of these resources are limited because most members of Congress can be reelected without the president's help, but doing favors at least creates a storehouse of goodwill. Although the president can also use these resources to punish nonsupportive members, such efforts are rare and of limited success.[9]

Although political parties are a source of presidential support in Congress, in comparison to political parties in most other Western democracies, American parties are quite weak and undisciplined. Even at its height, party loyalty in Congress barely reached levels found in most responsible party systems.[10] In addition, there is evidence of party decline in recent years.[11]

Thus a president whose party controls Congress has an advantage, but the benefits are limited. Furthermore, the rise of split-ticket voting has increased the likelihood that the president will face a Congress controlled by the opposition.[12] Presidents who seek to provide policy leadership in the American system of separated powers and weak parties must find other ways to link their preferences to those of members of Congress.

4. John Kingdon, *Congressmen's Voting Decisions*, 2d ed. (New York: Harper & Row, 1981), p. 180.

5. Gary C. Jacobson and Samuel Kernell, *Strategy and Choice in Congressional Elections*, 2d ed. (New Haven, CT: Yale University Press, 1983).

6. George C. Edwards, "Presidential Party Leadership in Congress," in *Presidents and Their Parties: Leadership or Neglect?* ed. Robert H. Harmel (New York: Praeger, 1984), pp. 184-87.

7. Richard Neustadt, *Presidential Power: The Politics of Leadership* (New York: John Wiley, 1960), p. 187.

8. Edwards, "Presidential Party Leadership," pp. 191-92.

9. Sidney M. Milkis, "Presidential Party Purges: With Special Emphasis on the Lessons of 1938," in *Presidents and Their Parties: Leadership or Neglect?* ed. Harmel.

10. David W. Brady and Phillip Althoff, "Party Voting in the U.S. House of Representatives: Elements of a Responsible Party System," *Journal of Politics*, 36:753-75 (Aug. 1974).

11. Joseph Cooper and David W. Brady, "Institutional Context and Leadership Style: The House from Canon to Rayburn," *American Political Science Review*, 75:411-25 (June 1981); Barbara Sinclair, "Coping with Uncertainty: Building Coalitions in the House and the Senate," in *The New Congress*, ed. Thomas E. Mann and Norman J. Ornstein (Washington, DC: American Enterprise Institute, 1981); Mellisa P. Collie and David W. Brady, "The Decline of Partisan Voting Coalitions in the House of Representatives," in *Congress Reconsidered*, 3d ed., ed. Lawrence C. Dodd and Bruce I. Oppenheimer (Washington, DC: CQ Press, 1985). Note, however, that party unity has increased during the Reagan presidency.

12. Morris P. Fiorina, "The Presidency and the Contemporary Electoral System," in *The Presidency and the Political System*, ed. Michael Nelson (Washington, DC: CQ Press, 1984).

Political ideology

Political ideology is a second variable that influences congressional support for the president. Whereas the effects of parties result primarily from electoral forces, the effects of ideology derive largely from shared values. Because political ideology is a major influence on roll-call voting in Congress, the president attracts higher levels of support from ideologically sympathetic members of both parties who share his policy preferences.

Party and ideology, of course, are related, and for most members of Congress, they are mutually reinforcing, but each party encompasses individuals who are cross-pressured by an ideology that is outside their party's mainstream. The weak party system allows members great latitude to cross party lines and vote in response to their own ideological preferences. Hence, on most controversial issues, the president will attract support from some cross-pressured members of the opposition, but he will also lose some cross-pressured members of his party.

The influence of ideology on roll-call voting in Congress is well established. Kingdon found that, for many members of Congress, ideology is an important voting cue that structures their decisions. While ideology is less useful for moderates than for ideologues, its influence "is nearly always present."[13] Similarly, Schneider presents evidence that "ideology plays a preponderant role in congressmen's voting decisions."[14]

Ideology influences roll-call voting for several reasons. First, the recruitment process brings to Congress individuals who have strongly held attitudes on major policy issues. Representatives' attitudes are relatively stable over time, and once in office, their behavior reflects their personal values. Kingdon quotes a congressional staffer who made the point as follows: "Most members come here with well-formed predispositions. They're very opinionated and their minds are made up beforehand. There's very little you can do to change their minds."[15]

Second, an incumbent's position along a liberal-conservative continuum may affect his or her reelection prospects. The conventional wisdom is "if you get too far from your district, you'll lose it." Getting "too far from the district" is a function of overall performance indicated by the incumbent's ideological voting pattern.[16] Quantitative research tends to support the conventional wisdom. Studies of House elections found that incumbents with ideologically discrepant voting records relative to their districts were more likely to attract well-financed, experienced challengers and were more likely to be defeated.[17]

Finally, patterns of cue taking in Congress interact with selective perception to cause ideological voting blocs to form on floor votes. To make politically correct decisions in the limited time available, members turn to each other

13. Kingdon, *Congressmen's Voting Decisions*, p. 271.

14. Jerrold E. Schneider, *Ideological Coalitions in Congress* (Westport, CT: Greenwood Press, 1979), p. 30.

15. Kingdon, *Congressmen's Voting Decisions*, pp. 269-70.

16. Richard F. Fenno, *Home Style: House Members in Their Districts* (Boston: Little, Brown, 1978), p. 144.

17. Jon R. Bond, Cary Covington, and Richard Fleisher, "Explaining Challenger Quality in Congressional Elections," *Journal of Politics*, 47:510-29 (May 1985); John R. Johannes and John C. McAdams, "The Congressional Incumbency Effect: Is It Casework, Policy Compatibility, or Something Else?" *American Journal of Political Science*, 25:512-42 (Aug. 1981).

for information. The most important criterion used in selecting cue givers is ideological agreement, and selective perception causes members to view reinforcing information as persuasive and "to dismiss the rest as coming from the wrong crowd or as not convincing."[18]

Presidents' policy positions tend to reflect their party's ideological mainstream. Because ideology influences decision making in Congress, it serves as a source of support for the president's positions. Previous research demonstrates that ideological forces exert a significant influence on support from members of Congress.[19]

Although ideology often causes the formation of bipartisan coalitions to support or oppose the president, its effects are limited for several reasons. First, because the typical American voter is not strongly ideological, most representatives' electoral self-interest is best served by avoiding ideological extremes. As noted earlier, ideology is a less important voting cue for moderates than for ideologues.[20] Second, distributive or pork-barrel issues typically do not produce ideological divisions. Presidents who attempt to tamper with these programs are likely to find few friends in Congress, as President Reagan discovered when he vetoed the highway bill in 1987. Finally, ideological voting blocs are relatively informal coalitions of members with similar values. Although there are several ideologically based caucuses in Congress, these organizations are less institutionalized than are parties, and their leaders do not command the same status and respect as do party leaders.

Party and ideology influence support for the president from within Congress. In addition, external forces such as public opinion may affect presidential support.

Public opinion

Partisan and ideological divisions in Congress are relatively fixed between elections. Public opinion, on the other hand, is highly fluid. Because members of Congress are elected representatives who are supposed to respond to popular preferences, the president's popularity might influence congressional decisions to support or oppose his positions between elections.

Edwards suggests two reasons why public opinion might influence congressional decisions to support the president.[21] First, the desire for reelection might lead members to adjust their support in response to changes in the president's popularity—members of Congress support the president when it is in their self-interest to do so. Neustadt argues that the president's "public prestige" affects congressional decisions to support the president because "most members of the Washington community depend upon outsiders to support them. ... What their public may think of them becomes a factor, therefore, in deciding how to deal with the desires of a President. His prestige enters into that decision; their publics are part of his."[22]

Second, role theory provides a plausible explanation of why presidential popularity might influence support in Congress. Many members of Congress believe that their role as a representative

18. Kingdon, *Congressmen's Voting Decisions*, pp. 75-82, 270-71.

19. Bond and Fleisher, "Limits of Presidential Popularity."

20. Kingdon, *Congressmen's Voting Decisions*, p. 268.

21. Edwards, *Presidential Influence in Congress*, p. 88.

22. Neustadt, *Presidential Power*, p. 86.

is to reflect constituency opinion. For example, Davidson found that about one-third of House members in his study agreed that "a Representative ought to work for what his constituents want even though this may not always agree with his personal values."[23] Representatives who hold this role orientation should increase or decrease their support for the president in response to his standing with the public.

Edwards was the first to test this theory with quantitative data. His analysis revealed strong correlations between presidential popularity and congressional support. The most important finding is that members of Congress are more responsive to the president's popularity among partisan subgroups than to his overall popularity—that is, Democrats in Congress respond to the president's popularity among Democratic voters; Republicans respond to his popularity among Republican voters. Edwards concludes that the president "should be concerned with his prestige among members of both parties, because all members of Congress respond to this prestige, particularly among their electoral supporters."[24]

Recent studies using different data and measures also purport to find that public approval is an important source of support for the president.[25] Other studies, however, raise doubts about the effects of public approval. Light, for example, found much weaker relationships than those reported by Edwards. The correlations between popularity and congressional action on presidential programs are .28 for spending programs, .27 for large programs, and .19 for new programs.[26]

Similarly, Bond and Fleisher's study revealed limited and indirect effects for public opinion. The data and measures are similar to Edwards's, but the research design incorporated three changes. First, the model includes a measure of "ideological conflict" between the president and members of Congress.[27] Thus the model estimates the effects of public approval on presidential support while controlling for the effects of an important variable omitted from previous studies. Second, rather than analyzing the partisan influence in terms of party names—Democrat or Republican—Bond and Fleisher measure party as the more general concept of president's party/opposition party. Third, the model estimates the effects of presidential popularity as a context that interacts with party. The results of this analysis reveal that, controlling for ideological conflict, overall popularity is related to support, but partisanship conditions the relationship. Popular presidents tend to receive more support from members of their

23. Roger H. Davidson, *The Role of the Congressman* (Indianapolis: Pegasus, 1969), pp. 118-19.

24. Edwards, *Presidential Influence in Congress*, chap. 4; the quote is in ibid., p. 109.

25. Charles W. Ostrom and Dennis M. Simon, "Promise and Performance: A Dynamic Model of Presidential Popularity," *American Political Science Review*, 79:334-58 (June 1985); Douglas Rivers and Nancy L. Rose, "Passing the President's Program: Public Opinion and Presidential Influence in Congress," *American Journal of Political Science*, 29:183-96 (May 1985).

26. Paul C. Light, "Passing Nonincremental Policy: Presidential Influence in Congress, Kennedy to Carter," *Congress and the Presidency*, 9:61-82 (Winter 1981-82).

27. Bond and Fleisher, "Limits of Presidential Popularity." Ideological conflict is the distance between the president and each member on a liberal-conservative continuum, measured as the absolute difference between the president's and each House member's support for Conservative Coalition votes.

party and less support from members of the opposition.[28]

Two considerations might explain this initially surprising result. First, popular presidents may behave differently in their dealings with Congress. Believing that they have the support of the people, popular presidents may be less compromising. An unwillingness to compromise on partisan presidential issues is likely to lead to increased partisan voting in Congress and hence more support from the president's party and less support from the opposition.

Second is the question of credit. Polsby observes that "much of the sharpest kind of partisan conflict on Capitol Hill revolves . . . around the question of credit. Members of the party in opposition to the President must ask themselves whether they can afford to support programs that may help perpetuate the administration in office."[29] Because few voters have information about levels of presidential support in Congress, members of the president's party tend to receive credit for his policies even if they do not support them, and members of the opposition are not likely to receive credit even if they do. Consequently, members of the opposition are likely to follow their basic partisan predisposition and oppose the positions of popular presidents because they have little to gain from their support and much to lose if the president succeeds.

The regression model estimates from this study indicate that, ceteris paribus, if a president's popularity declines by the relatively large amount of 25.00 percent, presidential support scores of members of his party decline by an average of 6.75 percent and those of the opposition increase by an average of 4.00 percent. Except on very close votes, the effect of these changes on the probability of victory is likely to be marginal.[30] Moreover, while a 25-point change in popularity over the course of a four-year term is common, changes from month to month are seldom greater than 5.00 percent. Thus the effects of public approval may be statistically significant, but the substantive effects are relatively small.

In summary, the literature provides unambiguous evidence that party and ideology systematically influence presidential-congressional relations. Evidence of the effects of public opinion, on the other hand, are mixed and inconclusive. The confusion concerning the nature of the relationship between presidential popularity and support may be traced to limitations in the data and research designs of previous studies.

Critique

Studies of the effects of presidential popularity on support from members of Congress typically use the presidential support scores of Congressional Quarterly (CQ). Presidential support scores indicate the percentage of time during a calendar year that each member votes in agreement with the president's preference on roll-call votes on which the president expresses a public position. CQ includes all votes on which the president takes a position, with all votes weighted equally.

28. Ibid., p. 75.

29. Nelson Polsby, *Congress and the Presidency*, 4th ed. (Englewood Cliffs, NJ: Prentice-Hall, 1986), p. 207.

30. Bond and Fleisher, "Limits of Presidential Popularity," p. 75. Another study of presidential-congressional relations that analyzes votes rather than individuals finds that presidential popularity has only marginal effects on whether the president wins or loses. See Bond and Fleisher, "Presidential Popularity and Congressional Voting."

Only votes cast in agreement with the president count as support; failure to vote lowers the score.[31] Although CQ's support scores provide a generally reliable and valid measure, several limitations suggest the need for refinement.

One problem with CQ's approach is that it includes too much. Because CQ includes all votes on which the president expresses a position, the measure mixes important votes and routine votes, as well as different types of policy issues. Mixing such divergent votes may produce a misleading picture. A better understanding of presidential-congressional relations requires that we refine our measure to test for differences across different types of policy.

Second, CQ's measure may not be a valid indicator of presidential support. Presidential support scores indicate the degree of agreement between the president and members of Congress. Many votes, however, involve noncontroversial issues on which nearly all members vote in agreement with the president's position. Most of these nonconflictual wins probably result from two forces that have little to do with presidential support. Some are the result of the president's posturing to endorse what Congress is going to do regardless of his preferences; some are the result of the support of both the president and the members of Congress for a popular or routine issue. In either case, the causal relationship is not members of Congress supporting the president. In one case, the president is supporting Congress; in the other case, a third variable has influenced behavior in both institutions.

If the proportion of nonconflictual wins does not vary systematically across presidents, then including these votes does not threaten the measure's validity. Unfortunately, the proportion varies systematically with the party of the president: presidential support scores of minority presidents are inflated more by these nonconflictual wins than are those of majority presidents.[32] Part of this partisan bias may result because minority presidents have a greater incentive to posture, but much of the difference results because support scores of members of the opposition party are inflated more by nonconflictual votes than are the scores of the president's partisans and because the number of opposition members is larger for minority presidents. Regardless of the cause of the distortion, measures of presidential support need to exclude nonconflictual wins that introduce systematic error. Excluding these votes will not solve all validity problems, but it is an improvement that can be made without threatening the measure's reliability.

A third limitation results because CQ's presidential support scores aggregate individual behavior over a calendar year. This aggregation is not a problem if we want to analyze the effects of the individual characteristics—such as party and ideology—that vary across individuals but are constant for each individual over the period of aggregation. Available measures of presidential popularity do not meet this requirement, however.

Researchers who use CQ's support scores as the dependent variable are forced to use the mean yearly public approval of the president as the independent variable.[33] This procedure is

31. *Congressional Quarterly Almanac* (Washington, DC: Congressional Quarterly, annually 1959-83).

32. Bond and Fleisher, "Presidential Popularity in Congressional Voting," p. 294.

33. Edwards, *Presidential Influence in Congress*, chap. 4; Bond and Fleisher, "Limits of Presidential Popularity."

problematic for two reasons. First, public popularity and support in Congress vary over the course of a year. Because annual support scores and mean yearly approval fail to reflect this variance, there is no way to match individual behavior with the president's popularity at the time the behavior occurs. If we use average public approval for the same year as the presidential support score, then part of the possible cause is observed after some of the behavior we are trying to explain. If we use the measure of popularity of the year before, then it is too far removed from many of the votes to have an effect.

More important, presidential popularity measured as a national average is not the appropriate measure for an individual-level analysis. To analyze the effects of public approval on individual members' presidential support, we need to measure public opinion at the individual level—namely, in each representative's electoral constituency. Polls of presidential popularity for states and congressional districts, however, are not available. Substituting the national yearly average is problematic because the dependent variable—individual presidential support scores—varies across members of Congress, while the independent variable—public approval—is constant across individuals within years and varies only across years.

Although this problem may appear to be a technical statistical issue, it introduces a serious limitation into studies using analytical methods based on correlations. A correlation indicates the degree to which two measures covary. A primary principle of statistics is that variance cannot be explained with a constant. Because national average public opinion is constant for all individuals in a given year, correlations with presiden-

tial support scores do not reflect individual relationships. Instead, they reflect the extent to which variation in average public opinion over time is associated with the aspect of individual presidential support scores that varies over time—that is, the yearly average. In short, what appears to be an analysis of individuals is, in effect, a correlation of average popularity for the year with the average presidential support score for the year. The effective number of cases in such an analysis is not the number of individuals times the number of years, but only the number of years.[34]

Partisan public opinion might provide a more appropriate measure because it reflects the president's popularity among subsets of voters that are part of representatives' electoral coalitions. Edwards's finding that partisan public approval correlates much more strongly with presidential support scores than does overall approval appears to support this argument.[35] These correlations with partisan public approval, however, are largely spurious.

The spurious relationship results from correlating Democratic, or Republican, public opinion with Democratic, or Republican, presidential support scores across presidents of different parties. If

34. This discussion argues that correlating individual support scores with an independent variable aggregated across individual constituencies to a national average is conceptually the same as correlating averages with averages. It can be shown that the two procedures are mathematically equivalent. The slopes and intercepts of the regressions are identical; the correlations differ depending upon how much variance there is around the mean of the true individual-level variable within each year. As variance around the mean decreases, the mean more accurately reflects the variance of the individual behavior, and the correlations from the two procedures become closer.

35. Edwards, *Presidential Influence in Congress*, p. 93.

the president is a Democrat, then Democratic public opinion and Democratic presidential support scores both tend to be high, and Republican opinion and Republican support both tend to be low. If the president is a Republican, then both Democratic opinion and support scores tend to be low, and both Republican opinion and support tend to be high. Because partisan public opinion is a national average that is constant across individuals within years, the correlation reflects the relationship between mean partisan opinion and mean partisan support scores, as noted previously. In this case, however, the research design has ensured that high averages will occur together and that low averages will occur together—that is, the variables are spuriously correlated because the party of the president determines when each is high and low.[36]

If the party variables are measured as president's party and opposition party rather than Democrat and Republican to avoid spurious correlations, then overall public opinion performs about as well as partisan opinion. Because same-party and opposition-party public opinion are strongly related to overall public opinion (r = .86 and .94, respectively) as well as to each other (r = .81), we should not be surprised to find that overall public opinion performs about as well as partisan opinion when the variables are not spuriously correlated.[37] Thus the

evidence that partisan opinion has a greater effect on congressional support for the president is suspect.

This critique of previous research on presidential-congressional relations has illuminated several difficult problems. Although we cannot solve all of these problems, the following is a description of our research design that attempts to deal with some of them.

RESEARCH DESIGN

The analysis is based on a random sample of House members drawn from the population of all members who served from 1959 to 1983, with 100 members selected for each six-month period, yielding 200 per year. Party leaders were added, bringing the total sample size to 5043.

Dependent variable: Presidential support

The dependent variable is each member's support for the president. The measure of support is a presidential support score similar to CQ's but reconstructed to overcome some of the problems discussed earlier.

First, our presidential support score aggregates individual behavior for a six-month period, which permits a closer matching of the timing of public opinion polls and the behavior of representatives on presidential-issue roll calls. We would have preferred monthly or quarterly aggregation periods, but we discovered

36. Edwards also reports a partial correlation between partisan opinion and partisan support controlling for the party of the president. The partial correlation solves the spuriousness problem, but the interpretation of a partial is not the same as the interpretation of a bivariate correlation.

37. Bond and Fleisher, "Presidential Popularity and Congressional Voting," pp. 296-97. Edwards reports a correlation of -.48 between Democratic and Republican approval of the president. Edwards, *Presidential Influence in Congress*, p.

93. This correlation is misleading, however, because it results from change in the partisan evaluations of the president as the presidential party changes over time. Holding president's party constant, partisan opinion varies together, although the opposition party identifiers' approval rate is lower.

that there were often too few votes occurring during these shorter periods to provide a meaningful measure. Aggregating for a six-month period is a reasonable compromise that improves on CQ's annual aggregation.

Second, we exclude noncontroversial wins, defined as roll calls on which more than 80 percent vote in agreement with the president's position. In addition, we calculate support as the number of votes cast in agreement with the president divided by the total number of votes cast, so failure to vote does not affect the score. Individuals in each sample who missed a large number of roll calls were replaced by other members of the same party and state or region.

Third, we construct separate presidential support scores for economic and foreign/defense votes. CQ's measure, based on all votes on which the president takes a position, mixes support across a diverse range of policy issues. Our approach permits a more focused analysis of two important policy areas. We chose economic and foreign policy for practical and theoretical reasons. From a practical standpoint, these are the only policy areas for which there are likely to be enough roll-call votes to calculate a meaningful support score.[38] The choice may also be justified theoretically. Cronin observes that modern presidents tend to concentrate on foreign and national security policy and that the "second-largest portion of the president's policy time is spent on aggregate . . .

economic policy."[39]

Votes used in our economic support score deal with such issues as stimulus tax cuts, general attempts to limit federal spending, wage and price controls, unemployment compensation, job creation, minimum wage, and raising the public debt limit. Not included are votes dealing with welfare, agricultural price supports, and transfer payments to states. These latter policies may affect the performance of the economy, but they are not purely economic. Votes used in the foreign/defense support score include such issues as foreign aid, arms sales, weapons systems, war-related measures, and the International Monetary Fund. Embargoes, veteran's benefits, and the sale of agricultural products abroad are examples of the types of votes excluded because such votes mix domestic politics with the foreign or military issue.

Independent variables: Popularity, party, and ideology

The independent variable of primary concern in this study is the president's popularity with the public. Presidential popularity is measured as the percentage of the public that "approve . . . of the way —— is handling his job as president."[40] The Gallup Poll has asked this question between 10 and 26 times in each of the years in our study, providing almost monthly indicators of presidential popularity. Our measure is the average popularity during each six-month period. In calculating average popularity, we used polls taken in the

38. We did not calculate support scores if fewer than five votes of the policy type occurred during the six-month period. Periods for which support scores could not be computed were dropped from the analysis of that policy type. Because there were more periods with fewer than five economic scores, the analysis of economic support scores is based on a smaller number of cases than is the analysis for foreign policy support.

39. Thomas E. Cronin, *The State of the Presidency*, 2d ed. (Boston: Little, Brown, 1980), pp. 145-50.

40. George Gallup, *The Gallup Opinion Index* (Princeton, NJ: Gallup Poll, annually 1959-83).

months during or before the occurrence of most presidential roll calls in the period in order to match the timing of the dependent and independent variables appropriately.

Following previous work, we analyze the effects of overall approval and partisan approval on presidential support.[41] As noted earlier, however, using these measures is problematic because they are both national averages that do not measure presidential popularity at the relevant level—across individual congressional districts. Because opinion polls at the district level are not available over time, we cannot solve this problem, but we attempt to alleviate part of the problem by using presidential popularity broken down by region: East, Midwest, South, and West.[42] Regional public opinion, of course, is not district opinion, but it is closer than national averages, thereby reducing measurement error. Analyzing all three indicators at least will permit us to see if the relationships become stronger as we refine our measures to approach the relevant public opinion.

We also analyze the effects of party and ideology. Member's party is measured relative to the president's as same party or opposition party. Similarly, members' ideology is measured relative to the presidents's as ideological conflict. Ideological conflict is the absolute difference between the president's and each member's support for the Conservative Coalition.[43]

Methods

We use multiple regression to estimate the effects of presidential popularity, party, and ideological conflict on presidential support. The basic model is the one used by Bond and Fleisher.[44] This model permits one to test for different relationships within party. Based on evidence from this research, we expect presidential popularity to have different effects across parties, but the effects of ideological conflict should be essentially the same in both parties.

41. Edwards, *Presidential Influence in Congress*; Bond and Fleisher, "Presidential Popularity and Congressional Voting."

42. Gallup reports regional breakdowns several times each year. The states included in each category are as follows. The East comprises Connecticut, Delaware, Maine, Maryland, Massachusetts, New Hampshire, New Jersey, New York, Pennsylvania, Rhode Island, Vermont, and West Virginia; the Midwest: Illinois, Indiana, Iowa, Kansas, Michigan, Minnesota, Missouri, Nebraska, Ohio, North Dakota, South Dakota, and Wisconsin; the South: Alabama, Arkansas, Florida, Georgia, Kentucky, Louisiana, Mississippi, North Carolina, Oklahoma, South Carolina, Tennessee, Texas, and Virginia; and the West: Alaska, Arizona, California, Colorado, Hawaii, Idaho, Montana, Nevada, New Mexico, Oregon, Utah, Washington, and Wyoming.

43. Bond and Fleisher, "Limits of Presidential Popularity," p. 72. Conservative Coalition scores for members of Congress are from *Congressional Quarterly Almanac* (1959-83). The positions of the Conservative Coalition of Republicans and Southern Democrats are what we typically associate with a conservative stand in American politics. Although CQ does not report a Conservative Coalition support score for the president, we calculated one based on his publicly expressed positions on Conservative Coalition votes. We recognize that this measure introduces an element of circularity into the analysis. Because some presidential support score votes are also Conservative Coalition votes, some of the same votes are used to construct measures on both sides of the equation, which inflates the correlation between ideology and support. Because ideology is relatively stable for members of Congress, however, other measures purged of presidential votes would be highly correlated and would not produce substantially different results.

44. Bond and Fleisher, "Limits of Presidential Popularity."

In his discussion of "presidential prestige" as a source of presidential power, Neustadt emphasized that it "is a factor operating mostly in the background as a conditioner, not the determinant, of what Washingtonians will do about a President's request."[45] Using Neustadt's theory as a guide, the specification of this model does not assume that public opinion exerts direct effects on presidential support. Instead, it tests the effects of public opinion as a context that interacts with party.

RESULTS

Table 1 reports estimates of the effects of national overall popularity on economic and foreign policy support scores controlling for party and ideological conflict. In general, the model performs well, explaining 60 percent of the variance in economic policy support and 46 percent of the variance in foreign policy support.

Ideological conflict exerts the expected negative effect on support. The relationships are similar for both parties and in both policy areas, although the effects of ideological conflict are slightly stronger on foreign policy issues. This result is consistent with other studies that have found strong ideological influences on foreign and defense policy roll calls.[46]

The effects of overall popularity vary across parties and policy areas. In general, presidential popularity has a stronger effect on members of the president's party and on foreign policy votes. Although we fail to find the negative relationship for opposition-party members as in our earlier study, the weaker relationship for opposition-party members is generally consistent with the argument that the president's popularity has less effect on the opposition than on members of his own party. Moreover, the substantive effects of popularity on support are marginal in both policy areas. A 10.0 percent increase in public approval is associated with a 2.2 percent increase in economic support from members of the president's party and no significant increase from members of the opposition.[47] On foreign policy votes, a 10.0 percent increase in popularity is associated with a 3.8 percent increase in support from the president's partisans and a 1.6 percent increase from the opposition.

Thus partisan and ideological forces in Congress are the primary determinants of congressional support for the president's preferences on economic and foreign policy. Although his standing in national opinion polls is related to support in both policy areas, the effects are marginal. National opinion may have

45. Neustadt, *Presidential Power*, p. 87.

46. Robert A. Bernstein and William W. Anthony, "The ABM Issue in the Senate, 1968-1970: The Importance of Ideology," *American Political Science Review*, 68:1198-1206 (Sept. 1974); James McCormick and Michael Black, "Ideology and Senate Voting on the Panama Canal Treaties," *Legislative Studies Quarterly*, 8:45-63 (Feb. 1983); James M. McCormick, "Congressional Voting on the Nuclear Freeze Resolutions," *American Politics Quarterly*, 13:122-36 (Jan. 1985); Richard Fleisher, "Economic Benefit,

Ideology, and Senate Voting on the B-1 Bomber," *American Politics Quarterly*, 13:200-211 (Apr. 1985).

47. Significance tests are appropriate in this analysis because the data constitute a random sample. Given the large sample size, however, significance tests are mainly useful as a basis to reject weak coefficients. Coefficients that fail to attain statistical significance can be confidently rejected, but we must be cautious before accepting a statistically significant coefficient as substantively important.

TABLE 1
EFFECTS OF NATIONAL POPULARITY, IDEOLOGY, AND PARTY ON
ECONOMIC AND FOREIGN POLICY PRESIDENTIAL SUPPORT SCORES

| | Presidential Support Score | | | |
| | Economic policy | | Foreign policy | |
	b	B	b	B
National popularity				
Opposition party	.07	.06	.16	.13
	(.19)		(.00)	
Same party	.22	.19	.38	.32
	(.00)		(.00)	
Ideological conflict				
Opposition party	−.49	−.47	−.65	−.62
	(.00)		(.00)	
Same party	−.50	−.31	−.80	−.49
	(.00)		(.00)	
Intercepts				
Opposition party	52.57	−	68.57	−
Same party	75.24	−	69.39	−
R^2 =		.60		.46
N =		2,437		3,593

NOTE: The entries are unstandardized regression coefficients (b) and standardized regression coefficients (B). Significance level is in parentheses.

marginal effects because it does not measure the president's popularity among the relevant publics for members of Congress. Edwards argues that partisan public opinion is a more relevant measure.[48]

Table 2 reports estimates of the same basic model using partisan approval. Using partisan approval does not improve the explanatory power of the models. The multiple correlations are the same as or slightly lower than those in the model with overall popularity: R^2 = .60 for economic policy and .44 for foreign policy support. Furthermore, the pattern of relationships for partisan

48. Edwards, *Presidential Influence in Congress*, chap. 4.

public opinion is essentially the same as in the previous model. The relationship is slightly stronger for members of the president's party, but the substantive effects are marginal. In fact, the effects of partisan popularity are slightly weaker than the effects of overall opinion. Thus, unlike Edwards, we find that members of Congress are not more responsive to partisan opinion measured at the national level. Perhaps popularity measured at a level closer to members' electoral constituencies—the level of the region—might relate more strongly.

Table 3 reports estimates of the model using regional public opinion. Again, the results are essentially the same as with overall and partisan popu-

TABLE 2
EFFECTS OF PARTISAN POPULARITY, IDEOLOGY, AND PARTY ON
ECONOMIC AND FOREIGN POLICY PRESIDENTIAL SUPPORT SCORES

| | Presidential Support Score | | | |
| | Economic policy | | Foreign policy | |
	b	B	b	B
Partisan popularity				
Opposition party	.03	.02	.15	.09
	(.59)		(.00)	
Same party	.19	.20	.23	.25
	(.00)		(.00)	
Ideological conflict				
Opposition party	−.48	−.47	−.64	−.61
	(.00)		(.00)	
Same party	−.49	−.31	−.78	−.47
	(.00)		(.00)	
Intercepts				
Opposition party	54.97	—	71.43	—
Same party	73.63	—	72.23	—
$R^2 =$	.60		.44	
N =	2,437		3,416	

NOTE: The entries are unstandardized regression coefficients (b) and standardized regression coefficients (B). Significance level is in parentheses.

larity. The multiple correlations are not significantly improved and the pattern of relationships is unchanged, except that the effects of regional popularity on economic support are similar for both parties.

Our analysis reveals that the effects of presidential popularity are essentially the same regardless of whether we use national, partisan, or regional public opinion. The reason we find similar relationships is that, while the measures of popularity are different conceptually, they do not differ much empirically. The correlations of overall approval with partisan approval are .89 for opposition-party members and .82 for members of

the president's party; the correlation with regional approval is .91.

CONCLUSION

This study has sought to clarify the relationship between presidential popularity and support in Congress. The analysis reveals that variables within Congress—party and ideology—have the strongest effect on presidential support. Although public opinion exerts statistically significant effects, the substantive effects are marginal. Public opinion has slightly stronger effects on foreign policy issues than on economic issues, and the effects are generally stronger on mem-

TABLE 3
EFFECTS OF REGIONAL POPULARITY, IDEOLOGY, AND PARTY ON
ECONOMIC AND FOREIGN POLICY PRESIDENTIAL SUPPORT SCORES

| | Presidential Support Score | | | |
| | Economic policy | | Foreign policy | |
	b	B	b	B
Regional popularity				
Opposition party	.14	.11	.09	.07
	(.01)		(.04)	
Same party	.17	.14	.34	.28
	(.00)		(.00)	
Ideological conflict				
Opposition party	−.50	−.48	−.69	−.66
	(.00)		(.00)	
Same party	−.50	−.31	−.82	−.50
	(.00)		(.00)	
Intercepts				
Opposition party	49.40	−	73.27	−
Same party	77.87	−	71.70	−
R^2 =		.60		.50
N =		2,238		3,302

NOTE: The entries are unstandardized regression coefficients (b) and standardized regression coefficients (B). Significance level is in parentheses.

bers of the president's party than on members of the opposition. The marginal effects do not become stronger as we refine the measure of popularity to approach the relevant public for members of Congress. To the contrary, the relationships are slightly weaker with partisan and regional popularity.

The finding that popularity has only marginal effects on presidential support suggests that we need to clarify what the theory actually leads us to expect. Edwards's argument and method of analysis suggest that public opinion should exert strong, direct effects on the behavior of members of Congress.[49] Studies of con-

49. Ibid.

gressional behavior, on the other hand, suggest that external forces such as presidential activity will have marginal effects at best.[50] Neustadt's theory emphasizes that "public prestige" operates indirectly "as a conditioner, not the determinant," of congressional behavior.[51] Thus our findings of marginal effects are what one would expect from studies of

50. Kingdon, *Congressmen's Voting Decisions*, chap. 6; Donald R. Matthews and James A. Stimson, *Yeas and Nays: Normal Decision-Making in the U.S. House of Representatives* (New York: John Wiley, 1975), chap. 5; Aage R. Clausen, *How Congressmen Decide: A Policy Focus* (New York: St. Martin's Press, 1973), chap. 8.

51. Neustadt, *Presidential Power*.

congressional behavior and Neustadt's theory.

Finding marginal effects is not to deny that for some individuals on some votes the president's popularity with the public is a crucial—perhaps even deciding—consideration. In general, however, for most members on most votes, variation in presidential popularity is not likely to alter fundamentally the behavior of individuals already in Congress. Instead, public opinion affects congressional support for the president indirectly, through the electoral process, which alters the distribution of partisan and ideological forces within Congress through membership changes. Thus governmental institutions in the American system may respond to popular preferences over the long run, but adjustments between elections are unlikely.

ANNALS, *AAPSS*, **499**, September 1988

The President and
Congress in the Media

By STEPHANIE GRECO LARSON

ABSTRACT: The nature and determinants of presidential and congressional media coverage are described in this article, and the untested assumptions concerning political consequences of coverage are discussed. The argument that media coverage inherently enhances power, so that the president's influence is unconditionally increased at the expense of Congress's, is challenged through logic and example. The need to investigate the dynamics of media impact beyond public opinion, the nature of institutional coverage in various political settings, and the promise of congressional hearings for counterbalancing presidential coverage are discussed.

Stephanie Greco Larson is assistant professor of political science at the George Washington University, where she has taught since 1986. She received a B.S. degree from the University of Central Florida and an M.S. and Ph.D. from Florida State University in Tallahassee. Her main teaching and research fields are mass media and politics, and public attitudes toward political and governmental institutions.

THE conventional wisdom about press coverage of the national institutions is that when national politicians continually compete for news coverage, the president always wins. This media imbalance is then assumed to result in constitutionally equal branches being politically unequal. What we know about media coverage of the executive and legislative branch, however, is usually based on descriptive generalizations, war stories, and speculation. As a result, our understanding of the causes, nature, and consequences of national institutional coverage is quite limited. In fact, even the truisms are vulnerable and conditional when examined closely.

Research generally focuses on various media during specific time periods, looking at Congress and the president separately. The relationship between reporters and public officials and the type of coverage it produces are, therefore, like snapshots of specific instances rather than a continuous and comprehensive movie of the dynamics of media-institutional relationships and outputs. Apart from some public opinion data, the consequences of this coverage are left to speculation and seem to solidify into undocumented assumptions.

In this article, I will address the literature's acceptance of but lack of proof for the law of videopolitics that states that "television alters the popularly perceived importance of institutions and individuals in direct proportion to the amount of coverage provided—the greater the coverage, the more important the institution and its members appear to be."[1] This perceived importance is further interpreted as altering actual power in interinstitutional relationships. Although this balance-of-power issue is central to the discussion of media effects on public policy, it is not supported by large amounts of empirical data.

In this article, I will discuss the nature and determinants of presidential and congressional media coverage, usually treated separately in studies of this subject. Then the asserted consequences of this coverage for political power will be discussed and critiqued. Examples from the Watergate period will be used to challenge some of these assumptions and demonstrate important issues to consider for future research. Assuming that the president's political power is enhanced by his media coverage and that Congress's power is weakened, I will argue, is overly simplistic and instead depends upon the context in which the relationship is examined.

PRESIDENTIAL COVERAGE

Presidential press studies have generally focused on one of two topics: the length, tone, and subject matter of stories about the president; or the nature of the relationship between the president and the press. Press coverage is examined with content analysis, and press relations with elite interviews and historical participant observation, which are often anecdotal.

According to content analyses, coverage of the president is extensive, personal, and of variable tone.[2] Although

1. Michael J. Robinson, "A Twentieth-Century Medium in a Nineteenth-Century Legislature: The Effects of Television on the American Congress," in Congress in Change: Evolution and Reform, ed. Norman Ornstein (New York: Praeger, 1975).

2. Discussion of the extensiveness and tone of presidential coverage is provided in Martha Joynt Kumar and Michael Baruch Grossman, Portraying the President: The White House and the News Media (Baltimore, MD: Johns Hopkins University Press, 1981); Fred Smoller, "The Six O'Clock Presidency: Patterns of Network News Coverage of the Press," Presidential Studies Quarterly, 16(1):31-49 (Winter 1986); Doris Graber,

more prominent on television than in newspapers, stories from the White House beat are used almost automatically because the president is looked at as the great explainer and a personified demonstration of today in government. This executive branch coverage focuses on the president as an individual—family man, leader, man of the people—while deemphasizing bureaucratic policy implementation. The tone of presidential coverage is more favorable than unfavorable, especially when visual elements of the television news are examined. This is largely due to the limited access to the president, which provides the administration with the opportunity to control the settings for photo opportunities. The verbal interpretations of these pictures are more critical because they discuss the presidential motivations for the pictures. Diachronic analysis indicates, however, that this coverage has become more critical and interpretive over the last 20 years.

The relationship between the president and the press that creates this coverage embraces both adversarial and cooperative elements. Reporters want access to the president so that they can report the news, and the president wants to be in the news. These mutual needs lead to a certain degree of cooperation between the two sides. While the need for presidential coverage is agreed upon by both the presidential staff and the White House reporters, what that coverage should look like is not.

The president wants his message to be transmitted without alteration or interpretation so that he can control its clarity and persuasiveness. The reporters, in contrast, seek the inside story, which may include unflattering political motivations behind official statements and photo opportunities. The agendas differ inasmuch as the administration tries to minimize discussion of bad news and political blunders whereas the press tries to promote it.

These paradoxical ingredients—the need for interaction and the conflicting goals—have spawned an extensive communication network around the White House beat that includes a plethora of reporters and press assistants, each trying to maximize his or her goals. Various tactics and strategies used in this public relations war have been described by participants and observers as a combination of threatening, promising, attacking, and accommodating.[3]

Coverage of the president also varies over the course of his term of office. The beginning of a presidential term is referred to as the alliance, or honeymoon, stage. During this time, cooperative feelings between the president and the press are greatest and the tone of the coverage is most favorable. The second stage involves controversial decision making and resultant press criticisms. These may lead to a third stage: campaign-period retrenchment on both sides. The assumption is that the tone of presidential coverage reflects his accessibility. In other words, when the president is most responsive to the press's needs for his time and attention, then his coverage is favorable. When his personal attention to reporters wanes and is delegated to others, the coverage increases in criticism.[4]

3. Research on the interaction between the president and reporters is provided in Kumar and Grossman, *Portraying the President*; Graber, *Mass Media and American Politics*.

4. Martha Joynt Kumar and Michael Baruch Grossman, "The White House and the News Media: The Phases in Their Relationship," *Political Science Quarterly*, 94:37-53 (Spring 1979).

Mass Media and American Politics (Washington, DC: CQ Press, 1980).

CONGRESSIONAL COVERAGE

In studies of congressional media coverage, a major distinction is made between the local press whose coverage is produced for the representative's district or a senator's state, and the national press, which includes the prestige papers—such as the *New York Times* and the *Washington Post*—and the television network news. Both the coverage received and the interpersonal relationships between the legislator—or press secretary—and the reporter differ dramatically in tone and extensiveness when these two levels are compared.

The relationship between legislators and their hometown press is viewed as symbiotic and nurturing. No doubt this is due, in part, to their shared definition of newsworthiness: both the local reporter, with limited political contacts, and the senator or representative, who needs visibility to obtain votes back home, agree that the lawmaker is worthy of attention. Not only does reliance on a legislator's self-promotional material simplify the local reporter's job and save limited editorial resources; it is also parochially newsworthy. After all, legislators serve as the official government spokesperson for their state or district just as the president does for the nation.[5]

Press secretaries acknowledge that local coverage is more important, more sought after, and more dependable than national coverage. Newsletters, press releases, and radio and television actualities are produced in affordable congressional studios, with technically sophisticated office equipment, by specially trained staff members. When this prepackaged news is sent to the local media,

it is frequently used without alteration. The result is extensive and favorable coverage that is parlayed into unequaled district visibility that ultimately undermines challengers' competitiveness.[6]

Coverage at the national level is rare for individual members of Congress and generally negative with respect to the institution. Only a handful of senators and representatives are given national news coverage. These members are typically senior, leaders, policy spokespersons with specialized expertise, or members running for higher office. Individual effort in attracting press attention, once decried by congressional leaders as making a member a "show horse," may assist legislators in their policymaking; however, it is less important than internal sources of influence. In other words, who one is is more important than how one looks or sounds. The combination of being powerful within Congress and meeting the press's organizational needs is the best for obtaining national coverage.[7]

5. Michael Robinson, "The Three Faces of Congressional Media," in *The New Congress*, ed. Thomas Mann and Norman Ornstein (Washington, DC: American Enterprise Institute, 1981).

6. Research examining local news coverage and the impact that legislators have on this coverage include Timothy Cook, "Marketing the Members: The Ascent of the Congressional Press Secretary" (Paper delivered at the Meeting of the Midwestern Political Science Association, Chicago, IL, 1985); Stephen Frantzich, "Communication and Congress" in *The Communication Revolution in Politics*, ed. Gerald Benjamin (Montpelier, VT: Capitol City Press, 1982); Katherine Winston Evans, "A Capitol Hill Pro Reveals His Secrets," *Washington Journalism Review*, 3:28-33 (June 1981). The success of this coverage for reelection is discussed in Peter Clarke and Susan Evans, *Covering Campaigns: Journalism in Congressional Elections* (Stanford, CA: Stanford University Press, 1983).

7. James Payne, "Show Horses and Work Horses in the U.S. House of Representatives," *Polity*, 12(3):428-56 (Spring 1980); for opposing views, see Stephen Hess, *The Ultimate Insiders: U.S. Senators in the National Media* (Washington, DC: Brookings Institution, 1986); Timothy Cook,

While national coverage of Congress as an institution is generally neutral in tone, it is more often critical than favorable. Coverage focuses on conflict within the institution and with the president and on the slowness of the legislative process. The tone is said to be caused by Congress's being complex, dull, or simply too impersonal. It is argued that this decentralized institution is difficult to cover because it is hard to determine who or what is important.[8]

Although it is often held that Congress is covered less because it is harder to understand, this argument seems incomplete. Anyone who has tried to explain executive branch structure and operation to college freshmen knows that the legislature does not have an exclusive claim to organizational complexity. One could argue that Congress is easier to cover than the executive due to its openness and multiple sources of information. In fact, Congress is the most common source of information for Washington reporters even though it is not the most common subject.[9]

The press handles executive branch

complexity by assuming that the president controls the executive branch, thereby justifying their singular coverage of him. This flawed notion of executive centralization helps the president obtain coverage even for events labeled by Herbert Schmertz as "non-news news events," such as going on vacation or to church.[10] It can also cause problems for him because scandals in the executive branch imply presidential responsibility and knowledge.

CONSEQUENCES OF COVERAGE

Studying how reporters and officials interact and what coverage results can be valuable because these elements have political consequences. While it is difficult to assess these effects, many assume that the media have increased the power of the president because of his prevalence in the news. Television's alleged contribution to the president's image as the ultimate policymaker is said inevitably to have caused Congress to fall behind in political influence. Senators and representatives themselves tend to subscribe wholeheartedly to this argument. The following statements are typical:

Compared with the presidency, Congress as a whole has suffered a decline in image and power. This springs partially from stories that picture it routinely as lobby-ridden, incompetent, and slow and partly from the fact that the White House has provided more exciting copy.[11]

Television has done as much to expand the powers of the President as would a constitutional amendment formally abolishing the co-

"House Members as Rational Newsmakers: Effects of Televising Congress," *Legislative Studies Quarterly*, 11(2):203-26 (May 1986).

8. Discussions of the negative coverage of Congress and its possible causes include Michael Robinson and Kevin Appeal, "Network News Coverage of Congress," *Political Science Quarterly*, 94(3):407-18 (Fall 1979); Robinson, "Three Faces of Congressional Media"; Lynda Lee Kaid and Joe Foote, "How Network Television Coverage of the President and Congress Compare," *Journalism Quarterly*, 62(1):59-65 (Spring 1985); Larry Warren, "The Other Side of the Camera: A TV Reporter's Stint as a Congressional Aide," *PS*, 19(1):43-48 (Winter 1986); Susan Miller, "News Coverage of Congress: The Search for the Ultimate Spokesman," *Journalism Quarterly*, 55(3):667-63 (Autumn 1977).

9. Stephen Hess, *The Washington Reporters* (Washington, DC: Brookings Institution, 1981).

10. Herbert Schmertz, "The Media and the Presidency," *Presidential Studies Quarterly*, 16(1):11-21 (Winter 1986).

11. Graber, *Mass Media and American Politics*.

equality of the three branches of government.[12]

Television not only enhances the President's role as chief policymaker but also sustains him whenever he announces these decisions in prime time appearances.[13]

Perhaps the media coverage resulting in presidential strength is more a matter of perception than of reality. After all, a law of videopolitics states that "television alters the popularly perceived importance of institutions and individuals in direct proportion to the amount of coverage provided."[14] People may assume that exposure leads to power, ignoring the nature of the coverage and the real results of that coverage. The increased criticisms and interpretations undermine advantage from coverage, which may explain the infrequent reelection of media-age presidents. Increased attention to a political issue or conflict can lead to increased opposition and the mobilization of the opposing forces. In many ways, public scrutiny may help presidential opponents by pressuring the president to act, resulting in premature decision making, a reduction of viable options, or inevitable blunders.[15] Whether extensive coverage even facilitates presidential support among the public is debatable. After all, the rhetoric

of Ronald Reagan as the "great communicator" coincided with a less-than-average job-performance rating from the public.[16]

The notion that more coverage leads to more power, or the perception of more power, also ignores the type of coverage that results from an adversarial press. Because reporters view their role in the political process as being outside critics or watchdogs, the tone and subject matter selected for news stories is critical rather than catering to the preferences of the newsmakers. As reporters, especially those in television, grow more interpretive over time—no longer simply describing presidential actions but also second-guessing them by predicting motivations and consequences—the notion that coverage is inherently helpful is further weakened. While this weakening may be due to reporters' working definition of what is newsworthy rather than a political bias, the unfavorable picture of the president can result in a cynical public or an invigorated opposition.[17]

Concern over interbranch power is only part of the question of media effects. Whether television has changed institutional influence between and within the House of Representatives and the Senate, or within the executive branch, is also of concern. Beyond the use of publicity in the pursuit of reelection, does legislators' media coverage increase their legislative influence? Do differences in coverage between the House and Senate affect the relative clout of these two bodies? What is the result of the differen-

12. Senator William Fulbright, as quoted in *Congress and the News Media*, ed. Robert Blanchard (New York: Hastings House, 1974), p. 105.

13. Robertson, "Twentieth-Century Medium," p. 256.

14. Ibid., p. 252.

15. Austin Ranney, *Channels of Power: The Impact of Television on American Politics* (New York: Basic Books, 1983). For the negative impacts of critical coverage, see C. Don Livingston, "The Televised Presidency," *Presidential Studies Quarterly*, 16(1):22-30 (Winter 1986); Elmer Cornwell, "The President and the Press: Phases in the Relationship," *The Annals* of the American Academy of Political and Social Science, 427:53-64 (Sept. 1976).

16. Elliott King and Michael Schudson, "The Myth of the Great Communicator," *Columbian Journalism Review*, Nov.-Dec. 1987, pp. 37-39.

17. Arthur Miller, Edie Goldenberg, and Lutz Erbring, "Type-Set Politics: Impact of Newspapers on Public Confidence," *American Political Science Review*, 73(1):67-84 (Mar. 1979).

tial coverage of executive agencies?

The aforementioned adage—"more coverage equals more power"—supports the notion that individual members with more national coverage would have a larger impact on lawmaking. Some argue that any member who puts a priority on gaining media attention can do so by following a "media maximizing formula." Today's Congress, they remind us, is an "open system," where a new source of power comes from without.[18] Influence based on seniority, leadership, and expertise can presumably be counterbalanced by being considerate of press deadlines, turning a phrase, being photogenic, and addressing the hot issues of the day.

Studies of members of Congress in the news have severely weakened this argument, however, by demonstrating that people already in power within the chambers are the ones receiving the bulk of media attention outside of them. In separate studies of the House and the Senate, the seniors, leaders, and policy experts were found to be the ones in the national press.[19] Yet none of this clearly addresses the question of whether national coverage influences decision making. For example, being on television to say that a bill was sent to the president hardly influences the internal decision-making process in Congress, as action on Capitol Hill has already been completed. Empirical studies examining the linkages between media coverage and legislative results have not been forthcoming.

The debate over whether television coverage has altered the influence of the House vis-à-vis the Senate is equally speculative. Anyone who feared that the 1979 decision to allow cameras on the floor of the House—before the Senate followed suit—would reverse the status of the chambers was reassured by the lack of fallout. While televising proceedings may assist members in managing their time, provide them with clips to present at home, and reduce some networks artists' workloads, it has not rearranged the balance of power in the Capitol. It is still more likely that senators will receive national attention, be familiar to the public, and run for the presidency.

The impact of media coverage within the executive branch is even more elusive. Because there is little routine executive branch news reported, there are few studies that examine even the nature of department, cabinet, or agency coverage. Comparisons of the impact of visibility on relative agency influence are absent. We do know that agencies' press offices are more reactive to reporters' requests for routine information than manipulative of the media agenda.[20] The study of the impact of press coverage of department policymaking that relied on case studies and policymakers' perceptions noted that press coverage can speed up the decision-making process, move decision making up the organizational ladder, and, in rare cases, reverse decisions.[21]

The authority of the president within the executive branch would be expected to be overwhelming if the volume of media coverage were the determining

18. Norman Ornstein, "The Open Congress Meets the President," in *Both Ends of the Avenue*, ed. Anthony King (Washington, DC: American Enterprise Institute, 1983), pp. 185-211.

19. Hess, *Ultimate Insiders*; Cook, "House Members as Rational Newsmakers."

20. Stephen Hess, *The Government/Press Connection: Press Officers and Their Offices* (Washington, DC: Brookings Institution, 1984).

21. Martin Linsky, *Impact: How the Press Affects Federal Policymaking* (New York: Norton, 1986).

variable, as he receives the bulk of the administration's coverage. Again, this assumes that coverage equals power. Austin Ranney disagrees when he argues that the real winners in a power game influenced by media coverage are the largely invisible bureaucrats. They are not spending time seeking coverage but are instead working out public policy in the "political vacuum" left by elected officials who are concerning themselves with public relations.[22] Because the coverage of the president emphasizes his personality, daily ritualistic activities, and family life, it may increase his visibility as the symbolic or ceremonial leader of the nation rather than enhance one of his more influential roles.

Clearly, the discussion of media influence on relative power within or between branches of government is generally speculative without the systematic hypothesis testing prevalent in the study of the media's effect on public opinion. While public attitudes may be an important part of the power equation, assuming that policy decisions are representative and that government is responsive to citizens, it is a separate question from whether the media directly influence government. This preoccupation of searching for media effects on public rather than elite attitudes may be a function of the availability of polling data rather than a thoughtful theoretical decision.

THE CASE OF WATERGATE

Lessons from a case study of the Watergate period challenge one of the assumptions about the dynamics of press coverage and political power by demonstrating how media coverage can strength-en the position of Congress in its conflict with the president. *The Battle for Public Opinion*, written by Gladys and Kurt Lang, used content analysis of news coverage and public opinion polls during the Watergate period.[23] The Langs' primary goal was to enrich the media-effects literature by determining whether the public was influenced by the press and if, in turn, it influenced political elites. Nevertheless, their findings have important implications for the relevance of media coverage of political institutions to their power relationships.

In describing the agenda-building process, the Langs note that "media exposure and public attention generate responses at the elite level that produce still more news in a cycle of mutual reinforcement that continues until politicians and public tire of an issue or another issue moves into the center of the political stage."[24] They demonstrate that the press was only one of the many individuals who kept the Watergate story going. Politicians' actions—requests for tapes, release of transcripts, congressional investigations—attracted media coverage, which in turn stimulated public interest.

Congress was an important actor in this process, allowing members to attain personal attention and providing the institution with national power and prestige. For example, the 37 days of gavel-to-gavel coverage of the Senate Select Committee on Presidential Campaign Activities, the Ervin committee, received high viewership and contributed to doubts about Nixon, enhanced the saliency of the conflict, and raised respect

22. Ranney, *Channels of Power*.

23. Gladys Engel Lang and Kurt Lang, *The Battle for Public Opinion: The President, the Press and the Polls during Watergate* (New York: Columbia University Press, 1983).
24. Ibid., p. 50.

for the Senate.[25] Having already been convinced of the legitimacy of the investigation, the public was outraged at the president's actions in the Saturday Night Massacre; this response of the public was a turning point in the support for impeachment proceedings.[26]

Congressional media power was enhanced by the amount and type of coverage the institution received. "The opposition to Nixon was sufficiently prestigious and powerful to enjoy a degree of recognition the media normally accord only the Chief Executive."[27] The House Judiciary committee hearings later legitimized opposition to Nixon. This perception was due to the committee's style and activities and the type of coverage the hearings received. The committee, under the direction of Chairman Peter Rodino, Democrat of New Jersey, avoided partisan attacks and news leaks that would have undermined the appearance of a unified and fair committee. They tried to educate the public about the impeachment process; the issue being debated therefore took precedence over personal grandstanding on the committee.

The media coverage of the deliberations tended to allow the process and participants to speak for themselves. The press was "generally inclined to accept the members' self-flattering definitions" of being objectively concerned with legal constitutional issues rather than with "getting Nixon."[28] The public and political audiences' response was favorable for the legislature.[29] Public opinion polls demonstrated that the House Judiciary Committee "looked

good," did a good job, was fair, and made the right decision.[30] The prestige of Congress as a whole was enhanced by their Watergate activities.[31]

LESSONS FOR
FUTURE RESEARCH

The example of Watergate does more than illustrate one instance on which Congress received more favorable public evaluations than the president due in part to media coverage. It demonstrates how Congress, with other political actors, can undermine the authority of the president by publicizing situations that he would rather not address. It illustrates how the mass media can act as a catalyst and reporter of congressional oversight, enhancing the legislature's efforts to check and balance the executive branch.

Through committee action, Congress is able to command press attention and parlay it into interinstitutional influence. Congress is most frequently covered through its committees, when this "many-headed monster" loses a few hundred mouths.[32] After all, committees have fewer participants than the full Congress, stronger leadership, visually represented conflict, and more focus than floor debates have.

When congressional action is least ambiguous and the important actors and issues are obvious, then coverage is favorable and influence is enhanced. On the other hand, the Iran-contra hearing used a cumbersome committee, asked

25. Ibid., pp. 27, 73.
26. Ibid., p. 93.
27. Ibid., p. 133.
28. Ibid., p. 162.
29. Ibid., pp. 167, 174.

30. Ibid., p. 174.
31. Robinson, "Twentieth-Century Medium."
32. Mary Russell, "The Press and the Committee System," *The Annals* of the American Academy of Political and Social Science, 411:114-19 (1974); Kaid and Foote, "Network Television Coverage of the President and Congress."

unfocused technical questions, and stylistically deferred to the administration's public heroes, which undermined its initial advantage.[33] We need to separate the types of congressional actions that are covered—according to the means and effects of the coverage—to see if it can be demonstrated empirically that Congress's influence and prestige are enhanced by its use of oversight, a role that is probably magnified by the watchdog role of the press.

Historical examples illustrate how congressional power is exercised through press coverage of committee action. The Senate subcommittee investigations into organized crime in the 1950s increased attention to the issue of crime and to the subcommittee's leader, Estes Kefauver. The Army-McCarthy hearings contributed to the halt to legalized antidemocratic behaviors. According to Gallup polls, public approval for Congress's handling of its job was highest in August of 1974 and August-September of 1987, both during periods of publicized oversight by Congress.[34]

The interplay between media and congressional hearings changed public policy in the case of the Vietnam war. Daniel Hallin examined the content of war coverage and concluded that it was not until domestic dissent was voiced within the political elite that media coverage became critical of the war. Once the opposition to the war was

"within the sphere of legitimate controversy"—that is, the Senate—it became a necessary component of war coverage. The media's role was characterized as strengthening the political trends found in national institutions, reinforcing the breakdown in the elite consensus.[35]

It is not my intention to supplant one untested assumption—unqualified presidential media superiority—for another, congressional superiority due to committee oversight. One could challenge this argument by pointing to hundreds of committees and subcommittees that failed to receive press attention or public awareness or achieve policy impact. Additional attention to modeling the dynamic nature of the relationship between the press, the president, and Congress is needed. What conditions must be met for Congress to have the upper hand in press coverage and ultimate influence? Factors such as consensus within Congress, vulnerability of the president, type of issue, degree of congressional leadership, and degree of interinstitutional conflict, among others, should be used to examine the relationships between institutional behavior, media coverage, and policy decisions systematically. In this way, we could see if the examples of Watergate and the Vietnam war are indicative of how Congress's power is enhanced by the media or are just anomalies caused by atypical events or presidential flaws.

To reach beyond noting that the president typically receives more coverage than Congress, we need to investigate the dynamics of media impact on political power within different political settings. Measuring degrees of substan-

33. Barbara Matuson, "Made for TV," *Washingtonian*, 23(3):208-18 (Dec. 1987).
34. For studies of the impact of these historical hearings, see G. D. Wiebe, "Responses to the Televised Kefauver Hearings: Some Social Psychological Implication," *Public Opinion Quarterly*, 16:179-200 (Summer 1952); idem, "The Army-McCarthy Hearings and the Public Confidence," ibid., 22:490-502 (Winter 1958-59). Results of recent Gallup polls are found in *Gallup Report*, 264:29 (Spring 1987).

35. Daniel Hallin, "The Media, the War in Vietnam, and Political Support: A Critique of the Thesis of an Oppositional Media," *Journal of Politics*, 46(1):2-24 (Feb. 1984).

tive discussion, tone, and level of internal conflict by content analysis of congressional and presidential coverage during the same time periods rather than conducting separate studies is the first step. Because content analysis can demonstrate only the possible causes of influence inequity, the dependent variable—the impact of coverage—must be measured in other ways by examining the reaction of both the public and the policymakers to news stories.

ANNALS, *AAPSS*, **499**, September 1988

Congressional Oversight of the Presidency

By FREDERICK M. KAISER

ABSTRACT: Congressional oversight of the executive, including the presidency itself, has evidently increased over the past two decades. It relies upon a wide variety of techniques and occurs in a number of settings, not just select committee investigations or specialized subcommittee hearings labeled oversight. Other means range from hearings on authorizations and regular bills to informal meetings between legislators and executive officials; and from House impeachment proceedings to the use of offices outside Congress, such as inspectors general and independent counsels. Oversight does not exist in a political vacuum; the impetus behind it is often a conflict between the two branches over public policy or over competing institutional interests and powers. In addition, the apparent growth in the amount of oversight and the wide use of different means are the results of changes in Congress, including improved resources and incentives for members; changes in the presidency, especially the expanded operational role of its personnel; and changes in the polity, such as the rise of investigative journalism and electoral developments that have helped to divide party control of government.

Frederick M. Kaiser, a specialist in American national government at the Congressional Research Service, Library of Congress, is the author of "Congressional Control of Executive Actions in the Aftermath of the Chadha *Decision" and "Oversight of Foreign Policy," among other studies.*

NOTE: The views expressed here are the author's own and are attributable to no other source.

SOME of the most dramatic confrontations between Congress and the presidency over the past two decades have involved oversight—that is, Congress's review, monitoring, and supervision of executive activity and behavior. The Senate Foreign Relations Committee's televised hearings in the late 1960s helped to legitimize and mobilize opposition to the Vietnam war; the Ervin committee's 1973 investigation of Watergate showed how White House officials illegally used their positions for partisan gain and political advantage; the House Judiciary Committee's impeachment proceedings against Richard Nixon, the following year, ended his presidency; and select committee inquiries in 1975-76 identified serious abuses by intelligence agencies and, in 1987, detailed a range of illegal or questionable activities surrounding the Iran-contra affair.

Oversight, however, is more than highly publicized investigations by short-term select committees specially created to look into suspected executive abuses or into major policy failures. Indeed, investigations by such temporary panels are infrequent and, to a degree, misleading; establishing them indicates that routine monitoring and supervision through other, more conventional channels were nonexistent or inadequate to the task.

Congress, in fact, has adopted a wide range of techniques, nurtured a variety of devices, and fostered a number of opportunities to oversee the executive in general and the presidency in particular. Even with the so-called legislative veto declared unconstitutional,[1] many other

1. *Immigration and Naturalization Service v. Chadha*, 462 U.S. 919 (1983). For follow-up to the decision, see U.S., Congress, House, Committee on Rules, *Legislative Veto after Chadha*, 98th

avenues are available. In addition to the most easily identifiable—select committee inquiries and specifically designated oversight hearings by standing committees—these are

—hearings on appropriations, authorizations, regular bills, and other measures, including joint, concurrent, and one-house resolutions, and committee vetoes, which are the remnants of the legislative veto;
—formal consultation with and required reports from the executive;
—Senate advice and consent for executive nominations and for treaties;
—House impeachment proceedings and subsequent Senate trial;
—House and Senate proceedings under the Twenty-Fifth Amendment confirming a vice-president and potentially determining an acting president;
—informal meetings between legislators or staff and executive officials;
—congressional membership on governmental commissions and advisory groups;
—legislators' ombudsman role of handling complaints and questions from constituents and clientele groups;
—studies, reviews, and analyses by the staff of a committee or a member's office, congressional support agencies, and outside consultants; and
—investigations by noncongressional governmental units, such as statu-

Cong., 1st and 2d sess., 1983 and 1984; Louis Fisher, *Constitutional Conflicts between Congress and the President* (Princeton, NJ: Princeton University Press, 1985), pp. 178-83; Frederick M. Kaiser, "Congressional Control of Executive Actions in the Aftermath of *Chadha*," *Administrative Law Review*, 36(3):239-75 (Summer 1984).

tory offices of inspectors general and independent counsels, which can respond to congressional requests for investigations and are required to report to Congress.

This article looks at some of these techniques in action and offers reasons why oversight has undoubtedly increased over the recent past. First, though, the article examines the objectives of and obstacles to overseeing the presidency and the changing perception and meaning of oversight.

OBJECTIVES AND OBSTACLES

Congressional oversight applies not just to cabinet departments, executive agencies, or regulatory commissions operating under their own separate laws. Despite special obstacles facing it, oversight also applies to the presidency. In addition to the president, in whom "executive Power [is] vested" by the Constitution, the presidency encompasses a substantial institutional apparatus, a flexible organizational network, and a large number of advisers and assistants. The complex includes the vice-president, who operates under the president's instructions and public law—for instance, he chairs an antiterrorism task force and serves on the National Security Council (NSC); advisers in the Executive Office of the President (EOP); several statutory institutions, particularly the Office of Management and Budget (OMB) and the NSC and its staff; various ad hoc organizational arrangements, such as presidential councils or interagency groupings that are directed by EOP officials; and presidential commissions, such as the Grace commission, and other similar advisory bodies.

Objectives and rationale

Congress has implied constitutional authority, clear responsibility, and pragmatic, vested interests that support oversight of the presidency.

Constitutional powers. Although the Constitution grants no formal, express authority to oversee or investigate the executive, oversight is implied in Congress's authority to appropriate funds, enact laws, raise and support armies, provide for and maintain a navy, impeach and try the president and U.S. officers, and advise and consent on treaties and presidential nominations, among other powers.[2] Congress could not carry out these duties reasonably or responsibly without knowing what the executive was doing; how programs were being run, by whom, and at what cost; and whether officials were obeying the law and complying with statutory intent.

Also, the necessary-and-proper clause allows Congress to pass laws that mandate oversight, grant relevant authority to itself and its support agencies, and impose specific obligations on the executive, such as reporting or consultation requirements.[3] The Supreme Court, moreover, has legitimated Congress's investigative power, subject to constitutional safeguards for individual liberties.[4]

Democratic principles. The philosophical underpinning for Congress's power to oversee the presidency is the checks-and-balances system. As James

2. U.S. Const., art. I.
3. Ibid. For examples of reporting and consultation requirements, see Kaiser, "Congressional Control," pp. 263-65.
4. *McGrain* v. *Daughtery*, 273 U.S. 135, 176-89 (1927); *Watkins* v. *United States*, 354 U.S. 178, 187 (1957); *Barenblatt* v. *United States*, 360 U.S. 109, 111 (1959).

Madison described it in *Federalist* number 51, the system works

by so contriving the interior structure of the government as that its several constituent parts may, by their mutual relations, be the means of keeping each other in their proper places . . . [and] in all the subordinate distributions of power, where the constant aim is to divide and arrange the several offices in such a manner as that each may be a check on the other.[5]

Oversight, as a way of keeping the executive in its proper place, translates into detecting and preventing waste, fraud, and dishonesty; protecting civil liberties and individual rights from executive abuses; ensuring executive compliance with statutory intent; gathering information for lawmaking and educating the public; and evaluating executive performance.

Allied with the checks-and-balances notion is the constitutional preeminence of Congress, the first branch of government: "In republican government," again according to Madison, "the legislative authority necessarily predominates."[6] In tandem, the two principles—checks and balances plus legislative supremacy— endorse strong congressional oversight of the executive. This effort is certainly applicable to the presidency, a unitary office headed by an indirectly elected official, because of the potential for it to be captured by a "faction," usurp authority from other branches, abuse governmental power, and infringe on the rights of citizens.[7]

Other defenders of representative democracy have recognized the inherent value of oversight. Woodrow Wilson, writing about congressional government in 1885, counseled that "quite as important as legislation is vigilant oversight of administration"; noting the divergence between the ideal and real worlds, however, the future president concluded that "the means which Congress has of . . . exercising the searching oversight at which it aims are limited and defective."[8]

Congressional interests. Aside from its utility for democratic ideals, oversight plays a pragmatic role in protecting Congress's own institutional interests and political power from executive encroachment or abuse. An inability to monitor executive activity can allow subordinates of the president to undertake operations that the legislature has opposed and to run roughshod over Congress. The Iran-contra committees found, for instance, that executive personnel had evaded statutory reporting obligations, deceived congressional panels, and destroyed public documents, which could have implicated others and further incriminated the perpetrators.[9] Also, failure to supervise executive conduct can allow the White House to use law enforcement and intelligence agencies or its own personnel illegally and unethically, for partisan advantage or to

5. *Federalist* no. 51, in *The Federalist Papers* (New York: New American Library, 1961), pp. 320, 322.

6. Ibid., p. 322.

7. Ibid. See also Madison, *Federalist* nos. 47-50, in ibid, pp. 300-319; Alexander Hamilton, *Federalist* nos. 67-77, in ibid., pp. 407-63.

8. Woodrow Wilson, *Congressional Government* (New York: Houghton Mifflin, 1885), pp. 297, 270, respectively.

9. U.S., Congress, Senate, Select Committee on Secret Military Assistance to Iran and the Nicaraguan Opposition, and U.S., Congress, House, Select Committee to Investigate Covert Arms Transactions with Iran (hereafter called Iran-Contra Committees), *Report of the Congressional Committees Investigating the Iran-Contra Affair*, 100th Cong., 1st sess., 1987, S. Rept. 100-216 and H. Rept. 100-433, pp. 9-22.

intimidate and sabotage legitimate political opposition. The 1973 Watergate committee discovered efforts along these lines directed against legislators, among others, who were placed on an "enemies list" for opposing President Nixon's policies.[10]

Oversight is expected to serve yet another pragmatic purpose in the contemporary era. It is to be a principal means for Congress to regain lost power from the executive. As Allen Schick has noted, however, "It is from this perspective that members of Congress find oversight wanting. They sit at more hearings, commission more audits and studies, have access to more data, but do not feel that they really control what happens downtown."[11]

Despite this frustration surrounding oversight, other alternatives for gaining control over policy and the executive have their own built-in limits. For instance, passing highly specific, detailed laws often encounters strong objections from the executive, upset with restraints on its discretion; in any event, such laws are difficult to enact because of the usual need for bargaining and compromise to build majority support for a bill.[12] Indeed, partially because of the limitations of other devices, more is expected of oversight.

10. U.S. Congress, Senate, Select Committee on Presidential Campaign Activities, *Final Report*, 98th Cong., 2d sess., 1974, S. Rept. 98-981, pp. 3-22, 130-49.

11. Allen Schick, "Politics through Law: Congressional Limitations on Executive Discretion," in *Both Ends of the Avenue*, ed. Anthony King (Washington, DC: American Enterprise Institute, 1983), p. 166.

12. Ibid.; Kaiser, "Congressional Control," pp. 239-41, 247, 271.

Obstacles

Congressional oversight of the presidency can run into particular obstacles that make it more difficult—and more costly politically—to conduct than overseeing other executive establishments, such as a departmental bureau or a program office.

The president and, to a lesser degree, the institutional presidency are set apart from the rest of the executive branch through a number of formal and informal mechanisms. Among these are the president's express and implied constitutional powers, such as his position as commander in chief and his claims of executive privilege, respectively; the prestige and perquisites associated with the office of president; a nationwide electoral constituency and unequaled public visibility; and unparalleled ability to influence public opinion, to mobilize public support, and to set the policy agenda; and leadership of his party.

Congress's oversight efforts that challenge the president's powers—or his perception of them—and institutional supports, let alone the survival of an administration, can be met by a phalanx of defenses. Many of these arose in the Watergate investigation and the subsequent impeachment proceedings.

THE CHANGING PERCEPTION
AND MEANING OF OVERSIGHT

Over the past two decades, there has been a significant change in the way congressional oversight of the executive has been viewed. This change hinges on different understandings of what constitutes oversight, how much is actually conducted, and why it occurs. The transformation—from neglect to resurgence—is evident in oversight of the contemporary presidency.

From neglect to resurgence

Oversight—a word that lends itself to puns and possibly hyperbole—was labeled "Congress' neglected function" in the late 1960s.[13] The label has been hard to remove. During the next decade, legislators and observers were in agreement about "the inadequate oversight being done" and that it remained "one of Congress' most glaring deficiencies."[14]

Any lingering impression of neglect, however, has been seriously challenged in the interim. One study, for example, discovered a "very rapid recent growth in oversight" in the 1970s; the same author later added that the "amount of oversight done by Congress has increased substantially."[15] Another analysis boldly concluded that the "widespread perception that Congress has neglected its oversight responsibility is a widespread mistake."[16] Still another found that both

13. John F. Bibby, "Congress' Neglected Function," in *Republican Papers*, ed. Melvin R. Laird (Garden City, NY: Doubleday, Anchor Books, 1968), p. 477.

14. U.S., Congress, House, Select Committee on Committees, *Committee Reform Amendments of 1974*, 93d Cong., 2d sess., 1974, H. Rept. 93-916, p. 63; Roger H. Davidson, "Representation and Congressional Committees," *The Annals* of the American Academy of Political and Social Science, 411:55 (Jan. 1974).

15. Joel D. Aberbach, "Changes in Congressional Oversight," *American Behavioral Scientist*, 22:511 (May-June 1979); idem, "Congress and the Agencies: Four Themes of Congressional Oversight of Policy and Administration," in *The United States Congress*, ed. Dennis Hale (New Brunswick, NJ: Transaction Books, 1983), p. 285. See also idem, "The Congressional Committee Intelligence System: Information, Oversight, and Change," *Congress and the Presidency*, 14:51-76 (Spring 1987).

16. Mathew D. McCubbins and Thomas Schwartz, "Congressional Oversight Overlooked:

the House and the Senate evidenced a "heightened sensitivity to oversight" and that "the resurgence in oversight is reflected in Congress' assertiveness toward recent presidents."[17]

One of the reasons for the early, and lingering, impression of neglect is the high expectation associated with oversight, in terms of both philosophical principles and practical purposes. As noted earlier, oversight is expected to serve as a key to ensuring executive accountability and regaining lost legislative power. Frustrated with an inability to achieve such high expectations, legislators and observers may unfairly brand a less than perfect performance as neglect.

Competing definitions and their meaning

Changing definitions and understandings of oversight also help to explain its changing appearance.

If oversight, "strictly speaking, refers to review after the fact," as Joseph Harris defined it in the mid-1960s, then it is mostly composed of "inquiries about policies that are or have been in effect, investigations of past administrative actions, and the calling of executive officers to account for their financial transactions."[18] The minimalist school relegates oversight to a narrow range of purposeful activities and recognizes only a limited amount of oversight taking place.

This view is in decided contrast to

Police Patrols versus Fire Alarms," *American Journal of Political Science*, 28:176 (Feb. 1984).

17. Walter J. Oleszek, "Integration and Fragmentation: Key Themes of Congressional Change," *The Annals* of the American Academy of Political and Social Science, 466:200-201 (Mar. 1983).

18. Joseph P. Harris, *Congressional Control of Administration* (Washington, DC: Brookings Institution, 1964), p. 9.

more recent, broadly encompassing definitions, such as Morris Ogul's: "Legislative oversight is behavior by legislators and their staffs, individually or collectively, which results in an impact, intended or not, on bureaucratic behavior."[19] Based on this, oversight can be viewed as the review, monitoring, and supervision of past or ongoing executive activity and behavior, including plans for future operations or projects.[20]

This field of vision is substantially wider than simple review after the fact and takes in a larger amount of activity. It means that oversight is "polymorphic," as one author termed it; that is, it appears in different guises, forms, and varieties.[21] As demonstrated in recent studies,[22] the expansive understanding means the following:

1. Oversight can be manifest or latent, occurring by design, as in a focused investigation into misconduct by White House aides, or even when not specifically intended or recognized by legislators; the latter could occur during confirmation hearings that also look into the conduct of the presidency.

2. Oversight can occur in either official or unofficial settings, such as committee hearings or informal gatherings among legislators and presidential aides and sometimes the president himself.

3. Oversight can be direct or indirect, depending upon the location of the real target of an oversight inquiry. It is direct where the immediate subject and the long-range target are the same. For example, direct oversight of the presidency occurred when the Iran-contra committees examined the activities of the president's national security adviser and the NSC staff. Oversight is indirect where the immediate subject of an inquiry and the target differ. For example, indirect oversight of the presidency occurred when an appropriations subcommittee looked into a plan by OMB to consolidate inspection operations of the Customs Service and the Immigration and Naturalization Service; the subcommittee used hearings on Customs appropriations to question OMB's assumptions and projected savings, OMB's authority to implement the plan, and the presidential commission that generated it. The oversight target in this case was the absent presidency, not the present Customs Service.

4. Oversight can follow either a police-patrol or a fire-alarm approach. It can be a planned, active, and direct effort by congressional panels, searching out problem areas and information; or it can be an ad hoc, reactive, and indirect effort, waiting on charges in the press or complaints from parties adversely affected by administration policies.

5. Oversight can be either adversarial or supportive. Although it is usually stimulated by various conflicts between legislators and executive officials, oversight can also bolster a program or agency against its administration critics.

6. Oversight can have different pur-

19. Morris S. Ogul, *Congress Oversees the Bureaucracy: Studies in Legislative Supervision* (Pittsburgh, PA: University of Pittsburgh Press, 1976), p. 11.

20. Ibid., p. 7. See also Loch Johnson, "The U.S. Congress and the CIA: Monitoring the Dark Side of Government," *Legislative Studies Quarterly*, 4:477 (Nov. 1980); Frederick M. Kaiser, "Oversight of Foreign Policy: The U.S. House Committee on International Relations," ibid., 2:257 (Aug. 1977); Bert A. Rockman, "Legislative-Executive Relations and Legislative Oversight," ibid., 9:416-18 (Aug. 1984).

21. Rockman, "Executive-Legislative Relations," p. 387.

22. See studies cited in notes 15-17 and 19-20 of this article.

poses, either evaluation or control. It can be used to review and evaluate operations, programs, and activities of the presidency, thereby helping to ensure its accountability, or to check, control, and provide leverage over its specific actions, agencies, or officials.

OVERSIGHT IN ACTION

The various dimensions and characteristics of oversight are apparent in several contemporary illustrations of Congress's attempts to keep the presidency in its proper place, to paraphrase James Madison's view of the checks-and-balances system. On its oversight travels, which can include unforeseen detours and result in collisions, Congress can take:

—different vehicles, such as standing committees, temporary select committees, support agencies, and outside entities;
—different avenues or routes, such as hearings on appropriations and bills, investigations by select committees, informal contacts with executive personnel, and proceedings on nominations, treaties, and impeachments; and
—different directions, such as adversarial versus supportive, police-patrol versus fire-alarm approach, and evaluation versus control.

A couple of highly publicized investigations—of the intelligence community in the mid-1970s and the Iran-contra affair in 1987—demonstrate that oversight, when reinforced by other favorable conditions, can have a dramatic effect. It has helped to force officials out of office, change policies, and provide the catalyst for new statutory controls over the presidency and new oversight powers.

1975-75 intelligence community investigations

By the mid-1970s, the war in Vietnam, Watergate, and the reasons behind Richard Nixon's resignation had illustrated major failures and failings in the contemporary presidency. Further evidence of this condition, first disclosed in press accounts, was a range of long-standing illegal and unethical activities by intelligence agencies. Of particular concern were attempts by the Federal Bureau of Investigation (FBI) to "neutralize" civil rights leaders, infiltration by the Central Intelligence Agency (CIA) of dissident groups, planned assassinations of foreign leaders, and secret drug testing on unwitting subjects. In some cases, these problems were compounded by White House pressure to undertake the activities or capitalize on them; in other cases, they were compounded by negligence in the presidency, a failure to insist on accountability or to provide proper controls over the agencies.[23]

Examinations. In 1975, to investigate the charges, both the House and the Senate took the unusual step of setting up temporary select committees with nearly identical jurisdictions and mandates. Their efforts ran into barriers set up by the executive over access to clas-

23. U.S. Congress, Senate, Select Committee to Study Governmental Operations with Respect to Intelligence Activities, *Final Report*, 94th Cong., 2d sess., 1976, S. Rept. 94-755, book 1, pp. 127-52, 384-420, and book 2, pp. 5-20. For related developments, see Kaiser, "Oversight of Foreign Policy"; Johnson, "Monitoring the Dark Side"; Cecil V. Crabb, Jr., and Pat M. Holt, *Invitation to Struggle* 2d ed. (Washington, DC: CQ Press, 1984), pp. 161-87; Thomas M. Franck and Edward Weisband, *Foreign Policy by Congress* (New York: Oxford University Press, 1979), pp. 46-60, 115-34.

sified information. Policy disputes arose between Congress and the presidency, between Republicans and Democrats, and among Democrats, especially in the House.

The use of temporary select committees revealed a weakness within Congress. They were necessary because the regular system of oversight, particularly for monitoring executive activities and behavior, had been ineffective, insufficient, or nonexistent. The Senate investigating committee recognized this; it concluded that "Congress, which has the authority to place restraints on domestic intelligence activities through legislation, appropriations, and oversight committees, has not effectively asserted its responsibilities until recently."[24]

Other congressional inquiries supplemented the select committees'. The House Judiciary Committee, with the assistance of the General Accounting Office, occasionally called "Congress's watchdog," reviewed the FBI's domestic intelligence operations; this represented the first independent congressional investigation in the FBI's history. The House Foreign Affairs Committee, after receiving new authority, was able to monitor CIA covert operations abroad for the first time.

Effects. Shortly afterward, the House and Senate established Committees on Intelligence to consolidate oversight, funding, and legislative authority for the entire intelligence community. Congress also added new laws to restrict and control certain intelligence activities, to improve its own oversight capabilities, and to provide leverage over the agencies and their activities. These new arrangements and power cut into the substantial discretion over the CIA that administrations had enjoyed for nearly thirty years and cut into the sometimes symbiotic relationship between FBI directors and the White House that had proven harmful to democratic rights and to Congress.

1987 Iran-contra investigations

The Reagan administration has faced major congressional inquiries on secret arms sales to Iran and the diversion of arms profits to the contras in Nicaragua. These covert operations ignored or violated statutory prohibitions on funding the contras, and they avoided established channels of communication for notifying Congress as well as other executive officials, including members of the NSC and the Joint Chiefs of Staff. The operations were directed principally by the president's assistant for national security, personnel on the NSC staff, CIA operatives and officials, and private parties, both foreign and domestic.[25]

Congressional examinations. Oversight of this episode has been undertaken by a number of congressional panels looking into the affair itself, into proposed legislation to prevent similar occurrences, and into the president's nomination of a new director of central intelligence.

The Senate Intelligence Committee mounted a preliminary inquiry into the Iran-contra affair shortly after it broke in the press, in late 1986. The panel followed up on this effort when it examined the CIA deputy director's involvement in the whole affair, while it considered his nomination to become director of central intelligence, and when it held hearings on new legislation to cor-

24. Select Committee to Study Governmental Operations with Respect to Intelligence Activities, *Final Report*, p. 277.

25. Iran-Contra Committees, *Report*, pp. 11-22.

rect some of the underlying problems exposed by the investigation. The House Intelligence Committee reviewed aspects of the affair when it held hearings on a major bill to change presidential reporting requirements on covert operations. Still other House and Senate subcommittees inquired into possible drug-trafficking aspects of the Iran-contra affair and the adverse impact of the hostage-freeing effort on other executive agencies. Finally, a House Government Operations subcommittee, in part because of Iran-contra disclosures, has delved further into problems surrounding national security decision directives. These usually secret directives, issued over the president's signature and put into effect by his national security adviser, have been used to guide executive efforts in certain sensitive, classified matters, often without Congress's awareness.

Because of the widespread ramifications of the Iran-contra affair and jurisdictional overlap among congressional committees, both the House and Senate set up temporary select committees to consolidate the inquiry. The two panels, in what was apparently an unprecedented action, joined forces to conduct the inquiry, share information, hold hearings—including televised ones—and issue a report under both of their names. In addition to hiring outside counsel and other staff from the private sector, the Iran-contra committees relied upon congressional support agencies for additional personnel, studies, and reviews.

Independent counsel investigation. Another element in the Iran-contra investigation is the independent counsel, established in this case in part because of the initiatives of a House Judiciary subcommittee. An independent counsel can help Congress's oversight directly

and indirectly, particularly over the presidency.[26]

First of all, an independent counsel is required to report to Congress about its activities and to advise the House of any grounds for impeachment. Establishing an independent counsel also relieves Congress of the burden of trying to force an otherwise reluctant administration to conduct a criminal investigation of its own staff; Congress thus saves scarce political capital for other oversight investments.

Indirectly, an independent counsel's investigation lends credibility and legitimacy to Congress's separate endeavors. It may even help induce congressional testimony from recalcitrant witnesses. Eventually, the counsel's investigation could uncover other evidence and produce additional information that helps later oversight efforts. In addition, the independent counsel could bolster Congress's current—and future—oversight powers by prosecuting presidential staffers for deceiving Congress and destroying public documents.

In the short run, however, the existence of an independent counsel can impede congressional oversight inquiries. The Iran-contra panels, for instance, took precautions against exposing some findings and against granting limited immunity to witnesses prematurely, in order to avoid jeopardizing the

26. Ibid., pp. 686-88, 690. See also Charles Tiefer, "The Constitutionality of Independent Officers as Checks on Abuses of Executive Power," *Boston University Law Review*, 63:59-103 (Jan. 1983). The legal authority for the independent counsel, which has been recently reauthorized, is at 28 U.S.C. 591 et seq. In the meantime, moreover, the Supreme Court, in a 7 to 1 ruling, held the special counsel law to be constitutional. *Morrison, Independent Counsel* v. *Olson et al.*, Civil Action No. 87-1279 (U.S. Supreme Court, 29 June 1988).

counsel's potential prosecutions. Despite some assistance, moreover, the Iran-contra special counsel reportedly blocked congressional investigators' access to some Justice Department records that might be needed for eventual prosecutions.

Conflicts arise between an investigating committee and an independent counsel because differing perspectives, competing interests, and some incompatible goals guide the two. Success for a committee is measured in public exposure of executive wrongdoing—not necessarily criminal activity—and errors in policy judgments; in changes in administration personnel, procedures, and conduct of policy; and in legislative initiatives. Success for a counsel, by contrast, is measured in criminal indictments and, ultimately, convictions.

A plan to consolidate border inspections

In 1983, President Reagan's Cabinet Council on Management and Administration (CCMA) proposed to consolidate border-inspection operations of the Customs Service in the Treasury Department and the Immigration and Naturalization Service in the Justice Department.[27] CCMA, a progeny of then-White House counselor Edwin Meese, was set up to initiate and direct certain interdepartmental and interagency projects. The planned consolidation, endorsed by OMB, was reinforced by similar recommendations from the Grace commission, which

President Reagan established to survey the government and make recommendations for cost controls and cuts.

Examinations. The formal proposal, however, was not put into effect, largely because oversight inquiries brought out opposition to it. Centered in several House Appropriations and Government Operations subcommittees, this oversight effort was supplemented by a study by the Congressional Research Service and contacts between congressional staff and OMB personnel. All raised questions about the plan's impact; vast differences between various cost-saving estimates that came from the General Accounting Office, Grace commission task forces, agencies, and CCMA's senior staff; competing assumptions of which agency should do what; and the president's and OMB's authority to make such a change without new legislation.

Effects. Federal employee unions opposed to the plan were called to testify at congressional hearings. Despite the plan's official endorsement by the Immigration and Naturalization Service and Customs, moreover, differences between the two surfaced at the hearings. Conflict within the executive also included OMB. Congress's oversight effort revealed that OMB was perceived by agencies as "an advocate . . . and one of the contending parties"; because OMB could not coordinate the consolidation as an "honest broker," the job had to be taken over by another EOP office.[28]

INCENTIVES, STRUCTURES, AND CONDITIONS

The incentives to conduct oversight of the presidency, the congressional struc-

27. Cabinet Council on Management and Administration, *Congressional Briefing on Border Inspection Consolidation, Held on Nov. 16, 1983* (Washington, DC: Office of Management and Budget, 1983); U.S., Congress, House, Committee on Appropriations, Subcommittee on Treasury, Postal Service, and General Government, *Appropriations for Fiscal Year 1985*, 98th Cong., 2d sess., 1984, pt. 3, "Executive Office of the President," pp. 9-11, 342-45, 351-53, 391-401, 427-40, 463-69.

28. Subcommittee on Treasury, Postal Service, and General Government, *Appropriations for 1985*, p. 9.

tures supporting it, and the political conditions favoring it have improved in the recent past.

The earlier perceptions of neglected oversight were based, implicitly or explicitly, on the view that the incentives, structures, and conditions were not conducive to regular, systematic, or intensive oversight.[29] Most important for members of Congress, oversight took a back seat to the driving forces of reelection, constituent service, representation of clientele and constituent interests, and lawmaking. At the same time, Congress's ability and desire to conduct oversight were severely constrained when confronting a so-called imperial presidency, or at least one that dominated foreign policy. Congress also lacked sufficient resources and opportunities to challenge the presidency successfully on a regular basis. Despite notable improvements, the legislature's means of exercising "searching oversight," as Woodrow Wilson noted even in the era of congressional government, were still "limited and defective."

By the mid-1970s and into the 1980s, a great deal had changed in the polity, presidency, and Congress to foster and support independent oversight.

Political conditions

During the past twenty years, a number of political developments have reinforced congressional oversight of the presidency by separating the branches and by adding conflict over policies, priorities, and personnel.

Electoral and party changes. Changes in political parties, elections and campaigns, and candidates have been felt in the presidency and Congress. Two key developments are the continued decline of political parties and electoral allegiance plus the rise of the "personal" president, often attracting "outsiders" as candidates who have run anti-Washington and anti-Congress campaigns.[30]

Two key results have been frequent turnover in the White House and truncated party control of government. These have become the norm over the past two decades.

Only one president, Reagan, will have served two full terms; the others resigned (Nixon), lost election (Ford), or lost reelection (Carter). Only one president, Carter, enjoyed party control of both chambers of Congress for his entire administration, but his administration was limited to one term. Two, Nixon and Ford, failed to control even one house for a single two-year Congress. Finally, while the presidency has been regularly captured by Republicans—three of the last four presidents for 16 of 20 years—Congress has remained a bastion of the Democrats, the House for the entire 20 years and the Senate for all but 6.

The turnover among EOP staff is, of course, even higher than the change in presidents. President Reagan, for instance has had six national security advisers. The comparatively frequent change in personnel has been accompanied by changes in policies, programs, and priorities. These transfor-

29. See, esp., Morris S. Ogul, "Congressional Oversight: Structures and Incentives," in *Congress Reconsidered*, ed. Lawrence C. Dodd and Bruce I. Oppenheimer (Washington, DC: CQ Press, 1981); Morris P. Fiorina, "Congressional Control of the Bureaucracy: A Mismatch of Incentives and Capabilities," in ibid.; David R. Mayhew, *Congress: The Electoral Connection* (New Haven, CT: Yale University Press), pp. 110-40.

30. See, inter alia, Theodore J. Lowi, *The Personal President* (Itahaca, NY: Cornell University Press, 1985).

mations, especially when faced with divided party control, stimulate oversight efforts.

New presidential programs and priorities run into legislative opponents who sponsored the ones they are to replace. New presidential personnel run into legislators who are used to working with other officials; this change alone brings about uncertainty and may prompt closer scrutiny. The usual concern, however, has been exacerbated in the contemporary era, when the new appointees have also been seen as amateurs, unfamiliar with Congress and its procedures; as outsiders, unwilling to cooperate with it; or, especially, as hostile adversaries, contemptuous of the legislature and its members.

Presidential changes. A significant change in the institutional presidency that encourages oversight is the expanded operational role of various offices and the commensurate decline of their advisory status. Woodrow Wilson, examining the first century of presidential-congressional relations, suggested a similar tendency. He saw that department heads changed from being "simply counselors of the President [to becoming] in a very real sense members of the executive"; this transformation was accompanied by Congress's "extending its own sphere of activity" and "getting into the habit of investigating and managing every thing."[31]

In the Iran-contra affair, the NSC staff and the president's assistant for national security sacrificed their protected status as presidential advisers by becoming policy advocates and project operators. This shift lowered their immunity to congressional probes. In the

31. Wilson, *Congressional Government,* p. 46.

planned consolidation of border inspections, OMB was no longer an "honest broker" but had become a "contending party." The substitution also meant a further decline in its reputation for neutral competence, once a safeguard to critical congressional scrutiny.

Such changes in the institutional presidency as these foster oversight by Congress for two immediate reasons: the personnel lose their immunity, as presidential advisers, and they become important policy advocates, implementers, and operators. In effect, they move from the elevated presidential offices into more mundane executive or bureaucratic offices.

The transformation induces oversight for another reason. The expanded operational assignments for presidential offices encroach on the power and responsibilities of the executive agencies and departments; their heads are likely to protest—to Congress—the loss of policy control, as Secretary of State George Shultz did before the Iran-contra panels.

Agency and department heads, along with other top officials in their establishments, operate under important controls imposed by Congress and public law unlike, for example, the NSC staff and the president's national security adviser. Department and agency heads are confirmed by the Senate, are governed by specific statutory guidelines, have less administrative discretion available than does the president or his immediate subordinates, and appear regularly before oversight, appropriations, and authorization committees. The expanded operational use of EOP offices thus lessens congressional and statutory control over public policy. It also circumvents the usual working relationship between other executive officials and legislative panels. This harms not only congressional interests but also certain departmental and bureaucratic ones.

Seen in this light, congressional oversight of the presidency reflects disputes and rivalries that already exist within the executive. These include conflicts over policy, political power, and institutional interests that arise between the president and cabinet officers, White House staff and agency heads, political appointees and careerists, and policy advocates and opponents, among other competitors.

Societal changes. A number of changes in society have also contributed to increased oversight of the presidency. Investigative journalism, growing substantially since the early 1970s, feeds and feeds upon congressional investigations. A principal subject of these journalistic pursuits is the presidency.

Interest groups, both long-established traditional organizations and contemporary single-issue groups, prod congressional inquiries. As well, contemporary public interest organizations, such as Common Cause, not only monitor presidential activity but also tend to promote independent congressional scrutiny of the executive. There even exists a private organization, OMB Watch, that tracks and reports on the office's activities, frequently with a critical eye.

Congressional structure

The impetus for some of the long-term changes in oversight authority and structure came coincidentally from short-term oversight endeavors in the early 1970s, such as the Watergate hearings and the intelligence community inquiries.

Out of these efforts came new structures, powers, and statutory checks on

the executive, some directed especially at the presidency.[32] These included expanded reporting requirements, new intelligence committees, realignments of committee jurisdictions, and additional or improved subcommittees with increased autonomy, staff, resources, and mandates.

In the latter 1970s, independent counsels and statutory offices of inspector general were added to the arsenal of devices to check, and check on, the executive. Both conduct investigations of suspected executive misconduct, sometimes at the initiative of congressional panels, and both are required to report their findings to Congress.

All of these added resources and opportunities to oversee a White House weakened by the arrogance, failings, and abuses of its occupants and guests; their conduct eroded the credibility, respect, and trust that had been the foundation of the office of the president and his subordinates. The same developments laid a new foundation of increased control by Congress and for independent, assertive behavior by its members.

Trends in congressional activity in combination with certain policymaking conditions suggest a growth in oversight. The legislative emphasis "on adjustments, refinements, or cutbacks in current programs," rather than on designing new programs or agencies,[33] for instance,

32. See studies cited in notes 14-20 of this article; Roger H. Davidson and Walter J. Oleszek, "Adaptation and Consolidation: Structural Innovation in the U.S. House of Representatives," *Legislative Studies Quarterly,* 1:37-65 (Feb. 1976); James L. Sundquist, *The Decline and Resurgence of Congress* (Washington, DC: Brookings Institution, 1981).

33. Roger H. Davidson and Carol Hardy, "Indicators of House of Representatives Workload and Activity" (Manuscript, Congressional Research Service, 1987), p. 6. This feature plus other indica

indicates that more attention and effort go into reviewing existing operations and structures than planning new ones. In the contemporary era, actual and threatened budget cuts and competition for scarce resources foster both adversarial and supportive oversight. Legislators who want to reduce the number and costs of programs use oversight to assault program weaknesses and failings, while program promoters use it to defend their strengths or attack their administration critics.

Incentives

As a by-product of these many changes, legislative incentives are now

---

tors leads the authors to conclude that it "is likely that committee meetings are increasingly devoted to oversight and investigation as distinguished from developing and drafting legislation." Ibid., p. 24. For additional statistics on legislative activity and on indirect indicators of expanded oversight, see Norman J. Ornstein, Thomas E. Mann, and Michael J. Malbin, *Vital Statistics on Congress, 1987-1988* (Washington, DC: Congressional Quarterly, 1987), pp. 123-77.

more favorable to oversight than in the past. First of all, publicity has increased for such efforts. Also, various constituent, clientele, and some bureaucratic and executive interests also support oversight endeavors directed against the presidency. Consequently, oversight is not necessarily in competition with other functions—such as reelection, lawmaking, representation, or the ombudsman role—but can complement them.

In addition, legislators recognize that oversight, despite its difficulties and frustrations, offers the promise of retrieving lost power and regaining parity with the presidency. Public laws are only part of the answer to controlling public policy and conduct in the presidency. The Iran-contra panels concluded, for instance, that the serious abuses and illegalities "resulted from the failure of individuals to observe the law, not from deficiencies in existing law or in our system of governance."[34] Effective oversight—to ensure that the laws are being faithfully executed and to control the presidency—is an essential check.

34. Iran-Contra Committees, *Report,* p. 423.

ANNALS, *AAPSS*, **499**, September 1988

Gramm-Rudman-Hollings and the Politics of Deficit Reduction

By DARRELL M. WEST

ABSTRACT: Procedural change often has generated unanticipated consequences for the policymaking process. This article examines an effort in the United States Congress to institute a procedural mechanism for deficit reduction, the so-called Gramm-Rudman-Hollings procedure. Although the triggering mechanism for automatic spending reductions ultimately was declared unconstitutional by the Supreme Court, this case illustrates the strategic consequences that flow from procedural change. Negotiations over the content of Gramm-Rudman-Hollings dramatically shifted strategic advantages between Congress and the president as well as between Republicans and Democrats. A reform that started out with particular strategic consequences ended up being transformed into a procedure having quite different implications. This period, therefore, illustrates the crucial role that the strategic environment plays in legislative bargaining over deficit reduction.

Darrell M. West is associate professor of political science at Brown University. He received his Ph.D. from Indiana University in 1981. He has published Making Campaigns Count *and* Congress and Economic Policymaking *as well as numerous articles on public opinion and voting behavior in American elections.*

PROCEDURAL change is one of the primary constants of American political life. From the days of the Founding Fathers to contemporary efforts to deal with economic difficulties, dissatisfaction with the system has frequently led to reforms that altered the rules of the game and thereby sought to make it easier to achieve particular political objectives. Despite the frequency with which procedural prescriptions have been attempted, however, it has not been easy to predict the consequences of structural change. Reforms often have fallen short of intended goals, and they also have tended to generate unanticipated or undesired effects.

This article investigates a recent attempt in the United States Congress to use procedural change to achieve particular policy goals. Faced with ballooning budget deficits and an inability through more conventional means to reach agreements cutting these deficits, Congress and the president enacted a controversial procedure for deficit reduction—the Gramm-Rudman-Hollings mechanism of automatic spending cuts. Although the Supreme Court ultimately nullified the key triggering device behind this procedure, this case illustrates the crucial role that the strategic environment plays in legislative bargaining over policy matters. A reform that started out with particular ramifications for Congress and the president ended up being transformed into a procedure having quite different strategic implications. This article, therefore, illustrates the strategic consequences that flow from procedural change and also the dynamic nature of institutional conflict between Congress and the presidency.

PROCEDURAL REMEDIES FOR POLICY PROBLEMS: A STRATEGIC PERSPECTIVE

Political observers often presume that structural or procedural changes have policy implications. Given the regularity with which structural reforms are suggested and the intensity with which battles over procedural issues are fought, it is natural to assume that important ramifications arise from structural change. Yet it is clear, based on past reforms, that procedural changes have complex effects. It rarely is easy to discern direct links between structural change and policy consequences. The complexity of political processes and the tendency of reforms to generate unintended results make it difficult to discern effects with much precision.

To say that procedural changes have complex consequences is not to imply, however, that these effects are undecipherable. Procedural changes can have dramatic implications for the strategic environment in which policymaking takes place. This is particularly true in the case of institutions such as legislatures, where informal processes are central to policymaking and where the formal setting is characterized by a great degree of fragmentation and decentralization. The strategic environment in these settings can be an important intermediary factor between procedural reform and policy results.

There is little doubt that strategic processes are an essential ingredient of congressional decision making.[1] Leader-

1. Charles Jones and Randall Strahan, "The Effect of Energy Politics on Congressional and Executive Organizations in the 1970s," *Legislative Studies Quarterly*, 10(2):151-79 (May 1985);

ship strategies have always been a critical component of the legislative process, but they became unusually important after the congressional reforms of the 1970s. The declining influence of political parties made it difficult for leaders to ward off particularistic demands and build broad-based coalitions.[2] In addition, the substantial levels of public cynicism and mistrust that developed during that decade and the rise of budget limitations that constrained legislative policymaking placed a premium on strategic processes.

Few would claim that current economic conditions have eased the plight of legislators in this regard. Congressional inaction on the federal budget deficit has been one of the most widely discussed aspects of fiscal policy in recent years. With deficits that have risen to the multi-billion-dollar level and disagreements between representatives over the future course of fiscal policy, legislators have not yet been able to handle what most observers concede is a major policy problem.

There are several characteristics of the policy environment that have complicated efforts at deficit reduction. Though there is widespread agreement about the need to reduce the federal deficit— owing to its percentage of the gross national product and the large size of the interest payments on the debt—the costs and benefits of action in this area are not clear-cut. The economic costs of inactivity seem to be limited to future costs and they appear to come mainly in less visible forms, such as slower growth, higher interest rates, and the like. The

political benefits of deficit reduction meanwhile are rather diffuse. Because blame for the deficit problem currently is shared between Congress and the president as well as Republicans and Democrats, it is not clear that there are any partisan or electoral gains to successful action on the deficit.

There are also institutional barriers that have complicated deficit reduction: the divided control of political institutions at the national level, what some observers have described as the rising tide of partisanship in the contemporary Congress, and the volatility of legislative debates on the deficit.[3] All of these factors have complicated the strategic environment of legislative policymaking and have made it difficult for representatives to forge agreements on economic policy.

Yet these constraints did not prevent members of Congress in 1985 from taking forceful, albeit controversial, steps to deal with spiraling budget deficits. After several attempts to negotiate meaningful deficit-reduction agreements through conventional legislative means, Senators Phil Gramm and Warren Rudman, Republicans of Texas and New Hampshire, respectively, and Ernest Hollings, Democrat of South Carolina, introduced and eventually won enactment of a rather extraordinary spending-reduction procedure.[4] In the absence of voluntary congressional action to reduce the deficit, their procedure would have forced Congress and the president to cut the federal deficit by automatically triggering across-the-board reductions in government expenditures. Although the Supreme Court ultimately nullified the

Richard Fenno, *Congressmen in Committees* (Boston: Little, Brown, 1973).

2. Leroy Rieselbach reviews these developments in his *Congressional Reform* (Washington, DC: CQ Press, 1986).

3. Timothy Cook, "The Electoral Connection in the 99th Congress," *PS*, 19(1):16-22 (Winter 1986).

4. Elizabeth Wehr, "Congress Enacts Far-

triggering mechanism for Gramm-Rud-man-Hollings—that is, the sequestration order by the comptroller general—because of concern over its consequences for the separation-of-powers doctrine, the changes through which Gramm-Rudman-Hollings evolved between its introduction and its eventual enactment provide a fascinating case study of procedural efforts to deal with the deficit problem.[5] The legislative history of this period thereby illustrates how negotiations over the content of a procedural change had dramatic consequences for the strategic environment of congressional policymaking.

BACKGROUND ON DEFICIT REDUCTION: INITIAL EFFORTS

Reagan began his second term in an unusual position. Despite his 49-state sweep of Walter Mondale and an election vote total of more than 59 percent, Reagan faced major difficulties. In terms of political problems, Republicans gained only modestly in the House—they picked up only 16 seats—and actually lost two seats in the Senate. At the policy level, budget deficits were reaching crisis proportions. The deficit for fiscal year 1985

was projected at more than $200 billion; in following years, the figures looked even more grim. With unemployment hovering around 7.0 percent nationally and economic indicators projecting an uncertain future, Reagan started what should have been a triumphant second term in a position that did not look very promising.

This situation put great pressure on Congress to do something about federal spending, but the president's initial plan did little to develop enthusiasm among legislators. Announced publicly on 4 December 1984 by David Stockman, director of the Office of Management and Budget, and formally sent to Congress on 4 February 1985, Reagan's spending-reduction proposal was pronounced dead on arrival by representatives.[6] His plan proposed cutbacks of about $35.1 billion, with many of the reductions coming in politically sensitive programs benefiting middle-class or business interests, unlike the reductions of 1981, which fell disproportionately on less powerful, lower-class constituencies. Reagan's package, for example, proposed a one-year freeze in spending for many domestic programs, including Medicaid, Medicare, child nutrition subsides, farm price supports, rural electrification, and civil service retirement programs; selective cuts in others, such as sewage treatment grants, land management, and

Reaching Budget Measure," *Congressional Quarterly Weekly Report*, 14 Dec. 1985, pp. 2604-11.

5. The United States district court declared the automatic deficit-reduction process unconstitutional on 7 Feb. 1986, but it stayed the implementation of its order pending appeal to the Supreme Court. See the decision, "Economic Controls," *United States Law Week*, 18 Feb. 1986. The Supreme Court upheld this ruling 7 July 1986 on a 7-to-2 vote. See "Excerpts from High Court's Decision on Deficit-Cutting Act," *New York Times*, 8 July 1986; Elizabeth Wehr, "Court Strikes Down Core of Gramm-Rudman," *Congressional Quarterly Weekly Report*, 12 July 1986, pp. 1559-63. For a review of the background on this case, see "Synar Sues to Block Automatic Cuts," ibid., 14 Dec. 1985, p. 2607; Elizabeth Wehr, "Constitutional Test Hangs over Budget

Plan," ibid., 7 Dec. 1985, pp. 2547-49.

6. See Dale Tate, "Reagan's Budget Plan Subject to Hill Revision," *Congressional Quarterly Weekly Report*, 8 Dec. 1984, pp. 3062-63; idem, "FY 1986 Budget-Trim Options Aired by Senate GOP Leaders," ibid., 12 Jan. 1985, pp. 61-64; Pamela Fessler, "Shape of Fiscal 1986 Budget Eludes GOP Senate Leaders," ibid., 26 Jan. 1985, pp. 151-52; idem, "The Fiscal 1986 Reagan Budget: The Realities of Deficit-Cutting," ibid., 9 Feb. 1985, pp. 215-16; idem, "FY '86 Budget Projects Small Rise in Spending," ibid., 9 Feb. 1985, pp. 217-24.

Aid to Families with Dependent Children; and complete elimination of several programs, including the Small Business Administration, urban development action grants, Amtrak subsidies, general revenue sharing, the Job Corps, and the Export-Import Bank.

The president's proposal also generated controversy because of its glaring exclusion of defense spending from the cuts. Under Reagan's plan, military spending would be allowed to rise by an inflation-adjusted level of 5.9 percent. Finally, reflecting the general sensitivity of the issue plus the president's clear campaign pledge in 1984, Social Security would not be touched by the spending reductions. Although cost-of-living adjustments for several programs—such as civilian retirement and the military— would be delayed by one year, the president proposed no freeze or reductions in Social Security benefits.

The widespread dissatisfaction that developed over Reagan's deficit-reduction proposal led Congress to formulate its own budget package, but it soon became apparent that Republicans and Democrats as well as senators and House members had quite different spending priorities. The Senate Budget Committee took action first by approving on 14 March a budget resolution, the first step in the budget process, that would have cut the deficit by an estimated $55 billion.[7] Unlike the president's plan, which would have fallen completely on domestic programs, the Budget Committee froze cost-of-living increases during fiscal year 1986 for Social Security recipients and allowed defense spending to grow only with inflation—that is, there would be no real growth after

inflation. It also eliminated 13 domestic programs, including general revenue sharing, trade adjustment assistance, the Economic Development Administration, and community development block grants, among others. The Republican-led initiative produced a straight party-line vote of 11 to 10, just enough to send the legislation to the floor of the Senate. The full Senate considered and, after heated debate, approved this legislation on 10 May on a 49-to-49 tally, with Vice-President George Bush casting the tie-breaking vote.[8]

The House Budget Committee meanwhile passed a budget resolution on 16 May that cut spending by $56 billion.[9] This resolution, however, retained the 1986 cost-of-living adjustment for Social Security recipients, froze defense spending at 1985 levels, and eliminated only one program, general revenue sharing. The House plan, therefore, displayed quite different budgetary priorities from those of the Senate package. The Senate plan allowed for an inflation-adjusted increase for the military but not Social Security recipients, while the House version did the opposite, freezing defense and protecting Social Security. The committee vote was 21 to 12 with all Democrats favoring the bill and all Republicans, except W. Henson Moore of Louisiana, opposing it. The full House ratified this resolution 23 May on a 258-to-170 vote.[10]

7. Pamela Fessler, "Senate Panel's Party-Line Vote OKs Budget," *Congressional Quarterly Weekly Report*, 16 Mar. 1985, pp. 475-78.

8. Elizabeth Wehr, "Budget Squeaks through Senate Floor Vote," *Congressional Quarterly Weekly Report*, 11 May 1985, pp. 871-74.

9. Jacqueline Calmes, "House Panel Gives Quick OK to '86 Budget," *Congressional Quarterly Weekly Report*, 18 May 1985, pp. 915-22.

10. Jacqueline Calmes, "House, with Little Difficulty, Passes '86 Budget Resolution," *Congressional Quarterly Weekly Report*, 25 May 1985, pp. 971-79.

Not only were there clear differences in budgetary priorities between the House and Senate; there also were distinctive deficit-reduction coalitions in each chamber. The winning coalition in the Senate was almost entirely Republican. Only one Democrat, Zorinsky, voted in favor of the reductions, and only four Republicans—D'Amato, Hawkins, Mathias, and Specter—opposed them. The House deficit-reduction coalition, in contrast, was almost entirely Democratic. On the Republican side, 86.6 percent of members voted against their chamber's Democratically crafted bill, while 94.0 percent of Democrats favored their party's stance; only 15 Democrats defected from the party fold.

This conflict over budgetary priorities as well as the contrasting coalitions in the House and Senate obviously complicated the ability of Congress to undertake serious deficit reduction. House-Senate conferees had a difficult time resolving their substantive differences. The president torpedoed a preliminary agreement with Senate Republicans on reductions in Social Security benefits. Senate Republicans meanwhile accused House Democrats of padding their deficit-reduction estimates with unrealistic savings.

After an extended period of discussion, conferees agreed on 1 August 1985 on a deficit-reduction package. The House by a 309-to-119 vote and the Senate by a 67-to-32 margin approved a budget agreement that left the expected deficit for fiscal year 1986 at around $172 billion, which was about $55 billion lower than the projected figure. The compromise resolution contained no tax increases, as President Reagan had promised during the 1984 campaign, and no reduction in Social Security benefits, as Speaker O'Neill had wanted.

The greatest amount of deficit reduction took place on the expenditure side, with both defense and domestic programs— namely, Amtrak, mass transit, and economic development grants—sharing the burden.

Many observers, though, were skeptical of this deficit-reduction agreement. The rosy economic assumptions contained in the deficit-reduction estimates and the illusory nature of the proposed spending cuts led a number of independent analysts to conclude that the actual spending reductions would be much lower than predicted by the budget resolution.[11] In addition, because this package represented only a budget resolution, the first step in the budget process, it still needed to be followed up by appropriations legislation that would implement the actual cuts. Without additional action, real spending reductions could be problematic.

This fear soon turned to reality. By the start of the 1986 fiscal year on 1 October 1985, and for several months following, Congress had not taken any systematic action to implement its earlier deficit-reduction accord. There were a number of attempts to execute an agreement between the two chambers, but none of them won congressional support.

It was during this period of legislative inactivity on the deficit that members, growing increasingly frustrated with the snail's pace of deficit reduction, debated and ultimately enacted the Gramm-Rudman-Hollings procedure of automatic spending cuts. The Gramm-Rudman-Hollings proposal introduced in late September 1985 by Senators Phil Gramm, Warren Rudman, and Ernest Hollings, was designed to force Congress and the president to reduce government expendi-

11. "Congress Wearily OKs '86 Budget," *Providence Journal*, 2 Aug. 1985.

tures, but as we will see in following sections, this path to deficit reduction was fraught with difficulties.

THE INTRODUCTION AND EVOLUTION OF GRAMM-RUDMAN-HOLLINGS

Gramm-Rudman-Hollings was introduced by conservatives as a tool for reducing government spending across the board, but neither Gramm nor Rudman nor Hollings probably had any idea at the time that their procedure would be adopted by Congress.[12] It came as a great surprise when, shortly after the proposal was introduced, it swept through the United States Senate. Though described by one sponsor as "a bad idea whose time has come," the Senate passed this legislation 75 to 24 on 9 October 1985.

The legislation as enacted by the Senate required that elected officials eliminate the federal deficit in phased steps by 1991, either through conventional means or, failing to reach agreement, through automatic spending cuts.[13] Specific deficit-reduction targets would be established for each year—$180 billion for fiscal 1986, $144 billion for fiscal 1987, $108 billion for fiscal 1988, $72 billion for fiscal 1989, $36 billion for fiscal 1990, and zero in fiscal 1991—and failure to reach these targets, as determined by the Congressional Budget Office and Office of Management and Budget, would require across-the-board reductions in government programs.

This action proved to be quite controversial. Part of the problem was procedural in nature. Because the bill's sponsors bypassed usual legislative routines—committee hearings and the like—by attaching the bill as a rider to the debt-ceiling legislation on the Senate floor, skeptics worried about the lack of debate on such an important procedural change. Government officials, however, also worried openly about the substantive consequences of the automatic cuts. One opponent called the idea a "suicide pact" because of the pressure it would place on legislators to enact draconian cuts in domestic programs.[14] Others, including President Reagan, worried about the constraints this act would place on defense spending. Even proponents conceded that Gramm-Rudman-Hollings had serious flaws, but they argued that meaningful deficit reduction would not take place without procedural incentives to do so.

It was at this point in the debate that action shifted to the House of Representatives. Because the proposal had passed the Senate, House members had three possible responses: they could ignore it as a symbolic effort to embarrass the Democratic Party; they could explicitly reject the legislation as bad policy; or they could negotiate with the Senate in order to water down the bill's more

12. An insider's account of Gramm's deficit-reduction efforts is provided in David Stockman, *The Triumph of Politics: Why the Reagan Revolution Failed* (New York: Harper & Row, 1986). For a report on Gramm's perspective, see Jacqueline Calmes, "Gramm: Making Waves, Enemies and History," *Congressional Quarterly Weekly Report*, 15 Mar. 1986, pp. 611-15.

13. Elizabeth Wehr, "Senate Passes Plan to Balance Federal Budget," *Congressional Quarterly Weekly Report*, 12 Oct. 1985, pp. 2035-42. The quote comes from Senator Rudman and is cited in Elizabeth Wehr, "Congress Enacts Far-Reaching Budget Measure," p. 2604. Other articles that deal with Gramm-Rudman include idem, "Budget Conference Leaders Agree on Key Points," ibid., 7 Dec. 1985, p. 2548; Steven Roberts, "Many in Congress Say Session of '85 Was Unproductive," *New York Times*, 22 Dec. 1985.

14. This quote is from Senator Daniel Patrick Moynihan and is cited in Wehr, "Congress Enacts Far-Reaching Budget Measure," p. 2605.

deleterious features. Not wanting the stigma of being against the symbol of deficit reduction, though, House leaders chose to negotiate with the Senate. They thereby began discussions that eventually culminated in congressional passage of the revised Gramm-Rudman-Hollings procedure.

House Democrats initially had several concerns. One of their reservations was substantive in nature; they worried that the across-the-board nature of the automatic cuts would produce spending reductions that fell much more heavily on domestic than military programs. Given the greater preponderance of social welfare than military spending in the overall budget, they feared the original formulation of Gramm-Rudman-Hollings would fall disproportionately on Democratic programs and constituencies.

They also were aware that, from a strategic standpoint, Gramm-Rudman-Hollings put them in a difficult bargaining situation with Senate Republicans and President Reagan. In the formulation passed by the Senate, opponents of domestic spending would have powerful institutional advantages over supporters. The combination of automatic, across-the-board cuts and the disproportionate amount of social welfare dollars in the federal budget meant that either Reagan or Republicans in general could employ the strategy of delay and deadlock to their own partisan advantage. By doing nothing and failing to reach a voluntary deficit-reduction agreement, the president would be able to fall back on a procedural device that would reduce social welfare spending more than military expenditures. Gramm-Rudman-Hollings, in its original formulation, thus offered important advantages to Republicans over Democrats and to the president vis-à-vis Congress.

Recognizing the asymmetry of these advantages, House Democrats undertook a long series of discussions with the White House and Senate and were ultimately able to win several key concessions. Though straightforward in a procedural sense, these perfecting amendments had dramatic consequences for the strategic environment and also shifted more of the onus for deficit reduction away from Democratic programs and constituents. While the initial formulation of Gramm-Rudman-Hollings called for across-the-board reductions if Congress did not take action, Democrats were able to protect social programs and ensure that deficit reduction did not fall as heavily on nondefense programs by exempting nearly two-thirds of the budget from automatic cuts: Social Security, interest on federal debt, veteran's compensation and pensions, Medicaid, Aid to Families with Dependent Children, food programs for women and children, Supplemental Security Income, food stamps, and child nutrition. Limits also were placed on cuts in Medicare and other health programs.

House Democrats also required that the automatic cuts be divided equally between defense and nondefense accounts, again to prevent domestic programs from bearing a disproportionate share of the burden. Democratic leaders finally were able to convince a reluctant White House to place responsibility for administering the automatic cuts with the comptroller general, an individual who, though technically independent, is subject to removal by Congress.[15]

15. The office of comptroller general later became one of the critical constitutional issues in the lawsuit against Gramm-Rudman-Hollings as critics claimed Congress's power to remove the comptroller general violated the separation-of-powers doctrine.

These changes, while seemingly simple, had major consequences for leadership strategies. Democrats wanted to keep the president from being able to use delay and deadlock as a political strategy. If the original formulation of Gramm-Rudman-Hollings had been enacted, Reagan could have forced much larger cuts in domestic than military spending simply by doing nothing and waiting for the automatic, across-the-board reductions to take place. The exemption of leading social welfare programs from the legislation along with the requirement that defense spending share equally in automatic reductions gave Democrats strategic advantages vis-à-vis the president. Not only were they able to limit a proposal originally designed to scale back domestic spending; Democratic leaders were also able to turn Gramm-Rudman-Hollings into a procedure that could be used to force the president into reductions in defense spending and possibly even into accepting tax increases, which the president obviously was not eager to do.

House Democrats, though, were not the only ones trying to gain strategic advantages. Senate Republicans also used the amending process to try to protect their electoral flanks in 1986. Because twice as many Senate seats to be filled during the 1986 midterm elections were occupied by Republicans— 22 of the 34 seats—GOP leaders bargained to restrict sensitive deficit cuts before these elections. After extensive discussions on this point, House-Senate conferees agreed to limit budget cuts before the election to $11.7 billion. In winning House agreement with this plan, Republicans sought to reduce their risk of losing control of the Senate in 1986, although ultimately they still lost the Senate in these elections. Even if it

meant agreeing to House changes that shifted the original thrust of Gramm-Rudman-Hollings, Senate leaders were willing to approve these changes in order to reduce their electoral risks.

The negotiations over Gramm-Rudman-Hollings were important furthermore because they introduced new timetables and budget requirements into the fiscal-policy debate. Two changes that were especially important included specific budget numbers and timetables for deficit reduction, and a requirement that budget amendments be revenue neutral. Specific timetables initially were established to guarantee political accountability for legislators. By having visible and concrete goals for reducing the deficit—culminating in a balanced budget by 1991—voters and interested observers could easily evaluate deficit-reduction actions. These timetables, in fact, were noteworthy because politicians normally avoid specificity like the plague. Concrete standards create clear criteria of success and failure, and most leaders seek to avoid that kind of clarity.

In addition, economists worried that deficit reduction by formula was a recipe for disaster. Deficit reduction without regard to changing economic conditions could throw the country into a recession. If the economy needed a fiscal stimulus, automatic spending reductions could run counter to sound fiscal policy.[16]

The requirement that budget amendments be revenue neutral meanwhile placed serious constraints on new spending initiatives. Congress could not, according to Gramm-Rudman-Hollings, take any budget actions that increased the deficit. Spending changes that increased the red ink had to be accom-

16. Elizabeth Wehr, "Economists Warn Gramm-Rudman Threatens Stagnation," *Congressional Quarterly Weekly Report*, 26 July 1986, p. 1681.

panied either by decreases in other areas or by revenue increases. This change meant that along with the usual procedural and institutional restrictions on congressional policymaking, members now faced additional fiscal restraints.

The evolution of Gramm-Rudman-Hollings, in short, illustrates the important policy and strategic consequences that can flow from procedural changes. By exempting two-thirds of the budget and requiring that deficit reduction fall equally on defense and domestic programs, Democrats spread the political risks of unpopular spending cuts more evenly between Republicans and Democrats and between Congress and the president. They furthermore altered the automatic-reduction procedure in such a way that it no longer was as advantageous for the president to use delay and deadlock as a legislative strategy. Failure to reach a voluntary agreement on deficit reduction would invoke spending cuts that would not only harm programs of interest to Democrats; it also would hit programs cherished by a conservative president.

THE STRATEGIC DIMENSIONS OF DEFICIT REDUCTION

The Gramm-Rudman-Hollings case illustrates the strategic consequences that develop from procedural change. Negotiations over the content of Gramm-Rudman-Hollings had the effect of turning a procedure designed to scale back domestic spending into a process that could be used to cut both domestic and defense spending and that furthermore might be used someday as a vehicle for a future tax increase. These discussions also altered the strategic environment of deficit reduction. The perfecting amendments adopted by House-Senate conferees dramatically shifted strategic advantages between Congress and the president and between Republicans and Democrats.

At a more general level, however, this case allows observers to understand why strategic factors are an important, and sometimes underappreciated, part of the deficit-reduction process. There are a number of economic and structural factors that have complicated policymaking in the budget area: the perennial trade-offs between unemployment and inflation, the decentralization and fragmentation of legislative process, the lack of consensus about budget matters, and the like.

Yet it seems clear, based on recent deficit-reduction actions in Congress, that the subject is more complex than structural or economic perspectives would grant. Policymaking inherently is a political process, and one cannot completely understand policy decisions through structural arguments or resource limitations alone. Efforts at deficit reduction, in particular, have been more complex than generally realized because there is a strategic component to the subject that often has not been fully understood.

The need to develop a strategic model of deficit reduction has been readily apparent during the Reagan era. There has been growing speculation in the current period that, at different times, both President Reagan and Democratic leaders have adopted policy deadlock on the deficit as a political strategy. Senator Daniel Patrick Moynihan, for example, has argued that Reagan is using high deficits as a strategic tool to force further cutbacks in social welfare spending.[17] As long as deficits are high,

17. Moynihan made this argument in his column, "Placing the Deficit in Perspective," *Providence Journal*, 23 July 1985.

there can be no new social programs or no expansion of existing programs.

There also is considerable pressure in this situation to reduce spending on domestic programs further. This argument suggests that policy stalemate or conscious inaction on the part of Reagan and his legislative supporters may not necessarily represent negative outcomes from their standpoint and may, in fact, serve the partisan political interests of these individuals.

Others have pointed out that, from time to time, Democratic leaders also have used delays and the threat of deadlock on the deficit to force compromises with the president. Knowing that Reagan prefers to reduce domestic spending more than he wants to raise taxes or slow the growth of military spending, House Democrats occasionally have sought to protect their political interests by refusing to compromise with the president.

Because of the strategic component to legislative bargaining over the deficit, this period demonstrates why deficit reduction has been so difficult and also why representatives fell back on a procedural device—Gramm-Rudman-Hollings—about which few were enthusiastic and that ultimately turned out to be unconstitutional. In a situation of diffuse political costs and uncertain benefits, deficit reduction becomes a major part of the bargaining process between institutions. Failure to appreciate the strategic dimension of this situation makes it more difficult to understand both the politics of deficit reduction and the strategic consequences that flow from procedural change.

ANNALS, *AAPSS*, **499**, September 1988

The Consequences of
Budget Reform for
Congressional-Presidential Relations

ABSTRACT: The struggle between Congress and the president over spending and taxing was altered significantly by the Congressional Budget and Impoundment Control Act of 1974 and the Gramm-Rudman-Hollings Act of 1985. The purpose of this article is to evaluate the impact of these reforms on congressional-presidential budgeting. The analysis answers two questions: what are the major budgetary reforms that have influenced congressional-presidential relations, and what have been the consequences of these changes? The article concludes that the budget reforms have strengthened the congressional role vis-à-vis the president's role in the budget-making process. Macro-budgetary and macro economic trade-offs between Congress and the president are highlighted. In sum, the reforms have made budgeting between the president and Congress more difficult. They have increased the number of budgetary participants, made the budget process more open, forced the president to work more closely with Congress, and allowed Congress gradually to tighten control over executive spending discretion.

James A. Thurber is professor of government at the American University, Washington, D.C., and director of the Center for Congressional and Presidential Studies. He is former director of the Battelle Human Affairs Research Centers in Washington, D.C., and former legislative assistant to Senator Hubert H. Humphrey. He served as professional staff for the reorganization of the U.S. Senate committee system and for the Commission on Administrative Review of the U.S. House of Representatives. He was also an American Political Science Association congressional fellow.

NOTE: Research for this article was partially funded by the American University and the Everett McKinley Dirksen Congressional Center.

101

THE struggle between the president and Congress over the size and composition of government taxing and spending is at the heart of American politics. The power to establish the federal budget of the United States has been shared between the executive and Congress throughout American history. Congress is given the constitutional power of the purse, the authority to establish the necessary revenue policy and to authorize, appropriate, and budget money for the president as chief executive to spend on his programs. Budgets reveal the nation's priorities, problems, and processes of social choice; it is here that the checks and balances between Congress and the president are often glaringly apparent. After decades of conflict and increasing centralization of the budget by the president, Congress passed the Budget and Impoundment Control Act of 1974 (Public Law 93-344). After another decade of budgetary struggle and often deadlock with the president, Congress passed a second major reform, the 1985 Balanced Budget and Emergency Deficit Control Act (Public Law 99-177), commonly called Gramm-Rudman-Hollings (GRH). With both of these reforms, Congress sought to recapture presidential domination of the budget-making process. The purpose of this article is to evaluate the impact of these reforms on congressional-presidential budgetary relations.

CONGRESSIONAL BUDGET REFORM

Prior to 1974, Congress considered the president's annual budget in a highly decentralized manner. Authorizations for federal agencies and programs were considered separately by congressional authorizing committees. Appropriations of funds for these agencies and programs were considered by the House and Senate Appropriations Committees working through subcommittees. Revenue policies were handled by yet another committee in the House—Ways and Means—and the Finance Committee in the Senate. Congress considered the budget piecemeal and at no point did the House or Senate evaluate the relation between total expenditures and total revenues. These were only by-products of decentralized decisions made by committees and subcommittees strongly influenced by those interests groups and agencies with the resources and access to participate. The president's budget came far more from the power of interest groups and agencies than from congressional concern about the economic consequences of their collective decisions. At no point did Congress review the total budget through its committees or on the Senate or House floors. The full budget was not visible until all of the appropriations subcommittee bills were passed. To compound the problem, supplemental appropriations bills were often passed in the middle of a fiscal year, making the size of the budget a moving target. Congress had no budget committees, skilled budget experts, or a comprehensive budget-making process to bring discipline to the process and to challenge the president's budget.

The 1974 reform in the way Congress made budgetary decisions had the potential for remedying these problems and for changing the struggle with the president. The Congressional Budget Act, consisting of Titles I through IX of Public Law 93-344, established several major institutions and procedures that changed congressional-presidential relations.[1] The Budget Act had the potential to restore congressional power over fiscal policy. The act created separate House and Senate Budget Committees, responsible for setting overall tax and spending levels.[2] Most important, it required Congress each year to establish levels of expenditures and revenues and prescribed procedures for arriving at those spending and income totals. The procedures, later revised by GRH, include three important elements: (1) a timetable establishing deadlines for action on budget-related legislation, intended to ensure completion of the budget plan prior to the start of each new fiscal year; (2) a requirement to adopt concurrent budget resolutions—which do not require presidential approval—for total budget authority, budget outlays, and revenues for the upcoming fiscal year; and (3) a reconciliation process to conform revenue, spending, and debt legislation to the levels specified in the budget resolution.[3] The reconciliation process gives the budget committees power to direct other committees to determine and recommend revenue and/or spending actions deemed neces-

sary to conform to the determinations made in the budget resolution. The Budget Act also created a Congressional Budget Office, which provides Congress with independent information and analysis on the budget. Title X of the act includes the presidential impoundment control provisions of the reform.[4] The act sanctions two kinds of presidential impoundments: deferrals and rescissions.[5] Deferrals are presidential requests to Congress to postpone or delay spending for a particular program. Rescissions are presidential requests to abolish funding for a program permanently. If Congress wants to reorder the president's budget priorities, it can use these institutions and procedures to do so.

GRH and amendments made to it in 1987 changed the congressional budget process further by establishing a procedure to reduce deficits to annual maximum levels through mandatory sequestration of funds if the Congress does not reduce the deficit through legislation.[6] The law originally provided for annual reductions in the budget deficits from $171.9 billion in fiscal year 1986 to zero in fiscal year 1991 but was revised in 1987 to set 1994 as the balanced-budget year.[7] If the deficit limits are not met,

1. See James A. Thurber, "Congressional Budget Reform and New Demands for Policy Analysis," *Policy Analysis*, Spring 1976, pp. 198-214. See also James A. Thurber, "Assessing the Congressional Budget Process under Gramm-Rudman-Hollings and the 1974 Budget Act" (Paper delivered at the Annual Meeting of the American Political Science Association, Washington, DC, 1986).

2. See John W. Ellwood and James A. Thurber, "The New Congressional Budget Process: The Hows and Whys of House-Senate Differences," in *Congress Reconsidered*, ed. L. C. Dodd and B. Oppenheimer (New York: Praeger, 1977), pp. 163-92.

3. See Allen Schick, *Reconciliation and the Congressional Budget Process* (Washington, DC: American Enterprise Institute, 1981).

4. See James P. Pfiffner, *The President, the Budget, and Congress: Impoundment and the 1974 Budget Act* (Boulder, CO: Westview Press, 1979).

5. Dale Tate, "Reconciliation Breeds Tumult as Committees Tackle Cuts: Revolutionary Budget Tool," *Congressional Quarterly Weekly Report*, 23 May 1981, pp. 887-91.

6. See Elizabeth Wehr, "Congress Enacts Far-Reaching Budget Measure," *Congressional Quarterly Weekly Report*, 14 Dec. 1985, pp. 2604-11.

7. For two articles on the Supreme Court case regarding GRH, see Jonathan Rauch, "The Thickening Fog," *National Journal*, 12 July 1986, pp. 1721-24; Elizabeth Wehr, "Court Strikes Down

automatic spending cuts will be made by the Office of Management and Budget (OMB) using a congressionally mandated formula.[8]

In summary, the 1974 Budget Act and GRH have created several major institutions and processes that have the potential of greatly influencing congressional-presidential budgetary relations.[9] What has been the impact of these budgetary institutions and processes on the struggle between the president and Congress? To answer this question, the present analysis focuses on four hypotheses about the consequences of the budget reforms for congressional-presidential relations. These hypotheses are (1) that reforms have increased congressional influence over presidential budget priorities; (2) that the reforms have allowed Congress to control presidential impoundments; (3) that the reforms have changed the budgeting power of presidents, agencies, committees, congressional leadership, and interest groups; and (4) that the reforms have created greater congressional control of the budget.

Core of Gramm-Rudman," *Congressional Quarterly Weekly Report*, 12 July 1986, pp. 1559-63.

8. See Elizabeth Wehr, "Gramm-Rudman: Domenici Has His Doubts," *Congressional Quarterly Weekly Report*, 19 Sept. 1987, pp. 2234-35.

9. See Ellwood and Thurber, "New Congressional Budget Process"; Louis Fisher, "Ten Years of the Budget Act: Still Searching for Controls," *Public Budgeting and Finance*, Autumn 1985, p. 15. See also John Ferejohn and Keith Krehbiel, "The Budget Process and the Size of Budget," *American Journal of Political Science*, May 1987, the Budpp. 296-320; Kenneth A. Shepsle, "The Congressional Budget Process: Diagnosis, Prescription, Prognosis," in *Congressional Budgeting: Politics, Process, and Power*, ed. W. T. Wander, F. T. Hebert, and G. W. Copeland (Baltimore, MD: Johns Hopkins University Press, 1984).

Congressional-presidential budget priorities

Advocates of the 1974 Budget Act argued for "an improved congressional system for determining relative funding priorities."[10] Many felt reform was needed in order to unify the disaggregated budgetary process and to create a mechanism for challenging and changing presidential budget priorities. The first chairman of the House Budget Committee, Representative Brock Adams, stated it simply: "Perhaps the most important aspect of the budget resolution is the fact it contains the budget of Congress and not that of the President."[11]

Congressional-presidential budget relations are driven by a highly representative, fragmented, and decentralized decision-making system that is organized to make incremental distributive decisions in favor of strong interests groups, agencies, and congressional committees. The budget process is pluralistic and incremental, with each agency and association guarding its part of the budget. Past budget decisions are given preference over requests for new programs. GRH forces Congress to reaffirm existing budget priorities, leaving few resources and little congressional energy to tackle new programs. Automatic across-the-board cuts in the sequester-based outlays under GRH by definition do not change budget priorities; they simply set existing program preferences permanently in place. If change does come, it will likely be increment by increment or by exceptions, not through radical reordering of budget priorities based on newfound

10. Thurber, "Congressional Budget Reform."
11. Lance T. LeLoup, *Budgetary Politics: Dollars, Deficits, Decisions* (Brunswick, OH: King's Court Communications, 1977), p. 126.

congressional budgetary power.[12]

Federal budget outlays grew dramatically from 1974 to 1988, but only slight changes occurred in the way the budget was allocated across general functions of government. Spending grew in constant dollars from $538.7 billion in 1974 to an estimated $839.3 billion for 1988. As a percentage of gross national product spent by the federal government, the budget grew from 19.0 to 21.7 percent during the same time period. Change in the relative percentage of outlays in budget functions, however, was only slight during the same period; for example, expenditures for national defense dropped from 29.5 percent to 29.0 percent and those for human resources dropped from 50.4 to 50.0 percent of outlays. The most dramatic shift in spending preferences was caused by borrowing to pay for the increase in the depth budget, the interest on the federal government's debt. From 1974 to 1988, the interest increased by 5.6 percent. This was, of course, unrelated to Congress's exerting a budgetary power over the president's spending priorities.

This real growth in government spending happened primarily through pluralistic incrementalism, budgetary decision making that guarantees that strong interest groups, committees, and agencies coalesce to protect their base spending and secure their fair share of increase. No major group has been significantly disadvantaged by budget reform. No major programs have been cut. No congressional committees have tried to abolish programs under their jurisdic-

tion. There have been no major shifts in spending priorities as a direct result of the 1974 budget process or GRH.

The Budget Act did change the nature of the congressional policy agenda and the debate over the budget. Though the reforms give Congress the potential of more budgetary power, it is the power to check the president, not to change major spending priorities. Ironically, that is the same power gained by the president, the power to block but not to initiate major changes in spending outlays. Congress is forced to focus on cutbacks in proposed increases rather than on new initiatives and dramatic increases in existing programs. With the massive federal government debt and continual deficits, the setting of overall revenue and spending limits each year has caused a major change in the floor debate from how to solve new problems to how to save money and reduce the size of government expenditures. Congress has had to learn to say no to major increases and new programs and to say it to presidents, interest groups, and constituents.

The Budget Act of 1974 and the GRH acts have given Congress the means to compete with the president's policy agenda; however, the complexity of the process and the size of the federal debt have forced Congress to focus primarily on spending cuts and budget control rather than dramatically changing presidential spending priorities. Thus confirmation of the hypothesis that the reforms have increased congressional influence over presidential budget priorities is still an open question.

12. See Allen Schick, *Congress and Money: Budgeting, Spending and Taxing* (Washington, DC: Urban Institute); idem, "Budgeting as an Administrative Process," in *Perspectives on Budgeting* (Washington, DC: American Society for Public Administration, 1980).

Congressional control of presidential impoundments

Have the reforms allowed Congress to control presidential impoundments?

Is the president obligated to spend money appropriated by Congress? President Nixon claimed the legal and constitutional power to impound funds already authorized and signed into law. Nixon challenged the constitutional doctrine of separation of powers that delegates to Congress powers of the purse and to the president the duty of spending appropriated funds. Nixon's impoundment actions, although later found to be unconstitutional, were a major cause of the quick passage of the 1974 Budget Act. A major objective of the Congressional Budget and Impoundment Control Act of 1974 was to control presidential impoundments. Procedures were established in Title X of the act to review presidential proposals for two kinds of impoundment: deferrals, to postpone or delay spending, and rescissions, to cancel or take back authority to spend. When presidents propose deferrals of up to 12 months, Congress may approve an impoundment resolution compelling the release of the affected funds. The original deferral process called for a one-house legislative veto, which the *INS* v. *Chadha* decision found to be unconstitutional,[13] but Congress has circumvented the constitutionality issue by voting on deferral decisions in both houses primarily by adding them to appropriations bills.

When a president proposes a rescission, however, it is much more difficult to garner congressional support. Congress has a 45-day period during which it can pass a bill rescinding the funds,

13. See William P. Schaefer and James A. Thurber, "The Legislative Veto and the Policy Subsystems: Its Impact on Congressional Oversight" (Paper delivered at the Annual Meeting of the Southern Political Science Association, Atlanta, GA, 1980). See also Louis Fisher, "Impoundment: Here We Go Again," *Public Budgeting and Finance*, Winter 1986, p. 72.

thereby approving the presidential rescission. If Congress fails to act during this period, the president is required to make the funds available for expenditure.

The effect of the impoundment provisions on congressional-presidential relations has been significant. The provisions have regularized and set a legal foundation for presidential impoundments while allowing Congress to overturn these cuts when it desires. Congress has control over presidential impoundments, with a latent consequence that presidents can legally use them to cut back on spending they deem unnecessary.

Table 1 shows an overall high approval rate for deferrals—over 80 percent. President Reagan's success through 1987 was almost 82 percent on proposed deferrals, the same as President Carter's average. President Ford had 76 percent accepted. More than $127 billion in deferrals has been saved by presidents from 1975 to 1987. Ford successfully deferred $31 billion, Carter $25 billion, and Reagan $71 billion. The conclusion: when the president wants to delay expenditures legally, Congress generally agrees.

Table 1 also reveals that the use of the rescission process is extensive but varies sharply from year to year. In 1975 and 1976, President Ford proposed over $6 billion in rescissions, but Congress cut only $529.6 million, around 7 percent of the proposed money. During the Carter administration, the rescission rate increased to 38 percent, for a $2.6 billion savings. Reagan used rescissions to implement his budget cuts in 1981 and 1982 with great success. Reagan cut approximately $16 billion, an unprecedented amount of money, in his first two years in office, for a rescission success rate of almost 59.6 percent. After the first two years of the Reagan administration,

TABLE 1
DEFERRALS AND RESCISSIONS, 1975-87, UNDER THE
IMPOUNDMENT CONTROL ACT OF 1974 (Dollar amounts in millions)

	Deferrals		Rescissions	
	Amount	Approval Rate (%)	Amount	Approval Rate (%)
Ford				
1975	15,954.8	63.0	391.3	14.4
1976 and transitional quarter	7,762.3	95.3	138.3	3.9
1977	7,048.1	100.0	0.0	0.0
total	30,765.2	75.9	529.6	7.2
Carter				
1977	4,975.8	99.5	711.6	39.8
1978	4,910.3	98.9	593.7	46.0
1979	4,676.9	99.8	723.6	79.6
1980	5,027.0	47.8	550.8	34.0
1981	5,670.4	100.0	0.0	0.0
total	25,260.4	81.9	2,579.7	38.2
Reagan				
1981	3,452.7	90.5	11,715.2	76.3
1982	7,853.4	95.6	4,364.7	55.2
1983	9,624.0	70.7	0	0
1984	7,919.5	99.8	55.4	8.7
1985	16,044.7	95.6	165.6	8.9
1986	14,690.0	59.3	143.0	1.4
1987	11,320.0	98.5	36.0	0.6
total	70,904.3	81.9	16,479.9	38.1
Grand Total	$126,929.9	80.3	$19,589.2	34.1

SOURCE: Compiled by author; data provided by U.S. Office of Management and Budget, Budget Review Office, 29 Oct. 1985 and 28 Oct. 1987.

however, the number of rescissions proposed and accepted dropped dramatically to only $400 million for five years. In summary, from 1975 to 1987, almost $20 billion was cut through rescissions, for a 34-percent congressional acceptance rate, as shown in Table 1. Congress reviews the permanent cuts through presidential rescissions very carefully.

In conclusion, the impoundment provisions of the 1974 Budget Act have worked in a constitutional and predictable manner. The impoundment procedures check the power of the president and have been implemented without major political confrontations under both Republicans and Democrats. The impoundment controls help Congress to reassert its constitutional power of the purse. The president clearly has lost unilateral power to cut appropriated federal dollars. The president is now forced to cooperate with Congress and build bipartisan support for impoundments, and when that is not done, few funds are cut. There is strong supporting evidence for the hypothesis that the reforms have allowed Congress to control presidential impoundments.

THE ROLE OF POLICY SUBSYSTEMS IN THE BUDGET PROCESS

Has the implementation of the 1974 budget reform act and GRH resulted in significant consequences for budgetary relations between the president, agencies, committees, and congressional leadership? Before passage of the Budget Act, the stable roles, relationships, and routines of the president, OMB, executive branch agencies, congressional party leaders, congressional committees, and interest groups led to few surprises in the federal budget process. Predictable pluralistic incrementalism with a narrow scope and low level of political conflict predominated over distributive budgetary processes. Since the 1974 reform, two oil crises, stagflation, and high interest rates have changed the economy, contributing to destabilization of the budget process. Reagan-era tax cuts forced Congress to make decremental redistributive budget decisions that both increased the visibility of, and widened the number of participants in, the conflict over the budget. President Reagan achieved his purpose "to limit the growth of . . . government by limiting the revenues available to be spent."[14] Concurrently, both budget reforms have placed restraints on spending by openly relating outlays to revenues. A latent consequence of the Budget Act and GRH has been increased budgetary tension, confusion, and stalemate between Congress and the president.

The budget reforms have caused some

jockeying for jurisdictional turf between the budget committees and the other standing committees, especially the appropriations and taxing committees. The appropriations committees no longer protect presidential interests in Congress, and the president no longer exercises quiet budgetary control that allows congressional committees and agencies to conduct their own business. The authorization committees have lost power because of the appropriations committees' right to cap new backdoor spending. The appropriations committees have also expanded their use of backdoor authorizations by increasing the number and complexity of restrictive program provisions placed on the president and executive branch through appropriations bills.

The 1974 Budget Act requires all standing committees to submit estimates of their spending authority for programs within their jurisdiction early in the budget cycle. These estimates of authorizations tend to limit the committees' freedom and that of executive agencies and interest groups who have a natural tendency to push for new programs and higher authorizations. The committees are forced to state priorities and to make difficult choices between programs very early in the process, rather than authorizing high levels of funding and new programs as a result of strong, well-organized, twelfth-hour lobbying by agencies and interest groups. Before the 1974 reform, program authorization levels were commonly—and symbolically—double and even triple the final appropriations. The substantive committees would authorize at very high levels to placate strong pressures from outside Congress, knowing full well that the appropriations committees would implement the president's budget and push the actual funding

14. Leroy N. Rieselbach, *Congressional Reform* (Washington, DC: CQ Press, 1986), p. 100.

down to more reasonable levels. After 1974 and GRH, the authorization committees could no longer play this game. They are now required to estimate total program funding within the overall budget totals and within their jurisdiction, thus reducing the gap between authorizations and appropriations and putting a cap on the political pressures from agencies and interest groups.

Budget decisions arrived at openly by the budget committees have caused presidents to be more attentive to Congress. Presidents now have OMB staff attending all budget hearings and markups. White House staff now find it necessary to work the Hill more effectively. The process is relatively open and burdensome for the president and executives, forcing them to bargain and monitor the budget process carefully. OMB directors commonly sit at the bargaining table with budget committee leaders to negotiate the final budget resolutions.

Another impact of the 1974 budget reform on congressional committee relationships with the president has been the closing of two types of backdoor spending by the authorizing committees: contract authority and borrowing authority. Although either house of Congress may waive this restriction, eliminating new backdoors brings the potential for increased control over spending by the appropriations committees and thus less freedom for the authorization committees to circumvent the traditional appropriations process. Pre-1974 entitlement programs and net interest payments, however, continue to reduce the ability of both Congress and the president to control the budget.

As a result of the wide-sweeping reforms of the 1970s, power in the House of Representatives shifted from committee chairs to subcommittee chairs,

and changes in rules and procedures concurrently increased the influence of the Democratic caucus and Democratic Party leadership.[15] The 1970s brought both decentralization and centralization of power to the House. The 1974 Budget Act was a major reform that had the potential for centralization of power and integration of decision making. The budget process may be one of Speaker Jim Wright's primary tools for better coordination and integration of decision making in the House. House Democratic leaders are forced to mobilize members behind budget resolutions that do not always please committee and subcommittee chairpersons, interest groups, agencies of the executive branch, or the president. They must build coalitions and centralize decision making in the House that is often fragmented and undisciplined; these necessities have the consequence of challenging interest groups and presidents. Budgetary power in the Senate has generally been firmly in the hands of the committee chairs. House party leaders have played a stronger role in the budget process than their Senate counterparts.

The House Democratic leadership has been actively involved in setting budget figures and offering refining amendments in order to marshal support for the resolutions on the House floor. One primary impact of budget reform on the House majority leadership and the president is that it has forced centralization, coordination, and the construction of a Democratic coalition behind a

15. For a case study of the committee reform effort in the U.S. House of Representatives in the 1970s, see Roger H. Davidson and Walter J. Oleszek, *Congress against Itself* (Bloomington: Indiana University Press, 1977). For a summary of congressional reforms of the 1970s, see Rieselbach, *Congressional Reform.*

congressional budget. The Senate budget is more bipartisan, and the Senate is less confrontational in building budget resolutions, and this strategy often carries on to the floor of that chamber.

House and Senate leaders from both parties, however, have helped give the budget process an independence from the president but not always from the power and expertise of committee and subcommittee chairs who put pressure on the House Budget Committee for higher spending for their favorite programs. Be it defense spending, money for highways, water projects, or funds for social security, when constituency interests and budget-committee priorities confront each other, the substantive committees with strong support from interest groups and agencies usually win.

A major challenge to the independence of the congressional budget process came during President Reagan's first year in office. Reagan's first OMB director, David Stockman, a former congressman who had an excellent understanding of the congressional budget process, designed a strategy to use the reconciliation process to impose severe cuts in total permissible spending by congressional committees. Reconciliation is a device to instruct committees to cut spending on total permissible expenditures within the jurisdiction of each to some level below a specific ceiling. Because sufficient funds do not exist for all programs, there must be winners and losers, a redistribution of money. With an up-or-down, take-it-or-leave-it vote on the budgets in the years 1981-83, the budget debate shifted from the parts to the whole, thus partially overcoming the desire by members to represent constituents and special interests on their committee. Interest groups

and their friends on committees and in agencies were taken by surprise when Stockman and his allies on Capitol Hill locked in spending ceilings in the first concurrent resolution, thus changing the focus of the budget debate from line items to the highly centralized reconciliation resolution. Disciplined Republicans and conservative Democrats coalesced with President Reagan to pass higher defense spending and through the reconciliation process reduced nondefense expenditures over the three-year period of 1981-83. The cuts totaled $100 billion. Democratic opponents were unable to stop the cuts until they changed the conservative coalition in the House and eventually recaptured the Senate. The confrontation showed that the president could use the budget process to his advantage. Since 1983, the protectionist power and force of interest groups, committees, and executive branch agencies have regained their influence over the budget.

The reconciliation process was Reagan's way of achieving reductions in expenditures within the protected jurisdiction of the tax committees and the sacred turf of the appropriations committees. Fisher estimates that over half of the spending reductions in the reconciliation acts were within House Ways and Means and Senate Finance.[16] After 1983, Congress used the reconciliation process to challenge several presidential budgetary priorities.

In conclusion, there is evidence to support the third hypothesis, mentioned at the beginning of this article, that the reforms have the potential to limit the power of policy subsystems—that is,

16. Louis Fisher, "The Budget Act of 1974: Reflections after Ten Years" (Paper delivered at the Annual Meeting of the Midwest Political Science Association, Chicago, 1985).

interest groups, committees, and agencies with jurisdiction over specific programs—by giving presidents and congressional leaders the tools to coordinate and centralize budgeting on the Hill. Reform has changed the budget power of presidents, agencies, committees, congressional leadership, and interest groups, but there is also strong evidence that our pluralist democracy is still alive and well. Strong interests continue to win and weak interests continue to lose in the battle of the budget no matter how centralized and well coordinated the budget process has become.

Congressional and presidential budget control

Have the reforms created greater control of the budget? Before 1974, the budget process was out of control in the sense that Congress found itself without the mechanisms to work its budgetary will through the appropriations process, regardless of whether that will was in the direction of decreased or increased federal expenditures. In this sense, the lack of congressional control since 1974 has been growing. The percentage of expenditures that cannot be altered without changing the basic authorizing statute has increased since 1974.

Shortly after passage of the 1974 reform, about 70 percent of the budget was considered relatively uncontrollable under existing law and, primarily because of backdoor spending measures—indexed permanently authorized entitlements—could not be directly controlled by the president and the appropriations committees on an annual basis. In 1988, OMB considers 77.5 percent of the budget uncontrollable, a 6.8 percent increase since 1976. Most of the uncontrollability comes from payments for

individuals (43.5 percent), fixed program costs (15.1 percent), and prior-year contracts and obligations (18.9 percent). If interest payments are added to the OMB estimates, almost 85 percent of the budget is relatively uncontrollable.

These programs are uncontrollable primarily because of the political ramifications associated with the proposed cuts. Any spending program is ultimately controllable; however, the nature or degree of controllability differs depending on the political power of the recipients of the programs. The eligibility for various levels of benefit is normally established in authorizing law rather than through appropriations of budget authority. Efforts by Congress or the president to reduce spending on these entitlement programs require changing the authorizing legislation, which is politically very difficult. In the absence of such legislative changes, the payments are made automatically, and in many cases such payments are made from the budget authority that is available, without appropriations action to finance the program. The rise in permanent budget authority—resulting in most part from these various forms of pre-1974 backdoor spending—has contributed to a diminished relationship between congressional budgetary decisions in any given year and the actual outlays of that year. The budget reform has not significantly altered the capacity of Congress to improve its control of the budget.

GRH has put increased pressure on Congress and the president to focus on the uncontrollables; however, there is little evidence that members of Congress and the president have the political will to reduce spending for popular programs such as Social Security. Reagan's OMB director, James Miller, captures the presidential perception of the lack of congressional concern for the uncontrollables: "Deficits create many winners and few losers. . . . Every legislator is in a position to try to confer benefits on his or her favorite constituencies, and the incentive for any individual legislator to refrain from such behavior is virtually nonexistent."[17] Congress may be behaving as it was designed, as a representative assembly. Members of Congress find it difficult to oppose well-organized constituents, and presidents find it impossible to oppose well-organized national interest groups, such as associations protecting the interests of Social Security recipients. Congressional-presidential budgeting has been transformed from a relatively closed process for financing government agencies into an open process for providing benefits and contracts to Americans. The more open the congressional budget process has become, the more Congress and the president have increased the flow of benefits to outsiders.

One solution to reduce the deficit is for the formula for spending to be changed in the entitlements, another is to reduce defense spending, and yet another is to raise taxes. All of these solutions, however, call for more budget control and are perceived to be politically too dangerous, if not electoral suicide, for both Congress and the president. There is little evidence that the reforms have created greater control over the budget; thus the fourth hypothesis is disconfirmed. Congress does not have greater control of the budget, but neither does the president. They have lost the ability to control the budget by representing the natural pressures of a pluralist democracy.

17. James Miller, "Miller Says Deficits Beget Spending," *A.E.I. Memorandum*, Spring 1987, p. 8.

CONCLUSION

The Budget Act and GRH are two of the most important structural and procedural budgetary reforms to be adopted by Congress in the last fifty years. The two acts have had several important consequences for congressional-presidential relations. They have

— strengthened the role of Congress in the budgetary process vis-à-vis the president;
— required the president and his staff to work more closely with Congress;
— allowed Congress to control presidential impoundments and allowed the president to legally impound funds;
— shown a potential for limiting the power of policy subsystems in the budget process; and
— opened up the budget process and focused public attention on macrobudgetary and macroeconomic tradeoffs but have had little impact on the controllability of the budget.

In sum, the consequences of the 1974 act and GRH have made budgeting between the president and Congress more democratic and difficult. Reforms have increased the number of budgetary participants, made the budget process more open, created a congressional budgeting process more independent of the president, forced the president and his staff to work more closely with Congress, and established a coherent and constitutional method of congressional review over presidential impoundments. Thus the budget process is more complex, open, and democratic, but more conflictual and difficult for the president and Congress.[18]

18. For a further discussion of this, see James

Congress is fundamentally a representative and disintegrated decision-making institution. It is responsive to political pressures and public preferences and thereby puts efforts to improve the efficiency of the budget process in direct conflict with its constitutional design and natural political state. The struggle inside Congress between centralization and decentralization will continue to cause delay, deadlock, and even breakdown in congressional-presidential budgeting until the American people wish something different. New budget reforms will be problematic and unlikely to work unless there is a clear public consensus for change.[19]

A major objective of the 1974 Budget Act and GRH is to force consensus where none had exited before. Changes in the budgeting rules have not changed presidential and congressional motivations to represent and to be reelected. It is clear that the divisions over budget policy remain as entrenched as ever. Increased budgetary discipline by Congress and the president cannot be simply legislated. Congress and the president will continue to muddle through by bargaining and compromise over incremental funding changes no matter what new budget reforms are adopted.

A. Thurber, *Public Policy Making in America: The Role of Policy Subsystems* (Washington, DC: Congressional Quarterly, forthcoming).

19. For recommended solutions to the crisis of the federal budget deficit, see Charles W. Dunn, "The Crisis of the Federal Budget Deficit" (White paper, Strom Thurmond Institute, Clemson University, May 1987).

ANNALS, *AAPSS*, **499**, September 1988

The President, Congress, and
Tax Reform:
Patterns over Three Decades

By JAMES M. VERDIER

ABSTRACT: Both Congress and the president have taken the lead on tax reform at different times in the more than three decades between full-scale revisions of the tax code in 1954 and 1986. This article traces four forces that shaped executive-legislative relations on tax policy during that period: partisan politics, economics, public opinion, and policy experts and entrepreneurs. It concludes that Congress's ability to lead is greatest when economic forces—inflation, recession, and budget deficits—help push tax reform onto the agenda. Presidents retain a natural advantage in agenda setting, however; they are able to put tax reform on the agenda when pressures for reform are weak, and sometimes they can keep it off when pressures are stronger. Tax-policy experts can have a major impact when political and economic forces provide an opening and when skilled entrepreneurs forge links between their prescriptions and political needs and concerns.

James M. Verdier teaches at the Kennedy School of Government at Harvard University. He served in the Tax Analysis Division of the Congressional Budget Office from 1975 to 1983, heading the division from 1979 to 1983. Earlier, he was a legislative assistant for Representative Henry Reuss, Democrat of Wisconsin, from 1968 to 1972, and for Senator Walter Mondale, Democrat of Minnesota, from 1973 to 1975, working on tax and other issues. He is a graduate of Dartmouth College and the Harvard Law School and studied at Oxford University.

THE Constitution in article I gives Congress the power "to lay and collect taxes" and in article II gives the president the power to "recommend to their consideration such measures as he shall judge necessary and expedient."

Congress has retained its constitutional prominence in tax policymaking, despite the growth of presidential power and the president's inherent advantage in shaping the national policy agenda. Beginning with the Internal Revenue Code of 1954 and ending with the Tax Reform Act of 1986, Congress took the lead on tax-reform legislation passed in 1954, 1969, 1975, 1976, 1982, and 1984, while the president took the lead on legislation passed in 1962, 1964, 1971, 1978, 1981, and 1986.[1]

Once tax reform is on the legislative agenda, Congress often plays the dominant role, frequently ignoring or substantially reshaping administration recommendations and adding many new provisions. Presidents nonetheless retain unique advantages in agenda setting. They have kept tax reform off the agenda during periods when other pressures might have forced it on, and they have moved it onto the agenda at times when other pressures for reform were not strong.

What accounts for this pattern of alternating congressional and executive leadership on tax reform? What are the major forces that shape the tax-policy agenda and help determine the relative influence of the president and Congress?

By tracing four forces that were at work between the early 1950s and 1986—partisan politics, economics, public opinion, and policy experts and entre-

preneurs—and comparing their influence at different times, this article suggests answers to those questions.[2]

PARTISAN POLITICAL FORCES

Both Democrats and Republicans have sought to capture the issue of tax reform and define it in ways that help their major constituencies. Much of the ebb and flow of tax legislation over the last three decades can be explained in terms of this partisan struggle to reshape the tax code.

Liberal Democrats have traditionally sought tax legislation that would close loopholes and increase progressivity by making wealthy individuals and large corporations pay their fair share of taxes. Conservative Republicans have sought to keep taxes low and to provide greater incentives for savings, work, investment, and capital formation.

The 1950s

The Internal Revenue Code of 1954 was the first major rewrite of the tax law since 1939. The effort was begun in late 1952, when Representative Daniel Reed, Republican of New York and incoming chairman of the House Ways and Means

---

1. For a listing of the major bills during this period, see Joseph A. Pechman, *Federal Tax Policy*, 5th ed. (Washington, DC: Brookings Institution, 1987), pp. 40-41. •

2. For a good summary history of tax policymaking through the early 1980s, see John F. Witte, *The Politics and Development of the Federal Income Tax* (Madison: University of Wisconsin Press, 1985), pp. 131-243. For more detail, see Congressional Quarterly, *Congress and the Nation, 1945-1964* (Washington, DC: Congressional Quarterly Service, 1965), pp. 397-442: idem, ibid., vol. 2, *1965-68* (1969), pp. 141-82; idem, ibid., vol. 3, *1969-1972* (1973), pp. 77-96; idem, ibid., vol. 4, *1973-1976* (Washington, DC: Congressional Quarterly, 1977), pp. 83-106; idem, ibid., vol. 5, *1977-1980* (1981), pp. 231-51; idem, ibid., vol. 6, *1981-84* (1985), pp. 63-82. Unless otherwise noted, historical references in this article are based on these sources.

Committee in the newly elected Republican Congress, instructed the staff of the congressional Joint Committee on Internal Revenue Taxation to undertake a full-scale review of the tax structure.[3] The joint committee's staff—a nonpartisan professional staff of lawyers, economists, and revenue estimators set up in 1926 to serve both the House and the Senate tax committees—worked closely throughout 1953 with the Republican Treasury tax staff. By the end of the year, the congressional and Treasury staffs had developed comprehensive revisions that formed the basis for President Eisenhower's proposals to the Congress in early 1954. By mid-August, the provisions were law.

Little partisan controversy surrounded most aspects of the 1954 act; the fighting was confined mainly to a few issues—dividend relief for stockholders versus increases in the personal exemption, for example—that symbolized each party's stakes in tax reform. It was nonetheless largely a Republican bill, with Democrats casting almost all the opposing votes on final passage.

Although Democrats recaptured control of the Congress in the 1954 midterm elections and retained it throughout Eisenhower's presidency, their majorities were never large enough to overcome Eisenhower's opposition to further tax reforms. Democrats never had more than a two-vote margin in the Senate until the last two years of Eisenhower's term. While Democratic House margins were larger, hovering around thirty votes, conservative southerners made up a large share of the Democratic majority in both bodies.[4]

The 1960s

Democratic congressional majorities were much wider in the Kennedy and Johnson presidencies, averaging 66-34 in the Senate and 266-169 in the House from 1960 to 1968. With Democratic control of the presidency and large majorities in the Congress, President John F. Kennedy moved tax reform forcefully onto the agenda, resulting in major reform legislation in 1962 and 1964. President Lyndon Johnson, preoccupied with pushing his Great Society domestic spending programs through Congress and later with the Vietnam war, had little interest in tax reform after 1964, despite urgings from some in Congress and his own Treasury Department.

The Treasury tax staff was hard at work on tax-reform studies and proposals in the late 1960s, however. As President Nixon took office in January 1969, facing a still heavily Democratic Congress, these studies were delivered to Capitol Hill by the outgoing administration. Johnson's Treasury secretary, Joseph Barr, stoked the fires by testifying that 155 taxpayers with incomes of over $200,000, including 21 with incomes over $1 million, had paid no federal income taxes for 1967. He predicted a "taxpayers' revolt" unless something was done about it.

Something was. Moving quickly, the Democratic Congress produced the Tax Reform Act of 1969, which closed or reduced a number of tax loopholes and instituted a new minimum tax to prevent wealthy individuals from completely escaping taxation.

3. *New York Times*, 2 Dec. 1952.
4. The data on the political makeup of Congress in this section are taken from Norman J. Ornstein, Thomas E. Mann, and Michael Malbin, *Vital Statistics on Congress, 1987-1988* (Washington, DC: American Enterprise Institute, 1987), pp. 38-39.

The 1970s

The post-Watergate 1974 elections produced overwhelming Democratic majorities—61-37 in the Senate and 291-144 in the House. These majorities led to further congressionally initiated tax reform in 1975—repeal of the oil depletion allowance for major oil companies—and another comprehensive loophole-closing bill in 1976.

The Jimmy Carter administration took office in 1977 bent on further reforming the tax code, which Carter had called in his campaign "a disgrace to the human race." A conservative backlash was building, however, fueled in part by the increasing tax burdens on higher-income individuals and on business investment produced by prior Democratic legislative successes on tax reform. Heavy business lobbying helped transform President Carter's 1978 tax-reform initiative into a major setback for liberal tax reformers. Capital-gains taxes were sharply reduced, business taxes were cut in a variety of ways, individual tax cuts were aimed at middle- and high-income taxpayers, and a number of special tax preferences were created or expanded.

The 1980s

With Ronald Reagan's 1980 victory in the presidential election, Republican capture of the Senate, and a sharply reduced Democratic majority in the House, the way was paved for a successful conservative offensive on tax reform. The president's 1981 tax bill reduced individual income tax rates across the board, cut taxes for business by greatly increasing depreciation allowances, and created or expanded still more tax preferences or loopholes.

The landmark Tax Reform Act of 1986 departed from past partisan efforts by combining loophole-closing reforms long sought by liberal Democrats with rate reductions favored by conservative Republicans. Although put on the agenda by President Reagan, its prototype came from congressional Democrats Bill Bradley and Richard Gephardt. The formula finally agreed upon by Congress and the president—reduction in the top tax rate for individuals from 50 percent to 28 percent, offset by closing capital-gains and tax-shelter loopholes that benefited mainly the wealthy, and a $20-billion-a-year tax cut for individuals that was to be financed by a tax increase of the same amount on corporations—so neatly balanced the goals of Republicans and Democrats that the bill eventually proved unstoppable. "It breathes its own air," one senator said.[5]

ECONOMIC FORCES

While much of the story of tax reform over the last 35 years can be told in terms of partisan political pressures and the relative strengths of Republicans and Democrats in Congress and the White House, economic forces also have played a major role.

Inflation, recession, and budget deficits all have helped to move tax reform onto the legislative agenda during this period. While these economic forces have had some impact on the content of reform proposals, their main effect has been to provide legislative vehicles to which reforms could be attached.

Bracket creep in the 1970s

The most striking examples occurred in the 1970s, when inflationary increases

5. Jeffrey H. Birnbaum and Alan S. Murray, *Showdown at Gucci Gulch* (New York: Random House, 1987), p. 285.

in incomes repeatedly pushed taxpayers into higher tax brackets, requiring tax cuts every year or two to keep tax burdens from rising. The need to offset this bracket creep provided the major impetus for tax-cut bills enacted in 1975, 1976, 1977, 1978, and 1981. While the cuts were generally only enough to offset inflation, they looked like real cuts to many taxpayers, especially in the mid-1970s, when most people did not yet fully realize the impact inflation was having on their tax bills.

Each of these bills included significant reform provisions aimed at reducing or increasing tax preferences or providing economic incentives. The 1978 act, for example, eliminated the deduction for state and local gasoline taxes and began taxing unemployment compensation, while the 1976 act created incentives for the preservation of certified historic buildings and the 1977 act set up a new jobs tax credit. Most of these reforms were not urgent or popular enough to make it onto the legislative agenda on their own. Tax-cut bills, however, are legislative trains with power and room enough for plenty of extra baggage.

Recessions in the 1960s and 1970s

Tax legislation designed mainly to stimulate the economy and combat recession has also served as a vehicle for tax reform. Examples include

— the 1962 Kennedy tax bill, which sought to encourage business investment in new plants and equipment by instituting an investment tax credit;
— the 1964 Kennedy-Johnson individual income tax cut bill; and
— the 1971 Nixon tax bill, which included a number of investment

incentives for businesses and tax cuts for individuals.

Each of these bills included reform provisions that probably could not have passed on their own but that succeeded under the cover of tax cutting and economic stimulation.

Deficit reduction in the 1980s

The tax bills enacted in 1982 and 1984 were aimed primarily at reducing the federal deficit, which was hovering around $200 billion a year and threatening to go higher. Both bills included revenue-raising reforms that would have had little support without the deficit pressures.

Inflation, recession, and deficits in the 1950s

The Eisenhower years provide an instructive contrast, because the economic forces that provided vehicles for reform in later periods were either absent or had less impact during Eisenhower's terms in office. There was little pressure in that period from inflation or budget deficits, inasmuch as both remained low throughout the Eisenhower presidency. Economic growth was also low, however, with three recessions in eight years. In later times, this might have brought forth presidential proposals for antirecession tax cuts; but Eisenhower—no Keynesian—consistently resisted such temptations.

PUBLIC OPINION

Public opinion on tax issues rarely becomes focused enough to push tax reform onto the agenda. The exceptions have occurred in periods when overall tax burdens reached unusually high levels. Even then, the public has generally been more concerned with tax reduction than reform. Nonetheless, in a few instances, widespread publicity about specific examples of tax evasion and avoidance has led to reforms.

The Tax Reform Act of 1969

The clearest example of the impact of public opinion on tax reform came in 1969. Individual income taxes that year reached a post-World War II peak of 9.4 percent of gross national product (GNP). This followed a 17-year period in which income taxes fluctuated narrowly between 7.2 and 8.2 percent of GNP.[6] A major reason for the high tax level was the Vietnam war tax surcharge, which hit its peak in 1969.

As noted earlier, Treasury Secretary Barr's testimony about high-income tax avoiders inflamed an already surly taxpaying public, leading to the Tax Reform Act of 1969 and a tough new minimum tax.

Repeal of the oil depletion allowance

Another clear example of the influence of public opinion on tax policy came in 1975, when the oil depletion allowance for major oil companies was repealed. Repeal was tacked onto an emergency antirecession tax-cut bill, following widespread publicity about soaring oil company profits in the wake of the 1973-74 Arab oil embargo. The impact of public opinion was enhanced by structural and procedural changes in the House that made it possible for the Democratic Caucus to override the Ways

and Means Committee and force a full House vote on an amendment repealing the depletion allowance, which passed 248-163.

Tax cuts and tax reform in the 1980s

Individual income tax burdens began to rise again in 1979, reaching a new post-World War II high of 9.6 percent of GNP in 1981. President Reagan took advantage of public dissatisfaction with this high level of taxation to push through Congress the largest individual income tax cut in U.S. history, accompanied by a host of special relief and investment incentive provisions. These special provisions resulted not from any public pressure but from a bidding war between the president and Democrats in Congress as each party tried to attract special-interest votes to its own versions of tax reduction.

One such special provision—known as "safe-harbor leasing"—received wide publicity when companies quickly began using it to buy and sell tax breaks. The resulting public outcry led to its repeal in the 1982 deficit-reduction tax bill.

Widespread publicity on large corporations that paid no taxes helped lay the groundwork for the Tax Reform Act of 1986, and it accounted in large measure for the strict corporate minimum tax included in that bill.[7] Apart from this public concern over corporate tax avoidance, however, tax reform generated little public pressure in the period leading up to the 1986 act.

A big part of the reason for this lack of pressure was that overall individual income tax burdens were still declining

6. U.S., Office of Management and Budget, *Historical Tables Fiscal Year 1988*, 1987, p. 2.3(1).

7. "In Taxes, the Impossible Became the Inevitable," *Washington Post*, 29 June 1986.

as a result of the 1981 act—from 9.6 percent of GNP in 1981 to 8.1 percent in 1984. Public dissatisfaction with the federal income tax was no higher than it had been in the late 1970s, and by some measures it had begun to decline.[8] President Reagan's efforts to build grass-roots support for tax reform were notably unsuccessful.[9] There were other forces at work, however, as the next section details.

EXPERTS AND ENTREPRENEURS

Tax-policy experts—Treasury and congressional staffs, and the academics and policy advocates who write, testify, and consult on tax-policy issues—have been a continuing presence throughout the period we are examining. Their influence has varied, however, with larger political and economic forces sometimes offering them a window of opportunity and sometimes pushing them aside.

Even when events converge to create an opportunity for experts, something more is usually required: policy entrepreneurs, who create links between the prescriptions of experts and the needs and concerns of politicians and the public.[10] Experts had their maximum influence on tax policy in the bills

passed in 1954, 1969, and 1986. The ingredients of those successes will now be analyzed briefly and will be compared with two instances in which experts had much less impact.

Three successes

In each instance of successful expert influence, political and economic forces combined to create an opening; in each, policy entrepreneurs provided crucial links between experts and policymakers.

1954. Most of the Internal Revenue Code of 1954 was written by teams of staff experts from the congressional Joint Committee on Internal Revenue Taxation and the Treasury Department. Both the presidency and Congress were controlled by Republicans, minimizing partisan and executive-legislative conflict. Economic conditions were generally favorable for reform, with the 1953-54 recession and high Korean War tax burdens producing some pressure for action on taxes.

The linkage between experts and politicians was provided by Colin Stam, longtime chief of staff of the Joint Committee on Internal Revenue Taxation. Stam, who had joined the committee staff in 1927 and had served as its chief of staff since 1938, was relied on heavily by the largely conservative senior members of the two tax-writing committees, and he played a crucial role in developing the 1954 act.[11]

1969. As discussed earlier, the 1969 act also came at a time when wartime financing burdens had driven individual income tax burdens to unusually high

8. Advisory Commission on Intergovernmental Relations, *Changing Public Attitudes on Government and Taxes* (Washington, DC: Advisory Commission on Intergovernmental Relations, 1986), p. 1; Roper Organization and H&R Block, Inc., *The American Public and the Federal Income Tax System* (Kansas City, MO: H&R Block, 1986), pp. 7, 13.

9. See, for example, Timothy Clark, "At Grass Roots, Not Much Groundswell of Support for Reagan's Tax Reform Plan," *National Journal*, 27 Aug. 1985, pp. 1737-42.

10. For an elaboration of these concepts, see John W. Kingdon, *Agendas, Alternatives, and Public Policies* (Boston: Little, Brown, 1984), chap. 8.

11. E. W. Kenworthy, "Colin Stam: A Study in Anonymous Power," in *Adventures in Public Service*, ed. Delia Kuhn and Ferdinand Kuhn (New York: Vanguard Press, 1963), p. 134.

levels. Unlike 1954, however, deep partisan divisions separated President Nixon and the Democratic Congress. The close collaborative relationship between Treasury and congressional staff experts that had been such a prominent feature of the 1954 act was not feasible in this environment.

Such a relationship had been firmly established during the Kennedy-Johnson years, however, making it possible for congressional staff experts to draw on its fruits in 1969. Stanley S. Surrey, assistant secretary of the treasury for tax policy from 1961 to 1969, worked closely during the late 1960s with Laurence N. Woodworth, Stam's successor as chief of staff of the Joint Committee on Internal Revenue Taxation, on an extensive set of tax-reform studies and proposals.[12] As mentioned earlier, these studies and proposals were delivered to Congress as the Johnson administration left office, and they formed the basis of the 1969 act.

While Woodworth's position was nonpartisan, he was highly skilled at crafting proposals that met members' needs. Because Democrats controlled the congressional tax-writing committees, the outgoing Democratic administration's expert prescriptions could readily be adapted to its party's needs. Surrey and Woodworth's joint entrepreneurship thus blossomed after Surrey returned to his professorship at the Harvard Law School.

1986. As noted earlier, economic and political pressures for tax reform were not strong in the period leading up to the 1986 act. What paved the way was a crucial piece of policy entrepreneurship by Senator Bill Bradley, Democrat of New Jersey.

The tax reform bill Bradley introduced with Congressman Dick Gephardt, Democrat of Missouri, in 1982 drew on decades of research and analysis by tax-reform experts and relied heavily on help from the staff of the Joint Committee on Taxation.[13] With the presidency and the Senate controlled by Republicans and the House by Democrats, however, a partisan approach to tax reform held little promise.

Bradley thus decided to take the ideology out of tax reform by linking the low-tax-rate thrust of conservative Republicans with the base-broadening, loophole-closing thrust of liberal Democrats.[14] The Bradley-Gephardt bill had a top rate for individuals of only 28 percent—compared to 50 percent in existing law—but closed or reduced so many loopholes benefiting wealthy individuals that the overall tax burden by income class remained unchanged. It also neither gained nor lost revenue overall, thereby circumventing potential partisan conflicts over the overall level of federal taxing and spending.

The Bradley approach attracted President Reagan, who had long favored lower tax rates and who feared that Democrats might use the issue of tax reform to their advantage in the 1984 presidential campaign. He therefore ordered his Treasury Department to prepare a study of tax reform, to be delivered after the election.[15]

12. Stanley S. Surrey, "Tribute to Dr. Laurence N. Woodworth: Two Decades of Federal Tax History Viewed from This Perspective," *National Tax Journal*, Sept. 1979, pp. 227-39.

13. The committee's name was officially shortened from the longer version—Joint Committee on Internal Revenue Taxation—in 1976, its fiftieth anniversary.

14. Birnbaum and Murray, *Showdown at Gucci Gulch*, pp. 27-31.

15. Ibid., pp. 39-41.

The study, prepared by a team of Treasury experts working behind closed doors, drew on the same intellectual tradition as the Bradley-Gephardt bill and followed the same rate-reducing, loophole-closing approach. It was released in November 1984, forming the basis for President Reagan's reform proposals to Congress the following May. The president's proposals, together with the Bradley-Gephardt bill, laid the groundwork for the 1986 act.

Two failures

Expert prescriptions had much less influence in 1959 and 1978, in the first case because political and economic forces were generally unfavorable, and in the second because no one supplied a good linkage between expert prescriptions and political needs and concerns.

1959. Soon after Congressman Wilbur D. Mills, Democrat of Arkansas, took over as chairman of the House Ways and Means Committee in 1958, he decided to hold an ambitious set of hearings on tax reform to see whether he could build support for comprehensive reform. The committee commissioned 183 papers from a variety of tax-policy experts and then held 22 days of hearings over two months on a wide range of tax-reform issues, hearing testimony from nearly 200 invited witnesses.[16]

Chairman Mills had a bill drafted that would have eliminated all exclusions and deductions, with rates ranging from 5 to 25 percent. It would have raised more revenue than did existing law, which at the time had rates that ranged

from 20 to 91 percent. Mills ultimately never introduced the bill, concluding that he could not build enough support in Congress to pass it.[17]

The situation Mills faced was much less favorable than that faced by other policy entrepreneurs. There was little public discontent with the income tax system in the late 1950s. The percentage of people believing their federal income tax burden was too high was dropping sharply, from 66 percent in 1957 to 50 percent in 1961, the lowest level in over a decade.[18] While nominal tax rates were quite high, few people were concerned about the high rates because scarcely anyone paid them. In 1961, only 10 percent of all returns were taxed at rates above 22 percent and less than 1 percent at rates above 38 percent.[19]

There was also little prospect of a bipartisan coalition between the heavily Democratic Congress and President Eisenhower, then in the final two years of his presidency. Unlike President Reagan, Eisenhower was not intrigued by bold policy strokes.

Finally, the idea proposed by Mills was still new and unfamiliar. It had not been developed and refined for more than two decades—as when Bradley took it up.

1978. Shortly after his election in 1976, President Carter assembled in his Treasury Department a team of experts with long experience in Treasury, on Capitol Hill, and in academia. It was

16. U.S., House, Ways and Means Committee, *Tax Revision Compendium* (Washington, DC: Government Printing Office, 1959); idem, *Income Tax Revision* (Washington, DC: Government Printing Office, 1960).

17. "Mills, Conable Talk about Tax Reform," *Washington Post*, 4 Aug. 1985; author's telephone conversation with Wilbur Mills, 30 July 1987.

18. James M. Verdier, "The Prospects for Tax Stability," *Tax Notes*, 13 Apr. 1987, p. 173.

19. Eugene Steuerle and Michael Hartzmark, "Individual Income Taxation 1947-79," OTA Paper 48, U.S. Department of the Treasury, 1981, p. 36.

headed by Assistant Secretary for Tax Policy Laurence Woodworth, formerly chief of staff of the Joint Committee on Taxation. The team put together a reform package that continued the loophole-closing thrust of earlier Democratic proposals, and concentrated tax cuts on low- and moderate-income taxpayers.

The time was no longer ripe for Democratic-style reform, however, with inflation steadily pushing middle- and upper-income taxpayers into higher tax brackets, eroding business depreciation allowances, and increasing the tax burden on capital gains. The prescriptions of Carter's Treasury experts were quickly thrust aside by a Congress that found them unresponsive to its concerns.

CONCLUSION

The following conclusions emerge from this brief review of more than three decades of tax history:

1. Congress's ability to play a leadership role in tax reform is greatest when economic forces help push the issue onto the agenda. Record-high individual income tax burdens in 1969, bracket creep in 1975 and 1976, and budget deficits in 1982 and 1984 all gave a major boost to reform efforts.

2. The prospect of partisan political advantage may help stimulate congressional leadership, but it is not crucial. It was an important factor in 1969, 1975, and 1976, but not in 1954, 1982, and 1984.

3. Presidents retain a natural advantage in agenda setting; they are able to put tax reform on the agenda when pressures for reform are weak, and they can sometimes keep it off when those pressures are stronger. Presidents Kennedy (1962 and 1964), Carter (1978), and Reagan (1986) put the issue of tax reform on the agenda during periods when there was little public pressure for reform and when outside economic forces—inflation, recession, and budget deficits—had little effect. Presidents Eisenhower (1955-60) and Johnson (1965-68) kept tax reform off the agenda despite pressures from Congress and, in Johnson's case, his own Treasury experts; by contrast, Presidents Nixon (1969), Ford (1975 and 1976), and Reagan (1982 and 1984) were unable to resist congressional tax-reform initiatives.

4. Tax-policy experts, when aided by favorable external forces and skilled policy entrepreneurship, can have a major impact on tax legislation. Those favorable circumstances came together in 1954, 1969, and 1986. When expert prescriptions do not fit political needs or economic conditions, however, as in 1978, or when political and economic forces combine to keep tax reform off the agenda, as in 1959, experts must pack up their papers and files and wait for another day.

Congress, Presidents, and
the Arts:
Collaboration and Struggle

By MARGARET JANE WYSZOMIRSKI

ABSTRACT: In the 23 years since the establishment of the National Endowment for the Arts (NEA), an arts-policy subgovernment has emerged. It comprises the agency, its congressional oversight and appropriations committees, and arts interest groups. During the first decade of the NEA's existence, both presidential leadership and congressional support were essential to the agency's development. Meanwhile, an arts constituency mobilized. During the second decade, the triangular alliance of agency administrators, congressional supporters, and arts interest groups matured and proved capable of either collaboration or conflict with the president. The record of arts policy since 1975—and especially during the Reagan years—reveals this new subgovernment's ability to protect the status quo from threatening presidential action. But because relatively low political stakes are involved in arts policy and the various members of the subgovernment alliance are themselves weak, positive policy action appears to require the active collaboration of Congress, presidents, constituency, and agency.

Margaret Jane Wyszomirski is a guest scholar with the Public Policy Education Program at the Brookings Institution. Formerly, she was director of the Graduate Public Policy Program at Georgetown University.

IN September 1965, with Public Law 89-209, Congress established the National Endowment for the Arts (NEA). Until that time, no federal agency had held the primary mission of administering public policies concerning the arts. Previously, various agencies and policies—such as tax and copyright laws or labor programs—had had significant but indirect effects on the arts. The creation of the NEA, however, marked the first direct and potentially long-standing federal commitment to the arts.

In the subsequent 23 years, an arts-policy subgovernment system developed, imparting a degree of political structure to the interrelations of Congress, presidents, executive agencies, and interest groups in this issue area. During the initial 10-year development phase of the arts subgovernment system (1965-75), both presidential leadership and congressional support were vital to the establishment and growth of the NEA and the attendant mobilization of the arts constituency. Since that time, an iron triangle of interrelationships between the agency, its congressional oversight and appropriations committees, and the organized arts constituency have matured into what Barbara Hinckley has more generally characterized as "a government for a policy area . . . that exists separately from presidential government."[1] Once such a subgovernment has coalesced, the potential arises for relations between it and the presidency to be either collaborative or conflictual with regard to the specific policy area in question.

The following discussion chronicles the development of the individual components of the arts subgovernment system and analyzes how these have been affected by and, in turn, have affected the relationship of Congress and presidents concerning the arts.

DEFLECTED ATTEMPTS AT LEADERSHIP

Prior to the mid-1960s, the high point of federal support for the arts had occurred as part of Franklin D. Roosevelt's New Deal and had been administered through the Treasury Department's Section on Fine Arts and the Art Relief Project of the Works Progress Administration (WPA). Although these programs had significant positive effects upon the state of the arts and of artists in the United States, their primary purpose was unemployment relief rather than the advancement of the arts. Additionally, the political legacy of New Deal arts programs was highly problematic. Ideological, partisan, and intraorganizational conflicts as well as the lack of a tradition of public support for the arts all proved detrimental to the operation of the WPA arts programs, particularly the Theater Project. In 1939, Congress drastically cut back the WPA programs in anger over what it considered to be radical plays and subversive artists.[2]

Indeed, the arts-policy controversies of the 1930s and 1940s gave rise to three maxims that would guide the character of any subsequent federal arts commitment. These included (1) a recognition of the importance of artistic quality in legitimizing public patronage; (2) an appreciation of the importance and potential difficulty of accommodating local

---

1. Barbara Hinckley, *Problems of the Presidency* (Glenview, IL: Scott, Foresman, 1985), p. 154.

2. For a history of the WPA Theater Project, see Jane DeHart Mathews, *The Federal Theater 1935-1939* (Princeton, NJ: Princeton University Press, 1967).

input on artistic programs; and (3) the danger of direct governmental responsibility for works of art, especially in the absence of a broad public consensus about their content and/or style.[3] Concomitantly, the political controversies and congressional investigations of the 1930s, 1940s, and early 1950s concerning the alleged subversive activities and beliefs of artists left the artistic community wary of government involvement in the arts. Thus at mid-century, both government and artists viewed one another with mutual suspicion.

Beginning with a 1949 joint resolution calling for a federal arts assembly, a small group of congressmen tried to lead the nation toward a renewed public commitment to the arts.[4] Throughout the 1950s, the House Committee on Education and Labor the Senate Committee on Labor, and Public Welfare, or various of their subcommittees, repeatedly held hearings on arts-related bills at the instigation of Congressmen Charles Howell and Frank Thompson, Democrats of New Jersey, and Senators Jacob Javits, Republican of New York, and Hubert Humphrey, Democrat of Minnesota. While these attempts at policy leadership failed to establish a federal arts policy or even a formal commitment, they did succeed in developing, refining, and promulgating a set of

arguments that gradually built support for this issue. In short, congressional arts-policy leadership efforts during the 1950s were insufficient to achieve anticipated goals but nonetheless proved helpful in incubating the issue.

The subsequent phase of attempted presidential leadership had tenuous roots in the late Eisenhower administration. The president supported congressional action to authorize the donation of public lands near the Potomac River for the building of a national cultural center with private funds. In addition, a chapter on the arts, "The Quality of American Culture," was included as part of the report of the President's Commission on National Goals issued in 1960.[5]

President Kennedy was the first president to take an active, albeit largely symbolic, leadership role with regard to a federal arts policy. The Democratic Party platform of 1960, on which he ran, contained the first major party arts plank[6] and called for the establishment of a federal advisory agency concerned with the cultural resources of the nation. Subsequently, inaugural invitations extended to 168 "creative Americans" resulted in the attendance of artists and authors such as Arthur Miller, Robert Lowell, Mark Rothko, and John Steinbeck. With this gesture, President Kennedy set a new tone for relations between government and the arts.[7] A sense of

3. For a fuller discussion of the lessons of the New Deal art programs, see Judith H. Balfe and Margaret J. Wyszomirski, "Public Art and Public Policy," *Journal of Arts Management and the Law*, 15:11-13 (Winter 1986).

4. For a history of efforts to establish a federal arts policy and of the opposition to that effort during the late 1940s and throughout the 1950s, see Gary O. Larson, *The Reluctant Patron, The United States Government and the Arts, 1943-1965* (Philadelphia: University of Pennsylvania Press, 1983).

5. August Heckscher, "The Quality of American Culture," in *Goals for Americans* (Englewood Cliffs, NJ: Prentice-Hall/Spectrum Book, 1960), pp. 127-46.

6. Terri Lynn Cornwell, "Party Platforms and the Arts," in *Art, Ideology and Politics*, ed. Judith H. Balfe and Margaret Jane Wyszomirski (New York: Praeger, 1985), p. 249.

7. On the role and activities of the Kennedy administration with regard to arts policy, see Milton C. Cummings, Jr., "To Change a Nation's Cultural Policy: The Kennedy Administration

opportunity and positive expectation arose both within the arts community and among White House staff members—such as Arthur Schlesinger, Jr., and Pierre Salinger—who favored the development of a national cultural policy.

During 1961, other executive actions served to underline the administration's interest in the arts. The president and the first lady not only attended a number of public art events but also hosted White House soirees in which artists often figured prominently, such as Pablo Casals's White House concert in November 1961. In October, Labor Secretary Arthur Goldberg, at presidential direction, stepped in to arbitrate an unprecedented musicians' strike that had closed down the Metropolitan Opera. In his remarks that accompanied the settlement accord, Secretary Goldberg called for a patronage partnership involving business, private philanthropy, and the government and thus laid out a rationale for later federal involvement.

Although failing to win congressional support for the creation of a federal advisory council on the arts, President Kennedy's leadership efforts continued with the appointment of Twentieth Century Fund director August Heckscher as special consultant to the president on the arts in February of 1962.[8] A year later, Heckscher presented his report, *The Arts and the National Government.*[9]

Heckscher's report renewed the call for a federal advisory council on the arts and proposed the appointment of a Federal Arts Foundation to make grants. Still unable to overcome congressional obstacles to the creation of an advisory council, President Kennedy finally established his own Advisory Council on the Arts via Executive Order 11,112, issued on 12 June 1963.[10] Ironically, on the morning of 22 November 1963, a White House press release was prepared to announce the appointment of Richard Goodwin as director of the advisory council and as presidential consultant on the arts. It also noted that the council itself was being formed, with a membership to be announced shortly.

Although President Kennedy's leadership toward a federal arts policy tragically ended at this point, his successor, Lyndon Johnson, carried the effort to more tangible fruition. The largely moribund effort to raise private funds for the construction of a national cultural center in Washington was reinvigorated and redirected toward creating a living memorial to the assassinated president, the John F. Kennedy Center for the Performing Arts. Congress appropriated $15 million in federal matching grant funds. Subsequently, in May of 1964, former Democratic National Campaign finance chairman and Broadway producer Roger Stevens was named special assistant to the president for the arts. That summer he succeeded, finally, in winning congressional approval for a Federal Advisory Council on the Arts.

---

and the Arts in the United States, 1961-1963," in *Public Policy and the Arts*, ed. Kevin V. Mulcahy and C. Richard Swaim (Boulder, CO: Westview Press, 1982), pp. 141-68, particularly pp. 143-48.

8. On Heckscher's appointment and reaction to it, see *New York Times*, 17 Feb. 1962.

9. *The Arts and the National Government: Report to the President*, submitted by August Heckscher (Washington, DC: Government Printing Office, 1963).

10. For the text of Executive Order No. 11,112 and of President Kennedy's accompanying statement, see U.S., Congress, Senate, *The Arts and the National Government: A Report to the President Submitted by August Heckscher, Special Consultant on the Arts*, 88th Cong., 1st sess., 1963, Senate Document 28.

TENUOUS COLLABORATION

Following his 1964 landslide election, President Johnson integrated the call for federal support for the arts into his educational-policy agenda, combining it with the effort to establish a National Foundation for the Humanities. On 10 March 1965, the administration submitted a legislative proposal to create a National Foundation for the Arts and Humanities comprising separate endowments for the arts and for the humanities. With strong presidential support, the arts and humanities bill quickly moved through committee consideration. In September, it was pried out of the House Rules Committee with an overwhelming discharge petition vote of 260 to 114. The bill was moved to floor debate two days later, and was thereafter approved by a voice vote. On 29 September 1965, President Johnson signed the bill into law in a Rose Garden ceremony where he called for an ambitious program of governmental patronage of the arts. Thus, after two decades of insufficient and disparate leadership efforts by Congress and by presidents, a federal commitment to the arts was finally established with the creation of the NEA. This accomplishment was possible only through an alliance between President Johnson and congressional arts supporters facilitated by the momentum of the landslide election of 1964, by a shared desire to realize some portion of the Kennedy legacy, by the effect of Johnson's emphasis upon a broad-gauged education-policy agenda, which included the arts, and by his legendary legislative skills.

The fate of the new arts agency for the remainder of the Johnson presidency illustrates the fragility of the alliance that had been instrumental in the agency's creation. After a start-up appro-

priation of $2.5 million for fiscal year 1966, the NEA's annual budget rose to but stagnated at approximately $7 million for the next three years. During that time, the president grew increasingly preoccupied with the Vietnam war and let much of the momentum for his Great Society domestic program dissipate. Without strong presidential interest and support, the development of the nascent arts-policy subgovernmental system floundered. Congressional supporters alone could not sustain the momentum, particularly not in the near absence of organized and positive interest-group activity from the arts community.

Indeed, by 1968, the war had not only severely weakened the president's political position but had also provoked congressional concern over its ability to fund both guns and butter. These factors had an impact upon the NEA's 1968 budget and reauthorization hearings. Coming, as they did, shortly after President Johnson's poor showing in the New Hampshire primary, the president was not in a good position to defend this new, small program. In the wake of this executive vacuum, old congressional opponents of federal arts support sought to make the NEA's appropriation a test vote about fiscal responsibility. Meanwhile, other congressional critics sought to revoke the agency's authority to make individual grants, citing concern for both quality control and fiscal accountability.[11] In the end, although arts supporters were able to preserve the agency's

11. See Fannie Taylor and Anthony Baressi, *The Arts at a New Frontier: The National Endowment for the Arts* (New York: Plenum Press, 1984), pp. 115-17; Kevin Mulcahy, "The Politics of Congressional Oversight of the Arts," in *Congress and the Arts: A Precarious Alliance?* ed. Margaret Jane Wyszomirski (New York: American Council for the Arts, 1988).

budget, they could not increase it from a very minimal level. Similarly, they managed to retain funding authority for individual artists, but only by agreeing to restrict its availability to those of "exceptional talent," thus effectively preventing the agency from nurturing emerging artists.

A final aspect of executive weakness accompanied the change of presidential administrations. Roger Stevens's four-year term as NEA chairperson expired in March 1969. The new president, Nixon, declined to reappoint him, thus allowing the agency to limp along with an acting chair for the next six months. It is not surprising that Congress hesitated to appropriate funds to an agency without a chair. During this interregnum, the agency lost considerable staff as well as members of its presidentially appointed advisory council. Although many possible appointees were considered, each proved to be either unavailable or unacceptable to key members of Congress and senators. In the absence of presidential leadership, the nascent arts-policy subgovernment could neither function effectively nor develop further.

POLICY CODETERMINATION AND THE DEVELOPMENT OF SUBGOVERNMENT

The tenure of Nancy Hanks as the second chair of the NEA was marked by the maturation of each of the components of the potential arts-policy iron triangle, as well as by the enhancement of presidential support for the new agency and its programs. As a precondition to accepting her appointment in October 1969, Hanks had required President Nixon's agreement to the general outlines of a proposed long-range plan. The plan called for presidential support

for agency reauthorization, a promise to propose substantial budget increases for the next three to four years, and a commitment to work for congressional appropriation of the proposed increases.[12] This promised presidential commitment was publicly confirmed with President Nixon's December 1969 special message to Congress on the arts and humanities, followed by his January 1970 budget request nearly to double the agency's current funding level.[13] Hanks further reinforced the presidential linkage by an alliance with presidential assistant Leonard Garment, by the development of friendly working relations with the Office of Management and Budget, particularly with deputy director Caspar Weinberger,[14] and by her personal service to the president and members of his family.[15]

Simultaneously, Hanks undertook efforts to mobilize the arts community in support of the president's proposals.

12. For a discussion of Hanks's leadership and strategy at the NEA, see Margaret Jane Wyszomirski, "The Politics of Art: Nancy Hanks and the National Endowment for the Arts," in *Leadership and Innovation*, ed. Jameson W. Doig and Erwin C. Hargrove (Baltimore, MD: Johns Hopkins University Press, 1987), pp. 207-45. Hanks laid out this plan in her "Memorandum for the President," draft 3, 17 Oct. 1969, found in the Nancy Hanks Papers, National Archives, Washington, D.C.

13. Richard M. Nixon, "Special Message to the Congress about Funding and Authorization of the National Foundation on the Arts and Humanities," in *Public Papers of the Presidents: Richard M. Nixon, 1969* (Washington, DC: Government Printing Office, 1970), pp. 1018-20.

14. See Wyszomirski, "Politics of Art," fn. 36.

15. For example, Hanks helped Tricia Nixon host a White House pumpkin-carving contest and succeeded in having a monumental modern sculpture that the president disliked removed from the lawn of the Corcoran Gallery. On the latter incident, see Michael Straight, *Twigs for an Eagle's Nest* (New York: Devon Press, 1979), pp. 31-33.

Sequentially, she identified those elements of the arts community most in economic need and solicited them to lobby for increased appropriations in return for the promise of more federal grant assistance. First orchestras and museums were approached. Because these had the most numerous, most widely distributed, and best-organized constituencies in the arts, they could, and did, mount extensive lobbying efforts. In turn, dance, theater, literature, film, architecture, and the growing complement of state arts agencies were enlisted in the common interest. Indeed, it was observed that in 1971 "few requests for money for a government agency have been endorsed by so many constituents in letters, telegrams, telephone calls, and personal visits."[16]

Beyond evoking group action, Hanks took concrete steps to develop the weak and divided arts community into a coordinated and politically effective constituency. Under her leadership, the NEA became a "patron of political action," helping to sustain the mobilization of its constituency from the top down by encouraging groups that could "promote new legislative agendas and social values."[17]

In the arts, these groups were the arts service organizations—nonprofit associations that provided artistic, technical, managerial, and/or informational services to their respective fields and also engaged in political advocacy. Starting in 1970, the NEA annually awarded between 5 and 9 percent of its program funds to support and develop such organizations. Indeed, the agency not only

supported both old and relatively newly established service organizations but also promoted the creation of completely new organizations, including Opera America and the National Assembly of State Arts Agencies.[18] Thus "the NEA patronized the political action of a constituency which, in turn, supported the agency's quest for more resources that could be channeled back into the very constituency the agency had helped to expand and organize."[19]

Similarly, as different components of the arts community were enlisted into the agency's political support group and became the beneficiaries of its distribution of benefits, the agency itself grew and matured. During Hanks's tenure, the NEA budget increased over 1000 percent, rising from $8.2 million in fiscal year 1970 to $123.5 million in fiscal year 1978. Meanwhile, the staff grew by nearly 600 percent to sustain a 900 percent increase in grant applications and a 600 percent rise in grant awards. The NEA's programmatic organization expanded from 8 to 12 divisions, while its administrative structure had begun to specialize and diversify. In short, the agency was becoming institutionalized.

Just as the constituency and bureaucratic legs of the arts subgovernment developed during the 1970s, so did the congressional leg. Although at the start of the decade, the arts had a small and highly committed group of congressional supporters, there was little legislative consensus concerning arts policy or its new lead agency. By 1977, however, House Majority Whip John Brademas

16. *New York Times*, 29 July 1971.
17. This style of interest-group formation is discussed by Jack L. Walker, "The Origins and Maintenance of Interest Groups in America," *American Political Science Review*, 77(2):390-405 (June 1983).

18. National Endowment for the Arts, "National Council on the Arts: Policy and Planning Committee Report on Service Organization Support," mimeographed (Washington, DC: National Endowment for the Arts, 1980), pp. 50, 68.
19. Wyszomirski, "Politics of Art," pp. 230-31.

could declare the arts to be "politically saleable."[20]

Throughout the 1970s, the arts was largely championed by three strategically positioned subcommittee chairs. In the Senate, Claiborne Pell, Democrat of Rhode Island, sought the creation of the Special Committee on Education, Arts and Humanities, which later became a subcommittee. Through most of the 1960s and all of the 1970s, he chaired this subcommittee, which held jurisdiction over the NEA's authorization. In the House, Representative John Brademas, Democrat of Indiana, chaired the equivalent subcommittee, which was variously concerned with postsecondary or select education,[21] while Representative Julia Butler Hansen, Democrat of Washington, chaired the House Appropriations subcommittee that considered the NEA's annual budget. In each of these, the arts found staunch congressional supporters who were positioned to provide precisely the strategic influence necessary as Congress evolved from an institution dominated by committees to one in which subcommittees predominated.

Thus by the end of the Nixon and Ford years and the resignation of Hanks in October 1977, an arts subgovernment system had developed to maturity. The NEA had crossed its "initial survival threshold"[22] and achieved a degree of permanence. It had also developed symbiotic relations with its constituency, which in turn had become organized

and had mobilized into an effective interest group capable of advocating its interests both with the agency and with Congress. Finally, subcommittee jurisdiction and leadership concerning the arts had stabilized and a working alliance of interests had been joined with the agency and its constituency. Indeed, during the waning months of the Nixon presidency and through the largely otherwise preoccupied years of the Ford presidency, the subgovernment proved itself viable even in the absence of presidential support.

If the first half of the decade of the 1970s had seen a pattern of policy codetermination with presidential leadership, the latter part of the decade saw the assertion of congressional leadership in codetermining arts policy with President Carter. One of the first signs of this shift could be seen in the politics of appointing the third NEA chairperson.

Whereas the first two—Roger Stevens and Nancy Hanks—had clearly been presidential preferences, the third, Livingston Biddle, was equally clearly the congressional candidate, specifically of oversight subcommittee chairman Senator Pell. As such, Biddle "embodied the concerns of the agency's friendly congressional critics, sharing with them a different program orientation for the Endowment."[23] Consequently, Biddle moved to expand populism in arts policy both procedurally and substantively. He sought to foster greater decision-making participation for the state arts agencies as well as for the National Council on the Arts. He also diversified the composition of review panels and increased the rotation of program officers. By putting primary emphasis on issues of access and availability, he sought to increase support for folk, popular, and amateur

20. *New York Times*, 4 Sept. 1977.

21. On the activities and personalities engaged in congressional oversight of the arts, see Mulcahy, "Politics of Congressional Oversight of the Arts."

22. The concept is that of Anthony Downs. For its application to an analysis of the NEA, see Lawrence D. Mankin, "The National Endowment for the Arts: The Biddle Years and After," *Journal of Arts Management and the Law*, 14(2):60 (Summer 1984).

23. Mankin, "Biddle Years," p. 63.

art. In addition, he sought to shift additional support to new and minority-based arts activities and reduce the emphasis on established, elite institutions. While this general direction was amenable to President Carter, it was clear that the impetus for this redirection was coming from Congress, notably from supporters rather than opponents of federal support for the arts.

Another indication of congressional assertiveness could be found in the emergence of Representative Sidney Yates as the new House leader on arts policy. Yates had succeeded Representative Hansen in 1975 as chairman of the House Appropriations Subcommittee on Interior and Related Agencies. During his first two terms in that position, however, he was apparently preoccupied with mastering his new assignment and dealing with the newly redesigned federal budget calendar and process. In addition, Representative Brademas, as head of the authorization committee for the arts, was still Mr. Arts in the House. It was not until 1977 that Brademas gave up this chairmanship upon his election as majority whip. Thus it could be argued that Representative Yates was not in a position to claim the arts leadership role in the House until after 1977. This he did with his request that the Appropriations Committee's investigative staff conduct a study of the NEA's application review process.

The resulting report launched a barrage of criticism against the agency and put it on the defensive. In refuting the charges, Chairman Biddle called the report "so flawed . . . as to be almost without merit."[24] Yates himself saw the

staff report as overly critical and "one-sided."[25] Thus the congressman had the double advantage of asserting his jurisdiction over the agency's activities as well as defending them in the face of an overzealous staff report.

Just as both the agency and the congressional elements of the arts sub-government were experiencing change and adjustment during the late 1970s, the character of the arts constituency also evolved during these years. As the NEA's budgetary growth slowed to an incremental pace after 1976, various elements of the arts constituency found themselves competing with one another for additional funding. The sense of unity and common purpose that had prevailed earlier in the decade began to erode.

Furthermore, the more effectively the various arts interests organized, the more they came to expect a greater and more equal role in policy formation. This was particularly true of the state arts agencies, which formed their own service organization in 1976 and lobbied the NEA for a partnership arrangement with the federal government rather than simply patronage from it.[26] A final development saw the establishment of the first arts organization explicitly devoted to advocacy rather than membership service—the American Arts Alliance. Seeking an "assertive voice" in Washing-

24. The statement was contained in the NEA's written response to the investigative staff report. See U.S., Congress, House, Appropriations Committee, Subcommittee on the Department of In-

terior and Related Agencies, *Department of Interior and Related Agencies Appropriations for 1980, hearings*, 96th Cong., 1st sess., 1979, pt. 2, p. 952.

25. As quoted in Ward Morehouse III, "Arts Groups to Keep U.S. Funding: Just the First Act," *Christian Science Monitor*, 25 Feb. 1981, p. 9.

26. See Taylor and Baressi, *Arts at a New Frontier*, pp. 178-88; Laurence Leamer, *Playing for Keeps in Washington* (New York: Dial Press, 1977), pp. 46-47; Wyszomirski, "Politics of Art," pp. 234-35.

ton, service organizations representing museum directors and dance, opera, and theater companies, as well as symphony orchestras joined together to form the American Arts Alliance in 1977 to advance their interests through lobbying.[27]

Thus, by the end of the 1970s, it could be said that each element of the arts policy triangle had achieved a level of political influence and/or organizational development such that its subgovernment was capable of independent action. On the one hand, this held the prospect of a mutually reinforcing set of political alliances among the chairpersons of the relevant congressional subcommittees, the arts interest groups, and the NEA. On the other, it also had the potential for a triple alliance against a president if the arts subgovernment found its common interests threatened by presidential policy proposals.

THE ARTS SUBGOVERNMENT IN CONFLICT WITH THE PRESIDENT

The election of 1980 changed both the presidential and the congressional environment for the arts. On the congressional side, two developments were of importance. First, the change in the majority party in control of the Senate resulted in the replacement of Senator Claiborne Pell with Republican Senator Robert Stafford, of Vermont, as chair of the NEA's oversight committee. Although Stafford proved to be a friend of the arts, he was not the champion of the arts that Pell had been. Indeed, as a

Republican, he functioned under more of an expectation that he would support President Reagan's policy proposals, particularly during the initial phase of the new administration. Thus the arts began the decade with a weakened, less strategically positioned support system in the Senate.

Second, the House experienced both negative and positive changes. On the negative side, two key arts advocates— Democratic Majority Whip John Brademas and Post-Secondary Education Subcommittee member Frank Thompson—failed to win reelection. Hence the arts policy network lost two long-term, active supporters at a time when it had also lost influence in the Senate. On the positive side, other House arts advocates—taking note of the partisan shift in the Senate and losses among supporters in the House, and expecting to face an unsupportive administration— recognized a need to organize to "guide more arts legislation through Congress and to protect arts agencies from anticipated budget cuts."[28] Under the leadership of Representative Fred Richmond, Democrat of New York, the Congressional Arts Caucus was formed. Founded with 50 members in January of 1981, the caucus tripled in size within a year to become one of the larger House service organizations.[29] The emergence of the Congressional Arts Caucus expanded the support network for the arts

27. For coverage of the formation of the American Arts Alliance, see *New York Times*, 15 Nov. 1977. For a discussion of the development of arts interest groups, see Margaret J. Wyszomirski, "Art Policymaking and Interest Groups Politics," *Journal of Aesthetic Education*, 14(4):28-34 (Oct. 1980).

28. *New York Times*, 13 Jan. 1981.

29. On the establishment, membership, and leadership of the Congressional Arts Caucus during the 1980s, see Margaret Jane Wyszomirski, "Budgetary Politics and Legislative Support: The Arts in Congress," in *Congress and the Arts*, ed. Wyszomirski; on the cohesiveness and effectiveness of this arts support network, see Mary L. Weaver, "The Politics of Congressional Arts Policy: National Decisions, Legislative Needs and the Public Interest," in ibid.

in the legislature just as the network was preparing to face its most serious presidential challenge.

Meanwhile, the election of Ronald Reagan as president had brought to office the first executive since the establishment of the NEA who recommended a substantial cut in its budget—a proposed cut of 50 percent for fiscal year 1982. Damaging in itself, the reduction was widely viewed in the arts community as the first step toward something even more threatening: the eventual elimination of federal patronage altogether.

In the face of this common threat, the arts constituency that had become somewhat fragmented during the late 1970s rallied to protect its interests by supporting the NEA and the benefits that it distributed. In this effort, it was aided not only by the new mobilization of congressional support represented in the Congressional Arts Caucus but also by the holdover chair of the NEA, Livingston Biddle.[30]

Biddle devised and executed a defensive strategy that had both administrative and advocacy components. As chairperson throughout most of the first year of the Reagan administration, Biddle was in a position to allocate the effects of the Office of Management and Budget's overall cut among the various program subdivisions of the NEA. Instead of spreading the cutbacks evenly across the board, Biddle concentrated them on congressionally popular programs such as artists in the schools and the challenge

grants, with the expectation that Congress would restore funds for these activities. In addition, although ostensibly testifying before the House in defense of the administration's proposed budget cuts, Biddle effected a protest against them, expressing severe doubts that the NEA could adequately address its congressional mandate if funds were reduced so drastically.[31]

Eventually, the alliance of congressional supporters, the arts constituency, and agency administrators succeeded in defeating President Reagan's proposed budget reductions, limiting them to an approximate 10 percent cut, a rate common among many discretionary, domestic programs in that first year of the new administration. In addition, they also succeeded in co-opting and persuading the Presidential Task Force on the Arts and Humanities to endorse heartily the structure of the agency as well as to praise its role in spurring both artistic creativity and private patronage.[32] Although there was considerable concern and uncertainty over President Reagan's late 1981 appointment of Frank Hodsoll to replace Biddle as chairman of the NEA, these fears were soon allayed. Hodsoll proved to be politically cautious but not unfriendly toward the arts.

This pattern of subgovernment alliance, successfully counter to presidential opposition, has prevailed throughout the 1980s. Its effectiveness demonstrates that a mature and stable arts subgovernment has developed during the past twenty years and is fully capable of maintaining a policy course quite independent of presidential preferences.

30. For detailed discussions of Biddle's role during 1981, see Mankin, "Biddle Years," pp. 71-75; Margaret Jane Wyszomirski, "The Reagan Administration: The Early Indications" (Paper delivered at the Annual Meeting of the American Political Science Association, Washington, DC, Sept. 1981).

31. Quoted in Mankin, "Biddle Years," p. 72.
32. Presidential Task Force on the Arts and Humanities, *Report to the President* (Washington, DC: Government Printing Office, 1981), p. 3.

CONCLUSION

The evolution of an arts-policy sub-government can be seen as an instance of American pluralism, yet unlike other instances of policy pluralism, the arts subgovernment does not seem to have been dominated by any of its components. Neither presidential direction, congressional control, nor interest-group capture seems to characterize the politics of American arts policy. Collaboration rather than dominance seems a more appropriate general model, although it may operate somewhat differently for positive or negative effect.

Negatively, the arts subgovernment has proven itself effective in mobilizing against external and threatening presidential actions. In this, the arts subgovernment exhibits the policy veto capacity associated with special-interest politics. As manifest in the 1980s, such subgovernment veto behavior reflects the mutual and complementary interests of the system's component members. The constituency, seeking to preserve its benefits, calls upon the assistance of its congressional and bureaucratic allies, who, in turn, share these concerns as well as their own to preserve institutional prerogatives and to further partisan or philosophical preferences.

The prospects for positive action are more complex. In order to advance arts policy, all political actors must engage in active collaboration, as was the case during the early 1970s. Presidential indifference, neutrality, or merely lack of opposition, as seen during the Carter administration, seems to allow for incremental and intrasystem adjustment at best and for stagnation at worst. For positive policy action, it appears to be necessary that Congress, presidents, constituency, and agency all actively collaborate. One possible explanation for this necessity may lie in the relatively low political stakes involved in arts policy and in the relative weakness of each political actor with regard to arts policy.

As one measure of relative importance, consider the budgetary stakes involved in federal arts policy. Combined federal support for the arts—for NEA plus other programs—amounts to about one-half of 1 percent of federal expenditures. In the scheme of political affairs, Congress and presidents are unwilling to expend much effort or incur many political costs over such a small-stakes issue. Similarly, for the arts constituency, federal action, while symbolically important, is not a primary concern. At the individual level, few artists benefit directly from federal grants. For arts organizations, federal money accounts for less than 10 percent of their budgets and for no more than 2 percent in most arts organizations. Even for arts service organizations, concern with federal arts policy is but one of the services that they provide to their members. Only for the arts agency is federal arts policy a primary focus, and its interests cannot be maintained—much less furthered—without support from the other concerned political actors.

Thus the necessity to combine resources in support of shared interests is obvious. Given the present developed state of the arts subgovernment, domination by any one element seems unlikely; conflict between presidents and Congress would seem to benefit no one but rather to impose political costs on all players. Collaboration appears to be the most productive and effective alternative.

ANNALS, *AAPSS*, **499**, September 1988

Congress, the President, and Military Policy

By CHRISTOPHER J. DEERING

ABSTRACT: This article examines the changing role of Congress and the president in military policy. The argument is that the basic contours of the debate about executive versus legislative control of military policy have changed very little in 200 years, that, nonetheless, the balance of power in that relationship has shifted in favor of the executive, and that that shift is attributable largely to the substantial increase in the size of the standing military establishment under the direct command of the president. As a result, contemporary presidents, regardless of their inclinations, are in a substantially different position from that of their predecessors during the 200-year history of the Constitution.

Christopher J. Deering is associate professor of political science at the George Washington University. He has served as a Brookings Institution research fellow (1977-78) and as an American Political Science Association congressional fellow (1984-85). He is coauthor of Committees in Congress *(1984), editor of* Congressional Politics *(1988), and author of a number of articles and papers on congressional politics.*

WHEN George Washington was inaugurated president in 1789, he became, under the Constitution, commander in chief of the armed forces of the United States. At that time, the armed forces of the United States consisted of roughly 700 army regulars, Secretary of War Henry Knox, and a single civilian assistant.[1] Two hundred years later, the forty-first president of the United States also will become commander in chief. Upon that occasion, he will inherit from Ronald Reagan 2.2 million active-duty military personnel, more than 1 million civilians employed by the three military departments, and just over 90,000 other civilian employees in the Department of Defense.

How important is this difference? Is it simply a reflection of national growth? Or does it also reflect a shift in national priorities? More important, how does this change affect the balance of legislative and executive authority regarding military policy?

The Constitution's "invitation to struggle" was the product of several important factors: design, disagreement, and ignorance. By design, the Constitution set up a system of competition between the three branches of government. By preventing a concentration of power in a single branch and by encouraging the branches to guard jealously their prerogatives, the Founders sought to avoid tyranny. Disagreement prevented the Founders from clearly locating the bulk of power in the new government. By compromising, they ensured that the debate would persist. Finally, they simply left some parts of the Constitution vague because they could not foresee every circumstance. Given their experience,

and the state of the world at the time they wrote the Constitution, they left some aspects for others to complete. This vagueness is particularly apparent in the Constitution's treatment of the role of Congress and the president in military policy.

It is not my purpose to debate whether greater executive or legislative control of military policy is proper. Rather, the argument is, first, that the basic contours of the debate about executive versus legislative control of military policy have changed very little in 200 years. Second, however, the balance of power in that relationship has shifted in favor of the executive. Neither intellectual arguments nor policy debates have caused the shift. Rather, over time, one important underlying condition of the original balance of opinion has shifted: the size of the standing military establishment under the direct command of the president has increased substantially.[2]

Regardless of party, politics, experience, or inclinations, the next president will be in a fundamentally different situation from that of President George Washington 200 years ago. The difference marks a de facto change in the constitutional balance of power between Congress and the president regarding military policy. The result has been a shift away from the pronouncedly pro-Congress Constitution and toward ex-

1. Leonard D. White, *The Federalists: A Study in Administrative History* (New York: Macmillan, 1948), p. 146.

2. The term "standing army" is used here and elsewhere in this article in a generic sense and includes all of the armed forces. The Founders tended to think of the standing army as land forces—that is, those that could be quartered in citizens' homes and used to subjugate the people—not as naval forces and thus would not necessarily approve. The characterization here is meant to apply to the regular, standing military establishment, so the wider usage is appropriate and not as unwieldy as "the standing army, navy, marines, and, later, air force" would be.

panded executive power. There is nothing particularly novel about observing an increase in the president's national security powers, but to date, little or no attention has been given to the historical context that precedes that increase. That is, little attention has been given to the congressional side of that equation. This article addresses that issue.

CONGRESS, THE PRESIDENT, AND MILITARY POLICY: THE PERENNIAL DEBATE

On 18 August 1787, Elbridge Gerry of Massachusetts asked the Constitutional Convention to consider an amendment that would have limited the size of the army to no more than 2000 or 3000 troops. An outspoken opponent of standing armies, Gerry argued that the draft Constitution did not sufficiently circumscribe the conditions for creating or maintaining an army. Chairing the convention, George Washington could not formally speak against Gerry's motion. Nonetheless, he was able to make his feelings known by facetiously suggesting to those within earshot that a corollary amendment should also be adopted that would limit any future invader to an army no larger than 2000-3000. Gerry's proposed amendment was unanimously rejected,[3] but the debate over the nature and extent of standing armies and the precise language limiting them—and by implication the future of military policymaking—was not laid to rest.

The American Constitution was written at an important historical turning point.[4] Despite the advent of the nation-

state in Europe at the middle of the seventeenth century, the monarchical and aristocratic states of Europe had not yet embraced the constitutional principles of citizenship that would subsequently link people to their national governments. Nonetheless, the American document was founded on principles of liberal individualism—life, liberty, and property—and required a means of implementing its foreign and military policy in ways that advanced and protected individual rights.

When they drafted the Constitution, the Founders had numerous bad experiences to react against but almost no positive experience and no historical examples of foreign and military policymaking in a democracy. They distrusted the military because it was an instrument of monarchical power rather than an instrument of democracy, but difficulties during the Revolutionary War, the patchwork quality of the Articles of Confederation, and Shays's Rebellion all helped convince the delegates to the convention that some attention to the military apparatus would be necessary. Thus, if not the center of debate, a new military apparatus certainly would be a leitmotiv faced by the delegates.

It is generally agreed that debate on foreign and military policymaking was of secondary importance during the Constitutional Convention.[5] Nonethe-

---

3. This story is recounted in, inter alia, Charles Warren, *The Making of the Constitution* (Boston: Little, Brown, 1928), pp. 482-84.

4. A good discussion of these last two points can be found in an interesting essay: Edward

Mead Earle, "Adam Smith, Alexander Hamilton, Friedrich List: The Economic Foundations of Military Power," in *Makers of Modern Strategy: Military Thought from Machiavelli to Hitler*, ed. Edward Mead Earle (Princeton, NJ: Princeton University Press, 1948), pp. 117-54.

5. See, for example, Louis Smith, *American Democracy and Military Power: A Study of Civil Control of the Military Power in the United States* (Chicago: University of Chicago Press, 1948), pp. 17-19.

less, such debate did occur during the convention and more heatedly during the ratifying conventions. As with other debates at the convention, the issue of military policymaking centered upon differing opinions about the strength of the new national government. Later these disputes would form the basis of perennial debates about the nature and extent of executive and legislative power.

Gerry—and other Republicans, such as Thomas Jefferson, Richard Henry Lee, and James Madison of Virginia— were frightened at the prospect of a standing army at the disposal of the national government. Consider, for example, the words of Richard Henry Lee in a 1787 letter to Madison:

You are perfectly right in your observation concerning the consequence of a standing army—that it has constantly terminated in the destruction of liberty. It has not only *been* constantly so, but I think it clear, from the construction of human nature, that it *will* always be so.[6]

Opponents of the standing army also believed that such an institution lacked democratic control, drained the treasury, burdened the people, and invited war. The new government should not emphasize military might but commercial development, neutrality, and the safeguarding of political liberties. These Republicans almost certainly also believed, even if they did not say it, that a national army would undercut their own local militias—in which most politicians held commissions. Indeed, it has been argued that the vested interests in local militia were as formidable a block to establishing a regular army as any of the philosophical arguments advanced at the time. Thus, in 1787, localism may

have been as powerful a motive as liberal individualism in combating the forces that favored a stronger national government.[7]

As we know, the Federalists, led by Alexander Hamilton during the convention, believed that the new nation required a strong national government in order to achieve some degree of stability and continued independence from England, France, and Spain. Hamilton believed that a professional army and navy of at least modest proportions would be necessary to secure American interests:

The steady operations of war against a regular and disciplined army can only be successfully conducted by a force of the same kind. Considerations of economy, not less than of stability and vigor, confirm this position. . . . War, like most other things, is a science to be acquired and perfected by diligence, by perseverance, by time, and by practice.[8]

In contrast to the local concerns of Republicans, Hamilton wished to be the architect of a competitive national economy, but as a realist, he knew that years would pass before America could seriously compete with the other trading and manufacturing nations of the world. In the interim, a regular army and navy would be needed to secure the country's financial interests from the intrusions of others.

In spite of the loss of Gerry's amendment, the Constitution on balance came out closer to his point of view than to Hamilton's. As in other things, the Founders erred on the side of limits rather than permissiveness. The resulting democratic

6. Quoted in Warren, *Making of the Constitution*, p. 484.

7. See Pendleton Herring, *The Impact of War: Our American Democracy under Arms* (New York: Holt, Rinehart & Winston, 1941), p. 30.

8. Alexander Hamilton, *The Federalist* (New York: Mentor, 1961), no. 25, p. 166.

military policy contained several components. First, the Constitution clearly established civilian control of the military. Second, the military was to be created by Congress, the popular branch of government. Third, except during wartime, the army would be very limited in size. Fourth, Congress would take the lead in determining when or if the United States should enter into war.[9]

In this context, the president's role as commander in chief takes on a much more limited mandate than is today commonly perceived. The president's duty was to command a military establishment if it became necessary, when provided by Congress, and pursuant to a declaration of war. But the linchpin in all this was the absence of a standing army, which, during peacetime, left the president nothing to command.

With this debate settled and the Constitution ratified, discussions shifted to the extent of executive and legislative control over military policy. Supporters of congressional control—again Madison, Jefferson, and Gerry—offered a series of arguments to support their position that the executive's role as commander in chief should be quite limited. Money spent on the military, they asserted, would rob the economy of its vitality at a time when growth was needed. A strong standing army would merely be an invitation for executives to seek foreign adventure. A strong standing army would threaten preemptive attacks and therefore invite such attacks by other nations. But Hamilton and the Federalists could not agree with these views. An investment in the military, they responded, would provide security

for commerce. A vibrant commerce, in turn, would invite jealousy and interference from abroad. Congress would be too slow to act in time of need, and, therefore, the executive required the tools and the flexibility to act.

Thus the basic contours of the debate about executive-legislative relations were already in place at the time the Constitution was written. In the intervening period, the terms of that debate have changed rather little. What has changed, of course, are the circumstances within which the debate takes place. More than anything else, the presence of a sizable standing army and the civilian military establishment have shifted the balance of power in favor of the executive.[10]

DEVELOPMENT OF THE
STANDING ARMY

For a little more than two decades after ratification of the Constitution—into the Madison administration—the Federalists and their opponents seriously debated whether to establish a regular and professional national army and navy. The debate, with contours very much like those previously outlined, settled nothing. Federalist Presidents George Washington and John Adams even won small increases in authorized troop levels—only to see most of the troops never recruited. But overall, the political battle in Congress was won by the Republicans and their presidents—Jefferson, Madison, Monroe, and Adams. It was not so

9. On the question of civil-military relations, see Smith, *American Democracy and Military Power: A Study of Civil Control of the Military Power in the United States* (1951), pp. 17-36.

10. This argument bears some relationship to the notion of the military-industrial complex, but rather than the version now offered by the Left, it is meant here to conjure up an argument closer to the bureaucratic politics model than the elitist model. The presence of a sizable military establishment creates an inertia in favor of continued existence, but its presence is also an invitation for its use.

much that no majority sentiment existed for a professional military. Instead, while the interior states opposed the navy and supported an army that could protect them from Indians, the coastal, commercially oriented Federalists stressed the need for a navy. In concert, these two factions might have formed a majority,[11] but they remained at loggerheads and the Republican opponents of either a strong army or navy were the beneficiaries. Whatever the immediate cause, the result was that throughout the nineteenth century, the United States established a pattern of keeping minimal military power during peacetime and hastily improvising for defense during war. That practice, of course, has been altered since World War II.

This significant change can be examined in a number of ways, but a brief examination of the number of personnel available for national defense will help to make the point.[12] Three characteristics for the standing military establishment are examined here: the growth in size of the active military, the size of the military relative to the growth in population, and the magnitude of the increase during times of war. (These data are presented in Tables 1 and 2.)

It is no great surprise that Congress has authorized an ever larger standing army throughout the last 200 years. As the country grew, so did the size of the standing military. For most of American history, until World War II, the level of peacetime, active-duty military provided by Congress kept pace with or somewhat exceeded the growth in U.S. population (see Table 1). The aggregate effect of this growth was to increase the size of the military some 68 times while the population multiplied less than half as much— 31 times. This relatively even growth ended at that point. Since World War II, the standing military has increased by almost another 8 times while the population has less than doubled. Thus the military is 500 times larger than it was in the decade of the 1790s while the population is just under 60 times greater. Put differently, one-tenth of 1 percent of the population in the 1790s was in the active military service of the United States;[13] today, just about 1 full percent of the population is engaged in active military service.

Clearly, expansion of the military has not been simply a function of national growth and expansion—at least as measured by population. In the opening decades of the Republic, many argued that the military was too small; some argue today that it is too large. Regardless of who is correct, the level of national commitment represented by the military has shifted rather dramatically during the twentieth century. In order to examine this shift more closely, it is revealing to look at the pattern and

11. Harold and Margaret Sprout provide an enlightening analysis of the voting patterns in Congress during this period, primarily with regard to naval bills. Harold Sprout and Margaret Sprout, *The Rise of American Naval Power* (Princeton, NJ: Princeton University Press, 1944), pp. 25-72.

12. It should be noted that one needs to focus on personnel actually available to the president. The various state militias were intended to be used for national defense, but in truth early presidents could not readily command them and frequently could not depend upon them.

13. This calculation excludes the state militias, which, in aggregate, were much larger than the garrison national army. Space prohibits analysis of the quality and quantity of militia forces. By most accounts, they were generally ineffective and did not represent a substantial contribution to national security. They were not directly funded by Congress or immediately in the control of the president so they do not alter the legislative-executive balance of power appreciably.

TABLE 1
U.S. POPULATION AND GROWTH OF THE PEACETIME,
ACTIVE-DUTY MILITARY, 1789-1986

Decade	Active Average*	U.S. Population[†]
1790-99	4,060	3,929,214
1800-09	6,540	5,308,483
1810-19	13,511	7,239,881
1820-29	11,527	9,638,453
1830-39	15,279	12,860,720
1840-49	21,544	17,063,353
1850-59	24,228	23,191,876
1860-69	59,527	31,443,321
1870-79	40,888	38,558,371
1880-89	38,525	50,189,209
1890-99	47,170	62,979,766
1900-09	116,515	76,212,168
1910-19	158,812	92,228,496
1920-29	276,230	106,021,537
1930-39	275,650	123,202,624
1940-49	1,626,544	132,164,569
1950-59	2,629,228	151,325,798
1960-69	2,635,083	179,323,175
1970-79	2,089,863	203,302,031
1980-86	2,118,534	226,542,580

SOURCES: Active-duty military data are from U.S. Department of Defense, *Selected Manpower Statistics: Fiscal Year 1986*, DIOR/M01-86 (Washington, DC: Government Printing Office, 1986). Population statistics are from *The World Almanac and Book of Facts 1988* (New York: Pharos Books, 1987).

*Mean level of active-duty military personnel during nonwar years for the period indicated.
†U.S. population based on the decennial census at the beginning of the decade indicated.

pace of growth with respect to periods of war. Because periods of wartime mobilization are infrequent, the best way to see the pattern of growth is to examine interwar years and war years separately. (These data are in columns one and two of Table 2.)

After each war up until World War II, the average level of peacetime, active-duty military personnel authorized by Congress roughly doubled. Thus, for example, average military strength from 1789 to 1812 was 7100, but between the War of 1812 and the Mexican war, the average level was 14,800. Active-duty levels between the World War II postwar period and the Korean War postwar period increased by about 50 percent,

but they have declined by roughly 25 percent since the Vietnam war. Put simply, despite two additional wars, the peacetime military became, in the half decade after World War II, about as large as it was going to.

These long-term trends, punctuated by wartime peaks, also show that Congress has tended to fit the army to the purpose at hand. Larger armies were created during such conflicts as the Civil War and World Wars I and II; relatively smaller armies were created for the War of 1812 and the Spanish-American War. Regardless of the duration or scope of the war, substantial increases were required and were provided on each occasion up through World War II—in-

TABLE 2
WAR AND THE GROWTH OF THE STANDING ARMY, 1789-1986

Years	Active Average*	Wartime Peak	War/Base Ratio†
1789-1812	7,100‡		
1814		46,858	6.6 (3.7)
1816-45	14,800		
1848		60,858	4.1 (2.9)
1849-60	24,500		
1865		1,062,848	43.4 (38.0)
1866-97	43,400		
1898		235,785	5.4 (5.4)
1899-1916	132,400		
1918		2,897,167	21.9 (16.2)
1920-40	284,600		
1945		12,055,884	42.4 (26.3)
1946-50	1,826,900		
1952		3,635,912	2.0 (2.5)
1954-65	2,729,600		
1968		3,547,902	1.3 (1.3)
1974-86	2,105,300		

SOURCE: Figures and calculations based upon data from Department of Defense, *Selected Manpower Statistics: Fiscal Year 1986.*

*Active average based upon mean interwar levels of active-duty military personnel.

†Ratio of peak war-year active-duty level to mean prewar level. Figures in parentheses are ratio of war-year active-duty level to the last interwar year.

‡Figures for 1790-93 and 1796-1800 are not available. Average is based upon the mean of the available years.

creases that had to be authorized by Congress. Thus the military increased by a factor of 6 during the War of 1812 but by 43 times during the Civil War.[14] In order to fight these wars, Congress was required to act in a positive fashion to create armies sufficient to the conflict at hand. By contrast, because the standing army of the post-World War II period was already quite large, the Korean War commitment required only a doubling of the army and Vietnam required an increase of only 30 percent. The larger the standing army, therefore,

14. The figures presented here are for the Union army only. It is estimated that a total of almost 2.2 million military personnel served with the Union during the Civil War, with a peak of about 1.1 million in 1865. U.S., Department of Defense, *Selected Manpower Statistics: Fiscal Year 1986*, DIOR/MO1-86 (Washington, DC: Government Printing Office, 1986).

the smaller will be any mobilization at the onset of war.

The data examined here suggest that Congress's willingness to raise and support a standing army is at least partially determined by wars. Rather than a smooth growth trend punctuated by wartime mobilizations, new plateaus were achieved with each war experience up through World War II. Demobilization inevitably occurred at the close of each conflict, but rarely to prewar levels.

As with all previous wars, World War II's close brought a rapid demobilization—from 12 million to 3 million troops in less than a year. By 1948, the armed forces numbered fewer than 1.5 million. For some members of the Truman administration, such as the recently departed Secretary of State James F. Byrnes and the first secretary of defense,

James V. Forrestal, the demobilization was too much too soon, but because the Republican Eightieth Congress (1947-48) pressed Truman for tax cuts, there was no way to finance a larger standing army.

In the end, the new plateau reached in this period was substantially higher than any previously witnessed in American history—even if it was judged insufficient by the secretaries of state and defense.[15] Prior to this jump, the largest increase had occurred at the Spanish-American War, with a postwar plateau 300 percent higher than before the war. By contrast, the post-World War II level increased 640 percent.

The maintenance of, and later increase in, the large standing army after World War II is typically traced to several related causes. First, the United States was the only major industrial nation to survive the war intact. Second, the maintenance of a large Soviet army forced the United States into a role as guarantor of peace in Europe. Third, in contrast to previous wars, world or otherwise, the United States had assumed a position of leadership among Western democracies that forced it to center stage in international affairs. Fourth, despite the end of the war, a series of hot and cold regional conflicts required the United States to maintain enough military might to fight limited wars without abandoning or

weakening its commitments to Europe. Regardless of the causes, the fact remained that the United States Congress authorized the retention of sizable land, air, and naval forces after World War II.

That was not all, however. In 1947, Congress also passed the National Security Act, which created a third military service, the Air Force, consolidated control of military affairs in the newly created Department of Defense, created the Central Intelligence Agency to gather national intelligence, and instructed the president to organize the National Security Council to coordinate executive branch policy affecting national security. Finally, Congress also consented to ratification of a series of treaties that, for the first time in U.S. history, committed the nation to a series of peacetime military alliances with other nations around the world and also consented, pursuant to those treaties and others, to stationing large numbers of American troops abroad.

This peacetime establishment of a substantial standing army with institutional and intelligence support in the context of firm treaty commitments marked a significant shift in Congress's 150-year practice of maintaining a small-to-moderate-sized standing army, adhering to a policy of neutrality, and creating only modest-sized civilian institutions for the military's support. Taken together, this set of circumstances has caused an important shift in the traditional balance of power between Congress and the president in military policy. The implications of this shift are examined next.

15. Ironically, at least by contemporary standards, it was the Republican Party that posed a block to a larger standing military force during this period. See George H. Quester, "Was Eisenhower a Genius?" *International Security*, 4:159-79 (Fall 1979). More generally on the politics of the postwar period, see Samuel P. Huntington, *The Common Defense: Strategic Programs in National Politics* (New York: Columbia University Press, 1961); Edward A. Kolodziej, *The Uncommon Defense and Congress, 1945-1963* (Columbus: Ohio State University Press, 1966).

THE PRESIDENT, MILITARY
POLICY, AND CONGRESS

As with many legislative acts of the twentieth century, the creation of a large standing army and its accompanying civilian establishment worked to the disadvantage of Congress.[16] Put simply, it has shifted the war-making power to the executive and has altered the long-standing constitutional balance of power between Congress and the president.

Through the middle of the nineteenth century, the burden of proof for using U.S. troops lay with the president. As we have seen, no standing army existed and the Congress was loath to provide it. In 1792, the House of Representatives created a committee to investigate the defeat of General Arthur St. Clair by Indians in the Northwest Territory, establishing in the process a Precedent for congressional investigation of executive military actions. In 1812, Henry Clay and the War Hawks pushed President Madison into a new war with the British. In the cases of *Little* v. *Barreme* (1804)[17] and *Gibbons* v. *Ogden* (1824),[18] the Supreme Court offered its own support for congressional superiority by, respectively, holding the president's duty to execute the laws subordinate to Congress's lawmaking power and establishing broad and limitless congressional control of foreign commerce.[19]

By the middle of the century, circumstances had begun to change. The federal courts reversed course and began to build judicial precedents favoring the executive. In *Durand* v. *Hollins* (1860), the Second District Circuit Court held that a president's decisions regarding the protection of citizens abroad are "final and conclusive."[20] In *The Prize Cases* (1862), the Supreme Court recognized for the president a de facto power and duty to make war and concomitant wartime decisions with or without Congress's formal assent.[21] The Civil War was accompanied by unprecedented mobilization and a wartime draft to support the efforts of the Union. The Lincoln presidency's "extra-constitutional" rule brought presidential war powers to a new high watermark.

From the middle of the nineteenth century until after World War II, few serious legal or political doubts existed about the president's freedom to use American troops, but in order to engage troops abroad, some means of raising the requisite number, their equipment, and transportation still had to be found. Even if presidents like Theodore Roosevelt could force the Congress's hand—with stunts such as sending the White Fleet to the South Pacific—congressional participation was still required.

Today those circumstances are reversed. The burden of proof now rests with Congress to demonstrate why executives should not be engaged in foreign military activities. Having already supplied the troops, bases, and equipment and having already consented to the alliance structures necessary to pursue military policies abroad, Congress is necessarily reduced to the role of spectator back home.

16. These acts would include, for example, the Budget Act of 1921, the Executive Reorganization Act of 1939, the Employment Act of 1946, and the Trade Expansion Act of 1962 plus the series of foreign policy resolutions that served to endorse the executive's military power: the Formosa Resolution of 1955, the Middle East Resolution of 1957, and the Tonkin Gulf Resolution of 1964. These legislative acts mark a continuous shift in power, by design and by default, to the executive during the twentieth century. See James L. Sundquist, *The Decline and Resurgence of Congress* (Washington, DC: Brookings Institution, 1981).

17. 2 Cranch 170 (1804).

18. 9 Wheat. 1 (1824).

19. More generally, see Louis Henkin's authoritative *Foreign Affairs and the Constitution* (New York: Norton, 1972).

20. 4 Blatch. 451, 454 (1860).

21. 2 Black 635 (1862).

The most important practical effect of this change is to reverse the traditional practice of Congress's supplying troops necessary to fight wars. In the absence of a standing army, Congress always had to make a positive commitment in time of war. Congressional participation in military policy is no longer primarily positive, but negative. Short of an all-out conventional war, the president now has enough resources at his command to commit the United States to substantial military engagements, with or without congressional consent. Congress, should it be so inclined, is placed in the unten-able position of having to take troops away from the president or withholding appropriations if it desires to limit execu-tive action.

Moreover, the president now has more flexibility than at any other time in American history in utilizing military force abroad. As of 1986, the United States had about one-quarter of its total troop strength stationed outside the country. Few dispute whether these troops may be used to defend American interests and that such discretion rests with the president, but serious questions arise regarding what conditions warrant that discretion and what Congress's role is in ratifying such decisions.

Congress thus found itself trapped when public opinion turned against the war in Vietnam. Because it had never made a conscious decision to participate in the war, it now faced the prospect of depriving the commander in chief of troops during a time of war. Fortunately for Congress, mounting political opposi-tion among some legislators and among the general public was sufficient to in-duce the executive to reduce U.S. partici-pation. Taking the step of actually deny-ing troops to the president proved to be too much for Congress. Not until after U.S. troops had been withdrawn did

Congress vote to cut off funds for the support of South Vietnam.

All this placed Congress in an unten-able position. It was reluctant to reduce American commitments abroad, inca-pable of exercising quick or coherent judgments regarding executive actions, and unwilling to deprive the president of needed troops once military action had begun. The result was the War Powers Resolution, a direct consequence of a confluence of political circumstances in 1973. Viewed in broader historical per-spective, however, the resolution was also an attempt to turn back the histori-cal clock without changing the existing circumstances. The War Powers Resolu-tion was intended to force Congress to do what it would not do otherwise: make a positive decision about U.S. military engagements. Because Con-gress, as a political matter, could not eliminate the armed forces, it decided to sequester their use by the president and require congressional approval beyond certain defined points.

For political and practical reasons, this plan has proved an unworkable solution. To date, no president has accepted the constitutionality of the act, arguing that it transgresses the presi-dent's role as commander in chief, and only one, Gerald Ford, has reported to Congress pursuant to its requirements.[22] In spite of the act, presidents have frequently utilized American troops abroad—in and near actual combat— but on each occasion Congress has been unable because of time, or unwilling due

22. It might be said that, in the fall of 1983, President Reagan also complied with the act when he signed a congressionally initiated resolution— S.J. Res. 159, 98th Cong., 1st sess. (Pub. L. 98-119)—that declared that the War Powers Resolu-tion was in effect and limited the presence of U.S. Marines in Beirut, Lebanon, to no more than 18 months on their so-called peacekeeping mission.

to political disagreements, to articulate its own position. Meanwhile, at its inception and since, the War Powers Resolution has rekindled the old debate. Some argue that it unfairly hampers the executive's prerogatives as commander in chief. Others say that it recognizes in the president a power meant to be retained by the Congress. Regardless, it is the same dispute that has occupied the two branches for more than 200 years.

CONCLUSION: THE SEARCH FOR NEW MECHANISMS

In late 1986 and early 1987, President Ronald Reagan decided that U.S. national security interests warranted an increased naval presence in the Persian Gulf, the reflagging to U.S. registry of 11 Kuwaiti oil tankers, and active convoy activities in the Gulf. On 17 May 1987, the American navy frigate *Stark* was hit accidentally by a missile fired from an Iraqi warplane causing serious damage and killing 37 American sailors. In July, a reflagged Kuwaiti tanker was damaged by a mine in the Gulf. Subsequently, U.S. forces in the Gulf captured an Iranian mine-laying vessel—killing three of its crew—received and returned fire from four Iranian gunboats while sinking at least one, and shelled two Iranian offshore oil platforms in retaliation for an attack on a U.S.-flagged oil tanker, the *Sea Isle City*. In spite of all this, President Reagan maintained his position that no formal report to Congress was required and that the War Powers Resolution did not apply to this situation.

It is not surprising that Congress was unable to act in a coherent and consensual fashion. Political divisions precluded a coherent position. Administration supporters continued to argue that the president's role as commander in chief precluded congressional interfer-

ence. Opponents continued to argue that a U.S. commitment to hostile action required congressional participation—with or without the War Powers Resolution. Meanwhile, a centrist coalition sought a compromise that would at least put Congress on the record with its support and its concerns about the operation.

In the end, Congress's predicament is caused by the shift that has been described here. So long as a sizable military establishment exists and is placed under the command of the president, Congress remains in the uncomfortable position of utilizing negative rather than positive powers to control military policy. Senator Patrick J. Leahy, Democrat of Vermont, put it quite succinctly: "Using the power of the purse to stop an undeclared war is just too difficult."[23]

The purpose of this article has not been to settle a debate but rather to observe a change in the context of that debate. Proponents of a strong standing army will continue to argue that sudden wartime mobilizations are undesirable, that we should maintain a professional military adequate to any reasonable threat, that such a practice would give the president the flexibility needed to meet crises, and that these precautions would tend to avert rather than cause wars. Their opponents will suggest that large military establishments drain the treasury, spur government growth, encroach on the liberty of the people, and give no guarantee against war. There is no reason to think that that basic debate will be settled. But so long as the tools required to engage in military activity are in the hands of the executive, Congress will remain at a disadvantage.

23. Pat Towell, "Senate Shows Its Ambivalence in Votes on Gulf," *Congressional Quarterly Weekly Report*, 24 Oct. 1987, p. 2595.

Foreign Policy Powers of the President and Congress

By LOUIS FISHER

ABSTRACT: The congressional hearings in 1987 concerning the Iran-contra affair provided a unique and unusual education for the general public. Month after month, American citizens became privy to how arms were shipped to Iran and funds diverted to the contras in Nicaragua. They learned about the Boland amendment, the Intelligence Oversight Act of 1980, and executive orders that provide the overall framework for covert operations. Witnesses included major cabinet officials, the former White House chief of staff, the flamboyant Colonel Oliver North, two national security advisers, and a host of generals, agency officials, and private citizens. Throughout the hearings, there was learned discussion of constitutional issues, including major Supreme Court cases and the specific powers and responsibilities of Congress and the president. This article focuses on two issues: how foreign policy is shared by the two branches, and how Congress tries to use its power of the purse to control executive activities.

Louis Fisher works at the Congressional Research Service of the Library of Congress. He received his doctorate in political science from the New School for Social Research in 1967 and joined the Congressional Research Service in 1970. In addition to teaching at several universities, he has published President and Congress *(1972),* Presidential Spending Power *(1975),* The Constitution between Friends *(1978),* The Politics of Shared Power *(1981, 1987),* Constitutional Conflicts between Congress and the President *(1985), and* Constitutional Dialogues *(1988).*

THE constitutional relationship between the president and Congress in foreign affairs was explored in an extraordinary set of hearings in 1987. In contrast to bicentennial celebrations of the U.S. Constitution that concentrated on events of 200 years ago, the congressional investigation of the Iran-contra affair focused on contemporary and highly sensitive issues. Congress examined the actions of the Reagan administration in selling arms to Iran and using profits from those sales to assist the contra rebels in Nicaragua.

For months at a time, citizens had front-row seats to a constitutional drama. Millions sat before their television sets to watch the unfolding of the story. Hundreds more were willing to stand in long lines to enter the hearing rooms. From those hearings, and the congressional report issued in November 1987, the American public received an unprecedented education in executive-legislative relations in foreign policy.

Although many of the hearings descended into the complexity of financial transactions and agency procedures, basic questions of constitutional law were addressed. How does the Constitution allocate foreign policy to Congress and the president? What may the president do without legislative authority? Is the power of the purse an adequate control on executive actions? May the president, deprived of appropriated funds, turn to private donations and foreign contributions to pursue his policies? Those questions form the boundaries of this article.

THE CONSTITUTIONAL FRAMEWORK

The Constitution does not isolate foreign policy in one branch of government. Portions of foreign policy are assigned to Congress, to the president, and to the president working in conjunction with Congress. This parceling of authority may suggest that it is impossible, under our system, to achieve any coherence or consistency in foreign policy. The framers deliberately dispersed functions, however, to avoid a concentration of power dangerous to individual liberties. Justice Jackson described the essential spirit that motivates and informs our system of government: "While the Constitution diffuses power the better to secure liberty, it also contemplates that practice will integrate the dispersed powers into a workable government. It enjoins upon its branches separateness but interdependence, autonomy but reciprocity."[1]

The Constitution divides the war power by giving Congress the power to declare war but making the president the commander in chief. The president commands the armed forces, and yet the Constitution empowers Congress to raise and support armies, provide and maintain a navy, and make regulations for the military forces. The power of the purse is vested solely in Congress: "No Money shall be drawn from Treasury, but in Consequence of Appropriations made by Law." The Constitution gives Congress the power to regulate foreign commerce. Recalling the political conflicts in 1787 over commerce between nations, this grant of power makes Congress a major participant in foreign policy.

The Constitution divides other parts of foreign policy. The president is empowered to make treaties and appoint ambassadors, but both powers are sub-

1. *Youngstown Co. v. Sawyer*, 343 U.S. 579, 635 (1952).

ject to the advice and consent of the Senate. Because treaties generally require appropriations before they can be implemented, the House of Representatives helps determine the scope of treaty commitments. This dispersal of power over foreign policy puts a heavy premium on consultation, coordination, and cooperation by the two branches.

Part of the Iran-contra affair had its source in serious misconceptions about executive-legislative roles in foreign policy. Key witnesses testified that foreign policy was the exclusive domain of the president. They regarded congressional involvement, by its very nature, as an illegitimate interference with executive branch responsibilities.

This belief invited consequences. If Congress withheld appropriations from the president to implement his foreign policy, advocates of executive power believed that the president could solicit funds from private parties and foreign governments. If Congress investigated activities within the administration, executive branch officials could withhold information and conceal operations. Lies and deception became part of the package of tools to protect presidential policy. Duplicity was practiced against not only Congress but cabinet officers as well. To preserve the imagined powers of the president, executive officials resorted to guile, deceit, dissimulation, and bad faith.

Such witnesses as Admiral John Poindexter, former national security adviser, and Colonel Oliver North, former staff member with the National Security Council, did more than profess theory. They acted on it. Their theory of government is hostile to the constitutional system of checks and balances. Congressional silence in the face of their theories and actions would in effect condone them.

Justice Frankfurter warned Congress about acquiescing to executive initiatives:

A systematic, unbroken executive practice, long pursued to the knowledge of the Congress and never before questioned, engaged in by Presidents who have also sworn to uphold the Constitution, making as it were such exercise of power part of the structure of our government, may be treated as a gloss on "executive Power" vested in the President by § 1 of Art. II.[2]

Justice Jackson made the same point: "Congressional inertia, indifference or quiescence may sometimes, at least as a practical matter, enable, if not invite, measures on independent presidential responsibility."[3]

Congress had challenged the Reagan administration in 1981 when the latter tried to act unilaterally in foreign affairs. Documents were denied to the House Committee on Energy and Commerce on the basis of Attorney General William French Smith's statement that the documents "are either necessary and fundamental to the deliberative process presently ongoing in the Executive Branch or relate to sensitive foreign policy considerations."[4] In fact, the dispute concerned the impact of Canadian investment and energy policies on American commerce, an issue clearly within the express power of Congress to "regulate Commerce with foreign nations." After a committee subpoena and a move by Congress to hold Secretary of Interior

2. *Youngstown Co.* v. *Sawyer*, 343 U.S. at 610-11 (concurring opinion).

3. Ibid., p. 637 (fn. omitted).

4. "Executive Privilege: Legal Opinions Regarding Claim of President Ronald Reagan in Response to a Subpoena Issued to James G. Watt, Secretary of the Interior," prepared for the use of the House Committee on Energy and Commerce, 97th Cong., 1st sess. 2 (Comm. Print Nov. 1981).

James Watt in contempt, the documents were made available to Congress.[5]

Judicial doctrines

On the infrequent occasions when questions of foreign policy are litigated, the courts treat foreign policy as shared by Congress and the president. In a decision in 1986, the Supreme Court said it was aware of the "interplay" between statutory provisions and the conduct of foreign relations, "and we recognize the premier role which both Congress and the Executive play in this field."[6]

Statements in some decisions, taken out of context, imply that the president has an especially broad power to invoke executive privilege in the area of foreign affairs and national security. For example, the Supreme Court has stated that even more privileged than executive confidentiality in communications is the president's "need to protect military, diplomatic, or sensitive national security secrets."[7] Yet the case from which that statement is taken, involving the Watergate tapes, concerned only judicial access to executive branch information. It did not relate in any way to congressional access. The Court specifically stated that the case had nothing to do with the balance between the president's generalized interest in confidentiality "and congressional demands for information."[8]

The decision of courts to defer to the president is no reason for Congress to do so. Unlike the courts, Congress has explicit responsibilities under the Constitution for foreign affairs and national security. The courts repeatedly recognize this legislative authority. In 1948, the Supreme Court declined to settle an issue on the ground that foreign policy decisions "are wholly confided by our Constitution to the political departments of the government, Executive and Legislative."[9]

Executive-legislative responsibilities in foreign affairs were emphasized by litigation in the 1970s concerning AT&T. The District of Columbia circuit court pointed out that the administration never claimed exclusive power in the area of national security and foreign policy. The Justice Department had acknowledged the legitimate interest of Congress by negotiating with a House subcommittee and giving it a substantial amount of information on national security wiretaps. With the assistance of the District of Columbia circuit, , the executive and legislative branches worked out an acceptable compromise. The court described national security as a joint executive-legislative enterprise: "There is constitutional power, under the Necessary and Proper Clause, in the federal government to keep national security information secret. This is typically a government power, to be exercised by the legislative and executive branches acting together."[10]

To support broad claims of presidential power, several witnesses during the Iran-contra hearings relied on *United States* v. *Curtiss-Wright* (1936). A proper understanding of this case does not justify sweeping assertions of executive

5. U.S., Congress, House, Committee on Energy and Commerce, *Contempt of Congress*, 97th Cong., 2d sess., 1982, pp. 385-94; H. Rept. 898, 97th Cong., 2d sess., 1982.

6. *Japan Whaling Assn.* v. *American Cetacean Soc'y*, 106 S. Ct. 2860, 2866 (1986).

7. *United States* v. *Nixon*, 418 U.S. 683, 706 (1974).

8. Ibid., p. 712, n. 19.

9. *C. & S. Air Lines* v. *Waterman Corp.*, 333 U.S. 103, 111 (1948).

10. *United States* v. *AT&T*, 551 F.2d 384, 393 (D.C. Cir. 1976) (fn. omitted).

power in foreign affairs, however. The dependence on *Curtiss-Wright* is misguided for three reasons: the case is misunderstood or misrepresented; much of it is dicta; and many of the dicta are erroneous.

Colonel North testified that the Supreme Court, in *Curtiss-Wright*, "held again that it was within the purview of the President of the United States to conduct secret activities and to conduct secret negotiations to further the foreign policy goals of the United States."[11] He quoted from the decision to argue that the president can act in foreign affairs without sharing information with Congress:

He has his confidential sources of information. He has his agents in the form of diplomatic, consular and other officials. Secrecy in respect of information gathered by them may be highly necessary, and the premature disclosure of it productive of harmful results. Indeed, so clearly [is this true] that the first President refused to accede to a request to lay before the House of Representatives the instructions, correspondence and documents relating to the negotiation of the Jay Treaty—a refusal the wisdom of which was recognized by the House itself and has never since been doubted.[12]

This is misleading, but the misrepresentation was compounded when North read from *Curtiss-Wright* part of the message that President Washington sent to the House of Representatives when he refused to submit certain documents to that body. By quoting only part of the message, North left the impression that presidents have a constitutional right to deny information to Congress in the

area of foreign affairs.[13] In fact, President Washington's full statement clearly shows that he never intended to withhold information from Congress as a whole. He excluded the House of Representatives on this occasion because it had no constitutional role in the treaty-making process. Far from withholding documents from Congress, Washington stated that he had already submitted them to the Senate:

I repeat that I have no disposition to withhold any information which the duty of my station will permit or the public good shall require to be disclosed; and, in fact, all the papers affecting the negotiation with Great Britain were laid before the Senate when the treaty itself was communicated for their consideration and advice.[14]

Curtiss-Wright does not justify the actions in the Iran-contra affair. The case concerned only the question of how broadly Congress could delegate its powers to the president in foreign affairs. In 1935, the Supreme Court had struck down two statutes because they delegated excessive legislative power to the president in domestic affairs.[15] *Curtiss-Wright* raised the issue of whether the same standard applied to external affairs. The case had nothing to do with independent presidential powers. To the contrary, the question was the extent to which Congress could delegate its own powers to the president. The power at issue was legislative, not executive.

11. Iran-contra hearings transcript, 13 July 1987, p. 18.

12. Ibid., 14 July 1987, p. 11, quoting from *United States* v. *Curtiss-Wright*, 299 U.S. 304, 320 (1936).

13. Iran-contra hearings transcript, 14 July 1987, p. 12.

14. James D. Richardson, ed., *A Compilation of the Messages and Papers of the Presidents* (New York: Bureau of National Literature, 1897-1925), 1:187.

15. *Schechter Corp.* v. *United States*, 295 U.S. 495 (1935); *Panama Refining Co.* v. *Ryan*, 293 U.S. 388 (1935).

The Court upheld broad delegations of legislative power to the president in matters of foreign affairs. Writing for the Court, Justice Sutherland said that legislation over the international field "must often accord to the President a degree of discretion and freedom from statutory restriction which would not be admissible were domestic affairs alone involved."[16] Sutherland went beyond the specific issue before the Court and added pages of obiter dicta, claiming for the president a number of powers in foreign affairs that are not mentioned in the Constitution:

It is important to bear in mind that we are here dealing not alone with an authority vested in the President by an exertion of legislative power, but with such an authority plus the very delicate, plenary and exclusive power of the president as the sole organ of the federal government in the field of international relations—a power which does not require as a basis for its exercise an act of Congress, but which, of course, like every other governmental power, must be exercised in subordination to the applicable provisions of the Constitution.[17]

As Justice Jackson later observed, the most that can be drawn from this opinion is the intimation "that the President might act in external affairs without congressional authority, but not that he might act contrary to an Act of Congress."[18] Jackson remarked that "much of the [Sutherland] opinion is dictum."[19] In 1981, the District of Columbia circuit also cautioned against placing undue reliance on "certain dicta" in *Curtiss-*

Wright: "To the extent that denominating the President as the 'sole organ' of the United States in international affairs constitutes a blanket endorsement of plenary Presidential power over any mat-ter extending beyond the borders of this country, we reject that characterization."[20]

Not only is the "sole organ" passage from *Curtiss-Wright* a dictum but it is a misleading dictum. Justice Sutherland explained that the phrase "sole organ" appeared in a speech by John Marshall: "As Marshall said in his great argument of March 7, 1800, in the House of Representatives, 'The President is the sole organ of the nation in its external relations, and its sole representative with foreign nations.' Annals, 6th Cong., col. 613."[21]

This passage suggests that Marshall promoted an exclusive, independent power for the president in foreign affairs. When the statement is read in full, however, it is evident that Marshall merely argued that the president carried out policy as established by statute or treaty. There was no claim that the president could make foreign policy single-handedly. Marshall's statement was made during a House debate on President John Adams's decision to turn over to England a person charged with murder. There were proposals to impeach Adams for encroaching upon the judiciary, because the case was already pending in court. Marshall defended Adams because he was carrying out a treaty with England. The "sole organ" comment appears in a passage that underscores the fact that foreign

16. *United States* v. *Curtiss-Wright*, 299 U.S. at 320.
17. Ibid., pp. 319-20.
18. *Youngstown Co.* v. *Sawyer*, 343 U.S. at 636, n. 2.
19. Ibid.

20. *American Intern. Group* v. *Islamic Republic of Iran*, 657 F.2d 430, 438 n. 6 (D.C. Cir. 1981).
21. *United States* v. *Curtiss-Wright*, 299 U.S. at 319.

policy is exercised jointly by Congress and the president:

The case was in its nature a national demand made upon the nation. The parties were the two nations. They cannot come into court to litigate their claims, nor can a court decide on them. Of consequence, the demand is not a case for judicial cognizance.

The President is the sole organ of the nation in its external relations, and its sole representative with foreign nations. Of consequence, the demand of a foreign nation can only be made on him.

He possesses the whole Executive power. He holds and directs the force of the nation. Of consequence, any act to be performed by the force of the nation is to be performed through him.

He is charged to execute the laws. A treaty is declared to be law. He must then execute a treaty, where he, and he alone, possesses the means of executing it.[22]

Sutherland claimed that foreign and domestic affairs were different "both in respect of their origin and their nature."[23] He said that the states "severally never possessed international powers" and that upon separation from England, "the powers of external sovereignty passed from the Crown not to the colonies severally, but to the colonies in their collective and corporate capacity as the United States of America."[24] By transferring external or foreign affairs directly to the national government and then linking foreign affairs to the executive, Sutherland supplied a powerful but deceptive argument for presidential power.

Sutherland's history was incorrect. External sovereignty did not bypass the colonies and the states. From 1774 to

22. *Annals of Congress*, 6th Cong., 1800, p. 613.

23. *United States* v. *Curtiss-Wright*, 229 U.S. at 315.

24. Ibid., p. 316.

1788, the colonies—or states—functioned as sovereign entities, not as parts of a collective body to be known as the United States of America. The American states were free and independent of one another. Following the break with England, they exercised the sovereign power to make treaties, borrow money, solicit arms, lay embargoes, collect tariff duties, and conduct separate military campaigns.[25]

This retention of sovereign power by the states immediately after independence has been acknowledged by the Supreme Court.[26] Even if Sutherland's thesis were correct that the power of external sovereignty passed intact from the Crown to a unified United States, the Constitution effectively provides that the power of foreign affairs is allocated between Congress and the president.[27]

Foreign policy as shared power

Because the Constitution divides foreign policy between Congress and the president, the two coequal branches must find ways to cooperate and fashion accommodations that meet their mutual

25. Claude H. Van Tyne, "Sovereignty in the American Revolution: An Historical Study," *American Historical Review*, 12:529 (1907).

26. *United States* v. *California*, 332 U.S. 19, 31 (1947); *Texas* v. *White*, 74 U.S. (7 Wall.) 700, 725 (1869).

27. For critiques of Sutherland's scholarship, see Julius Goebel, Jr., "Constitutional History and Constitutional Law," *Columbia Law Review*, 38: 555, 571-72 (1938); C. Perry Patterson, "In re the United States v. the Curtiss-Wright Corporation," *Texas Law Review*, 22:286 (1944); David M. Levitan, "The Foreign Relations Power: An Analysis of Mr. Justice Sutherland's Theory," *Yale Law Journal*, 55:467 (1946); Charles A. Lofgren, "*United States* v. *Curtiss-Wright Export Corporation*: An Historical Reassessment," ibid., 83:1 (1973).

needs. As President Reagan said on 27 April 1983 in his appearance before a joint session of Congress, "The Congress shares both the power and the responsibility for our foreign policy." After the Vietnam war, which featured efforts to concentrate power in the presidency, Secretary of State Henry Kissinger made these observations:

The decade-long struggle in this country over executive dominance in foreign affairs is over. The recognition that the Congress is a coequal branch of government is the dominant fact of national politics today. The executive accepts that the Congress must have both the sense and the reality of participation: foreign policy must be a shared enterprise.[28]

The need for cooperation was explained in testimony by Secretary of State George Shultz and Secretary of Defense Caspar Weinberger before the Iran-contra committees. Shultz told the committees:

Looking at it from the Executive Branch standpoint, we have to respect the fundamental duties of our colleagues on the Hill, but we have to expect them to respect ours and what that means is, as many have pointed out, that while we have a system of separation of powers in the way it is constituted, . . . we also have a system of sharing powers. . . .

You have to have a sense of tolerance and respect and a capacity to work together and a desire to do it, for us to share information, for you to put forward your ideas, not to keep telling us all the time how to run things. But keep tabs. To have a way of interacting. . .[29]

When Secretary Weinberger testified, Representative Thomas S. Foley, Democrat of Washington, asked about the

value of having the president consult with Congress on foreign policy. Weinberger replied that such consultations were necessary because "we can't fight a war on two fronts. We can't fight with the enemy, whoever it may be, and we can't fight with the Congress at the same time." For success over the long run, the two branches have to act jointly.[30]

The Iran-contra affair has stimulated a serious discussion about what it takes to make government work effectively. Steps are under way to restore a sense of trust and good faith, so essential in a government of divided powers. Comity, cooperation, and mutual respect are some of the necessary ingredients. This is good principle; it is equally good practice. Representative Dick Cheney, Republican of Wyoming, advised Poindexter: "The reason for not misleading the Congress is a practical one. It is stupid. It is self-defeating."[31]

THE POWER OF THE PURSE

The constitutional authority of Congress to shape foreign policy relies heavily on its power to appropriate funds. In *Federalist* number 58, James Madison said that the power of the purse represents the "most and effectual weapon with which any can arm the immediate representatives the people, for obtaining a redress of grievance, and for carrying into effect just and salutary measure." The Constitution places the power of the purse exclusively in the hands of Congress: "No Money shall be drawn from the Treasury, but in Consequence of Appropriations made by Law."

Several witnesses at the Iran-contra hearings denied that Congress could dictate foreign policy through its power

28. *Department of State Bulletin*, 72:562 (1975).

29. Iran-contra hearings transcript, 23 July 1987, p. 145.

30. Ibid., 3 Aug. 1987, pp. 26-27.

31. Ibid., 20 July 1987, pp. 54-55.

of the purse. They claimed that the withholding of appropriations did not prevent the president from pursuing his foreign policy goals. He was free, so they argued, to spend funds contributed by private parties and foreign governments. House counsel George Van Cleve discussed this issue with Colonel North:

Mr. Van Cleve: And it is also clear, isn't it, if Congress told the President he could not ask foreign countries or private individuals for financial or other assistance for the contras, there would be serious doubt about whether Congress had exceeded its constitutional power, correct?

Mr. North: You are asking for my opinion, I think there is no doubt. If the Congress had passed such a measure, it would clearly, in my opinion, be unconstitutional.[32]

Senator Mitchell asked Colonel North, "Is it your contention that the President could authorize and conduct covert actions with unappropriated funds? Is that the point you are trying to make?" Colonel North replied, "Yes."[33]

The capacity of the executive branch to conduct foreign policy operations without funds from Congress was seen in its most dramatic and far-reaching form when Colonel North described the interest of the director of central intelligence, William Casey, in creating an off-the-shelf, stand-alone, self-financed organization, accountable to no elected official of the U.S. government.

Admiral Poindexter agreed that the executive branch could circumvent Congress by using nonappropriated funds. He justified the withholding of information from Congress on the ground that the funds being spent to assist the contras did not come from Congress. Here is the exchange between Poindexter and House counsel John Nields:

Mr. Nields: My question to you is this: if that is what you were seeking to have happen, why was it, when the [National Security Council] was carrying out military support for the contras, you felt it necessary to withhold information from the Congress?

Mr. Poindexter: Because we weren't using appropriated funds. They were private, third-country funds.[34]

The North-Poindexter theory would destroy the system of checks and balances. Executive use of funds obtained outside the appropriations process would create a government the framers feared the most: union of sword and purse.

Congress constantly grants and denies funds for foreign policy. For example, through the Clark amendment in 1976, Congress cut off all assistance for conducting military or parliamentary operations in Angola.[35] That was the law of the land and remained so until the Reagan administration was able to have the Clark amendment repealed in 1985. Even since the repeal, assistance has been subject to congressional control. As the conference report on the 1985 repeal explained, "Provision of such assistance requires further legislative procedures—the appropriate authorization and appropriation bills or presentment by the President of a finding to the Select Committees on Intelligence."[36]

Presidential access to funds from private parties and foreign governments would create what the framers deliberately and carefully rejected: placing in the same branch the ability to make war

32. Ibid., 9 July 1987, p. 53.
33. Ibid., 13 July 1987, pp. 16-17.

34. Ibid., 17 July 1987, p. 49.
35. 90 Stat. 757, § 404 (1976). See also 90 Stat. 776, § 109 (1976).
36. H. Rept. 99-237, 99th Cong., 1st sess., 1985, p. 150.

and fund it. In *Federalist* number 69, Alexander Hamilton explained why the American president was less threatening than the king of England. Among other differences, Hamilton pointed out that the power of the king "extends to the *declaring* of war and to the *raising* and *regulating* of fleets and armies," whereas the Constitution placed those powers expressly in the hands of Congress.

James Madison, writing on the president's power as commander in chief, warned of the dangers of placing that power in the same hands as the power to go to war: "Those who are to *conduct a war* cannot in the nature of things, be proper or safe judges, whether a war ought to be *commenced, continued*, or *concluded*. They are barred from the latter functions by a great principle in free government, analogous to that which separates the sword from the purse, or the power of executing from the power of enacting laws."[37]

To preserve the system of checks and balances, foreign policy must be carried out with funds appropriated by Congress. Allowing foreign policy to be conducted with funds supplied by private parties and foreign governments would open the door to widespread corruption, compromise, and loss of public accountability. This type of outside financing would fundamentally subvert the Constitution and undermine the powers of Congress as a coequal branch.

Consider the damage that would be done if presidential policies could survive on extragovernmental funding. Recall the executive-legislative struggles over the Vietnam war. In 1973, after years of conflict, Congress finally passed legislation to cut off funds. At that point,

could President Nixon have appealed to South Korea, the Philippines, or other countries for financial assistance to continue the war? Would this assistance have been tied to promises of increased American economic and military aid? Could he have accepted donations from private parties to defy a congressional statute? To ask such questions is to answer them.

Our whole system of law and government rebels against the idea of basing foreign policy on nonappropriated funds. To sanction solicitations from foreign and private sources would destroy the integrity of the appropriations process. Departments and agencies could make exploratory, tentative efforts to obtain funds from Congress. Rebuffed, they could then turn to private parties and foreign governments for donations to finance their activities. The resulting abuse, inviting malfeasance on a massive scale, is almost too vast to calculate. No other activity would inflict such damage.

The prospect of quid pro quos

In October 1984, to a continuing resolution, Congress added the strict language of the Boland amendment, prohibiting any direct or indirect assistance to the contras. Later, Senator Christopher Dodd, Democrat of Connecticut, said that there "have been a number of rumors or news reports around this town about how the administration might go about its funding of the contras in Nicaragua. There have been suggestions that it would be done through private parties or through funneling funds through friendly third nations, or possibly through a new category of assistance and asking the Congress to fund the program openly."[38]

37. Gaillard Hunt, ed., *The Writings of James Madison* (New York: G.P. Putnam's, 1906), 6:148.

38. U.S., Congress, Senate, Committee on

Officials in the Reagan administration made repeated assurances to Congress that there would be no effort to circumvent legislative control by soliciting funds from private parties or foreign governments and using those funds for foreign policy. Langhorne A. Motley, assistant secretary of state for inter-American affairs, appeared before the Senate Committee on Foreign Relations on 26 March 1985. He gave his unqualified assurance that the Boland amendment was being complied with:

Nobody is trying to play games with you or any other Member of Congress. That resolution stands, and it will continue to stand; and it says no direct or indirect. And that is pretty plain English; it does not have to be written by any bright, young lawyers. And we are going to continue to comply with that.[39]

Similar assurances were provided to the House Committee on Appropriations in April 1985.[40] Without Motley's knowledge, at the very moment he was testifying before congressional committees, administration officials were soliciting funds from private parties and foreign nations to assist the contras.

Although National Security Council adviser Robert C. McFarlane helped solicit contributions from Country Two, he admitted it was not sound policy. Asked at the Iran-contra hearings if he was uncomfortable about receiving money from a third country, he replied, "Well, I believe strongly that we could not and should not expect to sustain the policy with this kind of support and that this had to be the last time." The danger, he said, was the creation of an implicit quid pro quo: "You always have to consider what is it that you may invite by way of reciprocal gesture or concession, what obligation do you incur for having had some contribution of this kind."[41]

The specific risks in receiving contributions from Country Two were explored in an exchange between McFarlane and Senator Daniel Inouye, Democrat of Hawaii. It was brought out during the hearings that Country Two was very dependent on the United States for sophisticated weapons. McFarlane admitted that "any responsible official has an obligation to acknowledge that every country in the world will see benefit to itself by ingratiating itself to the United States. . . . they will certainly gain leverage on us through that process."[42]

As Representative Ed Jenkins, Democrat of Georgia, explained concerning the time during the State Department solicitation of funds from Country Three,

I was involved in a tough legislative battle in this House. On October 12, I believe, of 1985, this House passed a textile bill, very controversial. At that very time, Colonel North apparently was soliciting, from a nation that was impacted by this bill, funds secretly and that country later delivered $2 million, according to the testimony. The president vetoed that bill in December 1985 and between December 1985 and August 1986, when the Congress decided to sustain

---

Foreign Relations, *Security and Development Assistance*, 99th Cong., 1st sess., 1985, p. 908.

39. Ibid., p. 910.

40. U.S., Congress, House, Committee on Appropriations Subcommittee, *Department of Defense Appropriations for 1986*, 99th Cong., 1st sess., 1985 p. 1092.

41. U.S., Congress, House, Select Committee to Investigate Covert Arms Transactions with Iran, and U.S., Congress, Senate, Select Committee on Secret Military Assistance to Iran and the Nicaraguan Opposition, *Testimony of Robert C. McFarlane, Gaston J. Sigur, Jr., and Robert W. Owen*, 100th Cong., 1st sess., 1987, p. 25.

42. Ibid., p. 201.

the president by an eight-vote margin, there were entreaties apparently made to many other nations that were impacted by this legislation.[43]

Given these conditions, Jenkins expressed concern that the foreign nation asked to contribute to the contras would be "placed in a compromising situation" if the legislation under consideration was important to it. McFarlane added, "What is worse, we would be."[44]

Witnesses before the Iran-contra committees described an extraordinary story of foreign policy initiatives that operated outside the regular channels of government. Policies were formulated and implemented without the knowledge of Congress or many of the principal cabinet officials. Instead of relying on funds appropriated by Congress, projects were financed by contributions from private parties and foreign governments. These operations posed major threats to democratic government, legislative control, and public accountability.

Private parties have been used in the past for foreign policy, but with proper accountability. Private envoys, as substitutes for public officials, are subject to special safeguards. They are appointed by the president; they represent the president; their duties are assigned by the president; they are paid from the president's contingency fund, which depends on congressional appropriations; and envoys return and personally brief or report to the president. This custom of using private envoys provides no support for the activities of such individuals as Richard Secord and Albert Hakim. In the Iran-contra affair, there

was no direct accountability to the president or even to the secretary of state.

Private activities in foreign policy and foreign contributions very seriously blur and undercut the accountability of government. Congress and the principal cabinet leaders did not know of Iran-contra operations that directly affected national policy. In many cases, the operations were in direct conflict with policies regarding Iran that the administration had announced to the public or policies restricting contra assistance that Congress had enacted into law.

The abuses in the Iran-contra affair have provoked Congress to draft legislation designed to minimize future occurrences. Bills have been introduced to tighten congressional controls on covert operations, especially by requiring the president to notify Congress and members of the National Security Council. If the president decides to authorize a covert action, he must prepare a written finding, distribute it to the proper parties, and take steps that all findings are preserved as official records. Findings are to be prospective, not retroactive. To prevent private parties from engaging in personal forays into foreign policy, Congress is considering amendments to strengthen the Neutrality Act. Enactment of new criminal penalties would remind executive officials and private citizens that violating congressional policy runs the risk of fines and jail sentences.

Beyond these steps, it is hoped that the damage inflicted by the Iran-contra affair will help to alter attitudes and create a healthier climate for executive-legislative cooperation. The two branches would benefit; so would the nation. What better way to celebrate the Constitution's bicentennial?

43. Ibid., p. 279.
44. Ibid., p. 280.

Book Department

INTERNATIONAL RELATIONS AND POLITICS

GREEN, DAVID G. *The New Conservatism: The Counterrevolution in Political, Economic, and Social Thought.* Pp. xi, 238. New York: St. Martin's Press, 1987. $32.50.

RAYACK, ELTON. *Not So Free to Choose: The Political Economy of Milton Friedman and Ronald Reagan.* Pp. xi, 215. New York: Praeger, 1986. $37.95.

Green and Rayack present contrasting views of the new conservatism purportedly at the base of Thatcherism and Reaganism. Both agree that these political leaders have at points significantly deviated from the prescriptions of contemporary conservative thought; they disagree in their assessments of the soundness of this theory and of the consequences of policy deviation.

David Green's *New Conservatism: The Counterrevolution in Political, Economic, and Social Thought* represents a sympathetic treatment of the major strands of new conservatism and its impact upon social and economic policy. Green, a research fellow at the Institute of Economic Affairs, a conservative think tank, describes the linkages between new conservatism and eighteenth-century liberalism, Nozick minimalism, Friedman monetarism, the public-choice school, and the works of Friedrich Hayek. To debates that often produce more heat than light Green adds clarity and informed advocacy. Not only does he deal with complex writers such as Murray Rothbard, Robert Nozick, John Rawls, and James Buchman; he attends to the central issues that distinguish new conservatism from the competing schools of thought, New Deal liberalism and socialism. Core concepts of liberty, justice, individual, and community provide the explicative medium through which theoretical variants are discussed. One comes away from the experience better understanding both the concepts and new conservatism. Green is one who recognized that it is the scholar's charge to separate the significant from the trivial and to promote understanding by sensitively and honestly simplifying the complex.

The policy section of Green's work is a study in contrast. Here his advocacy becomes intrusive and renders analysis shallow. Part of the problem stems from attempting too broad a policy coverage. Within seventy pages, he describes new conservatism's impact upon British and American education, social security, health, housing, roads, public transportation, agriculture, and economic and industrial policy. This frenzied treatment yields paragraphs such as the following, which describes British public acceptance of the National Health Service (NHS).

In Britain intellectual opinion remains predominantly socialistic and this is especially true of thinking about the NHS. The new liberal criticism of the NHS has aroused much passionate denunciation and has resulted in defenders of the NHS coming up with new arguments in its support, but few minds have been changed. The chief reason is that support for the NHS is rooted more in emotion than in reason. Some are attached to it because of their commitment to compulsory equalisation, but more are devoted to it because they associate the NHS with elementary decency or fair play.

Such glib assessments of major policies undermine the credibility of his entire work. He does not effectively or accurately describe selected policies or their relationship to new conservatism. Thus his comparison and critique of the Reagan and Thatcher administrations in terms of their reliance upon new conservatism is unconvincing.

Elton Rayack's *Not So Free to Choose: The Political Economy of Milton Friedman and Ronald Reagan* addresses policy dimensions head-on by carefully detailing the influence of Friedman's free-market economics upon Reagan's orientation to the role of the state in promoting peace and prosperity. In speeches and policy proposals, Reagan seems almost to plagiarize the works of Milton Friedman. His definition of freedom, equality, power, and governmental legitimacy run strikingly parallel to those of the dean of the Chicago school of economics, yet not close enough to satisfy Friedman fully. Rayack also describes the influence of the Chicago boys on the revolution, or counterrevolution, in Pinochet's Chile.

But Rayack's thesis does not hinge on the impact of Friedman upon Reagan and other national policymakers, nor is it based on their success in implementing Friedmanomics. Rather, he is concerned about the viability of free-market economic theory. His concern takes the form of empirically testing Friedman's sweeping descriptions of the past performance of markets and of the

applications of monetarism in the United States and Chile. Contrary to Friedman's central thesis that the free market is associated with economic growth, with international peace, and with meaningful individual freedom, Rayack finds little relationship between size of government and degree of regulation and economic growth or peace. Unfortunately, a characteristic economist, Friedman's empirical inattentiveness allows Rayack the prerogative of specifying the evidence and interpreting it. The result devastates Friedman's larger claim and plea for a value-free economic science in that his ideology rather than any tested reality produces continuity across his works. Therefore, like Rayack, one is led to question the relationship between free markets and individual freedom, namely, whether in a free-market system individuals are meaningfully "free to choose."

DAVID G. BAKER

Hartwick College
Oneonta
New York

HESS, GARY R. *The United States' Emergence as a Southeast Asian Power, 1940-1950.* Pp. xi, 448. New York: Columbia University Press, 1987. $45.00.

This is the first book-length study of U.S. policy toward Southeast Asia covering the wartime and early postwar years—a period of transition from Western colonial control and rivalry with Japan to cold-war polarization. Historian Gary R. Hess has marshaled an impressive array of original sources, ranging from British and U.S. government files to the personal papers of Presidents Roosevelt and Truman and other administration officials, to undergird his account of the evolution in U.S. policy toward major power responsibility in the region. One telling episode that is unaccountably omitted, however, despite the fact that it is well documented in State Department papers, is the United States' use of the prospect of military assistance to pressure a reluctant Thai government into recognizing the Bao Dai government in early 1950. Nevertheless, Hess's thorough and wide-ranging account will undoubtedly serve as a reference book on this period for a long time to come.

Where the book fails is in its exclusion of any critical interpretation of the U.S. failure to support anticolonial nationalist movements in Indochina and Indonesia in the early postwar years. Hess's major themes are standard observations made for decades about the motivations of U.S. policy during this transitional period: the United States compromised its wartime anticolonial principles because it needed strong European allies in order to contain the Soviet Union; it was later prevented from effectively moderating its European allies' colonial policies by "mounting communist insurgency," which the Soviets and Chinese "seemingly abetted."

These generalizations raise questions rather than answering them. Why was the United States not more afraid of colonial wars weakening France and Holland economically and militarily? Did the United States really face an effort by the Soviet Union to seize control of Southeast Asia, or was this notion fabricated from the thinnest evidence? And why were Acheson and the State Department ready to accept the possibility of "independent communism" in China but not in Southeast Asia, where real evidence of Moscow's hand in armed insurgencies was nonexistent? The preference for bland reporting of the official rationale to hard analysis of some of the underlying anomalies diminishes the value of a well-researched study.

GARETH PORTER

American University
Washington, D.C.

KNIGHTLEY, PHILIP. *The Second Oldest Profession: Spies and Spying in the Twentieth Century.* Pp. xi, 436. New York: Norton, 1986. $19.95.

The Second Oldest Profession is a book about intelligence activities and organizations in the United States, Soviet Union, and Europe in the twentieth century. It sketches the evolution of intelligence organizations in some of these countries, describes a few of their more salient activities, and above all attempts to analyze and evaluate their performance and contribution to the security and welfare of their countries.

The book consists of a somewhat perplexing collection of historical anecdotes, facts, and gossip and occasionally even book reviews. Above all, it contains a devastating critique of intelligence performance. But little of the material in the book is new or original. The book's discussion of the subject is neither systematic nor comprehensive. The book lacks any solid methodology and fails to substantiate in any acceptable manner most of the interpretations and assertions that it contains.

In fact, if there is anything that holds the book together, it is Knightley's burning desire to call, as no one had done before, the intelligence agencies' bluff. He seeks to expose in some detail many of the myths that intelligence agencies all over the world propagate to justify their existence, growth, and especially budget allocation. He thus describes the various intelligence organizations as highly bureaucratized and inefficient, unduly secretive, subversive, manipulative, and conspiratorial in nature. The principal preoccupation of intelligence services is said to be with their counterparts in other countries, to whom they owe their existence, whereas the loyalties of the intelligence professionals are argued to be transnational—more to their colleagues and rivals and within the trade than to their country or government.

The book is replete with biased exposure of intelligence failures, while the few intelligence successes that are mentioned in passing are explained away as irrelevant or accidental. No wonder, therefore, that Knightley concludes that intelligence services are unnecessary largely, but not exclusively, in peacetime. The threats that they are designed to counter are by and large imaginable, deliberately cultivated by intelligence services to justify their existence and rationalize their dismal performance despite their ubiquitous failures.

Intelligence failures and excesses are indeed frequent and intriguing. But not all of them are of their own making. In any event, the threats the states confront are in many cases real enough and sufficiently ominous to justify the continued existence of intelligence organizations. What is called for is, therefore, better understanding of their pitfalls and constructive suggestions for making them more efficient and accountable. *The Second Oldest Profession*, however, offers little of either.

ARIEL LEVITE
Tel Aviv University
Israel

MOORE, BARRINGTON, Jr. *Authority and Inequality under Capitalism and Socialism: USA, USSR, and China*. Pp. x, 142. New York: Oxford University Press, 1987. $28.00.

At a time when capitalist and socialist states are turning to markets, Barrington Moore, Jr., reminds us that their more basic commonality is bureaucracy. Based on his Tanner Lectures on Human Values delivered at Oxford University in 1985, this book argues that liberal capitalism in the United States and communism in the Soviet Union and China constitute reactions against the unjust authority and material relations of their historical predecessors. Yet the rise of bureaucracy and the institutionalization of inequality now limit the prospect for the further development of "free and rational" societies.

The thesis of inhibited human progress is substantiated by identifying patterns of authority and inequality in three leading nations. While America's liberal tradition originated as a reaction against absolute monarchy, bureaucracy became central to the management of a modern industrial society. In the Soviet Union, bureaucracy emerged as the chief weapon in the battle against the inequities of capitalism, facili-

tating the establishment of a totalitarian regime with a modern industrial base. Bureaucratic imperatives thwarted liberal impulses and triumphed in forced collectivization and rapid industrialization—along with Stalin's terror—and then in a consolidation of the now inefficient administrative apparatus. In China, Maoism reacted to colonial intruders and Koumintang corruption by asserting egalitarian and antibureaucratic ideals. Yet, soon after taking power, Mao created a large bureaucracy to oversee the economy and impose social control, backed by systems of mutual surveillance and indoctrination.

Further, capitalism and socialism have produced roughly similar patterns of inequality. The American idea of the equality of opportunity corresponds to significant inequalities of distribution, with the gap between rich and poor now increasing. If capitalism inequitably distributes rewards, so do the political and professional bureaucracies in communist systems. Brezhnev's rule provided greater consumption by those at the bottom and a rise in the numbers and importance of professionals. Like the USSR, China places political leaders at the top and poor peasants at the bottom, though, unlike the USSR, urban areas are wealthier than the countryside. With the limited introduction of markets, peasants are now better off and industrial workers are finding their wages dependent on output.

Both capitalism and socialism have lost their ability to inspire higher aspirations for human improvement. Unemployment, gross inequalities, and imperialism have tarnished capitalism; scarcity, oppression, and inequality have vitiated socialism's appeal. Yet the need to overcome scarcity, to impose discipline, to reward effort differentially, and to sustain a military organization make bureaucracy and inequality inevitable, limiting the possibilities of a just and egalitarian order.

Moore's explanation of diverse routes to minority rule and privilege constitutes a novel addition to elitist analysis. Even so, his argument that contemporary U.S., Soviet, and Chinese political systems are themselves attempts to overcome poverty and oppression contradicts his pessimistic conclusion that elite domination is inevitable. This suggests a need for more consideration of countervailing antibureaucratic movements, seen, for example, in the way the loss of credibility in the big models has fostered new opportunities for ethnic, moralistic, and regional demands for greater self-government.

JOEL D. WOLFE

University of Cincinnati
Ohio

*AFRICA, ASIA, AND
LATIN AMERICA*

EDWARDS, SEBASTIAN and ALEJANDRA COX EDWARDS. *Monetarism and Liberalization: The Chilean Experiment.* Pp. 231. Cambridge, MA: Ballinger, 1987. $29.95.

This study focuses on the macroeconomic policy of the Chilean government during the decade following the military assumption of power in 1973. The book is well documented, and Edwards and Edwards cover with thoroughness such topics as the creation of a dynamic capital market; the role of financial conglomerates and their irresponsible, if not illegal, conduct; the opening up of the economy accompanied by the pyramiding of foreign debt, encouraged by governmental authorities; privatization; deregulation; the establishment of free pricing; segmentation of the labor market; and tariff, exchange, and wage policies.

The title is misleading in that monetarism as taught by Friedman was not the principal element of the Chilean experiment or the main subject of this study. The key period began in June 1979 with the freezing of the peso-dollar exchange rate and ended abruptly in mid-1982 when the dam burst and the dollar once more resumed its ever-upward movement; the consequences of the measures taken during these three years are still being felt, both politically and economically. Edwards and Edwards correctly point out that

the failure of the "Pinochet economic miracle" cannot be attributed to only one factor, the exchange rate freeze, which the authors and I consider "a gross simplification."

Finance Minister Sergio de Castro, in establishing this freeze, correctly pointed out that "devaluations were completely ineffective since they would generate equiproportional inflation," but he erred grievously in ignoring the monetarist teachings of Friedman by treating the creation of money resulting from the massive inflow of foreign exchange as somehow different in kind from any other form or genesis of an increased money supply. Unfortunately, Edwards and Edwards do not attach sufficient importance to this point, which has generally been ignored by students of this period. Instead, they emphasize—correctly—the lack of governmental supervision over the financial sector, the incompatibility of 100 percent cost-of-living-allowance wage increases with a fixed exchange rate, a mistaken reliance on self-correction through automatic adjustment, and the absence of democratic institutions to serve as a check on erroneous measures of the executive branch.

Setting aside the obvious question of whether Chile could absorb such a tremendous influx of dollars, the fundamental error in Chile was, from a Keynesian point of view, that the government failed to build up through taxation sufficiently large surpluses during the artificial boom and, from a monetarist approach, their failure to sop up or sterilize the tremendous increase in money through governmental borrowing at attractive interest rates. Instead, the more than 100 percent increase in money in 1979-80 led to a three-year inflation of 70 percent and an inescapable dilemma: a rollback in wages and prices—"politically infeasible"—or devaluation and an end to the "guaranteed" exchange rate. Chile then lived through the worst of both possible worlds: the entire nation, indebted in dollars up to the hilt, flirted with bankruptcy when it did not actually fall into the abyss, causing Pinochet a severe political setback as triumphalism came to an end; at the same time, except in the case of a minority of organized workers and the military, real wages in 1987 were still enormously lower than they had been in June 1982.

The book is informative and sprinkled with some poignant and painful truths:

In Chile, the application of some simplistic and erroneous macroeconomic ideas with religious zeal created a major disequilibrium.

In the second half of 1981 international banks, taking an attitude that still puzzles most observers, agreed to pour vast amounts of resources into the sinking Chilean economy.

It is hoped that Edwards and Edwards will soon bring their story up to date. Certainly the subject matter has not been exhausted. Much has happened since 1983, most of it favorable, especially under the aegis of Finance Minister Hernán Büchi, who seems to know what monetarism is all about.

DAVID M. BILLIKOPF

Santiago
Chile

LEWIN, LINDA. *Politics and Parentela in Paraíba: A Case Study of Family-Based Oligarchy in Brazil.* Pp. xxv, 497. Princeton, NJ: Princeton University Press, 1987. $52.50.

Linda Lewin's book is an excellent contribution to the scholarly literature on Brazil's Old Republic (1889-1930). Focused on the state of Paraíba, the book analyzes oligarchic politics from a fresh perspective, that of the importance of the parentela. As Lewin explains, "parentela" refers to family-based groups; it is not restricted to consanguineous relationships, even though it primarily involves them. Political life in Paraíba during most of the Old Republic revolved around competition among different parentelas. This kind of competition precluded the emergence of political cleavages based on other lines, such as class. From the 1870s, when the last great peasant revolt in Paraíba was crushed, until

the 1920s, local landowners exercised virtually absolute political domination, challenged only by the brigands that roamed the countryside and by the gradually expanding, yet still very limited, power of the state. Until the 1920s, divisions within the elite were based largely on personal struggles to lead the oligarchy; the nature of oligarchic domination itself was unquestioned. Competition among the oligarchy was intense and violent, but it was not primarily based on ideological cleavages.

The parentela proved resilient as a means of organizing political life for a variety of reasons. The extreme poverty of the masses, coupled with their dependence on landowners, helped narrow political participation, making possible an oligarchic domination based on family connections. The open-ended nature of the parentela, as opposed to a strictly consanguineous political organization, allowed for greater adaptability to changing conditions.

In the absence of serious elite cleavages, why was competition for state power so violent? Part of the answer is that government positions increasingly assured access to state jobs and resources. Epitácio Pessoa, the head of the parentela that dominated Paraíba politics from 1912 until 1930, mastered this patronage game. As president of the Republic (1919-22), he created a federal agency that distributed resources to drought regions, making sure to benefit especially his own state. As political boss, he skillfully shuffled relatives and allies into a panoply of positions, ensuring their loyalty and his power.

One of the conditions and consequences of the personalization of the competition for power was the extreme fragility of representative institutions. There was virtually no party competition during the Old Republic. Governmental authority was precarious, especially in the least developed states. This legacy of institutional underdevelopment haunts Brazil to this day: the state has enormously expanded its authority, but parties and congress remain stunningly weak.

Yet even highly elitist and seemingly impermeable political systems change. Lewin shows that, in the 1920s, some of the bases of the parentela-led oligarchy eroded. Urbanization and economic growth created a small but important middle class, leading to a new urban-rural cleavage. The increase in patronage resources, greater governmental need for revenue, and widespread banditry all led to deeper state penetration in the hinterlands, where previously the oligarchy had reigned supreme. In the cities, new class associations were created in the 1920s, thereby diversifying the range of political interests that were articulated. Ideological issues became more salient, and strictly personalistic or clan bases of conflict eroded. Despite these changes, Lewin rightly notes in her conclusion that many patrimonial features of Brazilian politics remain intact until this day.

Lewin is not, of course, the first to call attention to the oligarchic nature of Brazil's political system, but she is the first who has extensively documented the centrality of the parentela in oligarchical politics. Paradoxically, however, it is the excellent analysis of oligarchical politics rather than the excessively lengthy discussion of the parentela that is the book's enduring contribution. Lewin's discussion of the interaction between economic, social, and political change is first rate, indicating an analytical acumen that matches her successful quest for interesting new data.

SCOTT MAINWARING
University of Notre Dame
Indiana

MacKINNON, STEPHEN R. and ORIS FRIESEN. *China Reporting: An Oral History of American Journalism in the 1930s and 1940s.* Pp. xxx, 230. Berkeley: University of California Press, 1987. $20.00.

JOFFE, ELLIS. *The Chinese Army after Mao.* Pp. ix, 210. Cambridge, MA: Harvard University Press, 1987. $20.00.

Judging by their titles, the two books under review appear to have little in common. Each title deals with a different theme: the qualities of American journalistic reportings on China in the first, and the modernization of China's Communist military establishment in the second. The combination, however, provides us a better, or deeper, understanding of modern China.

The first book, by MacKinnon and Friesen, represents an oral-history narrative of the American journalistic experience in China during the 1930s and 1940s that results from the transcripts of a gathering of old China hands at Scottsdale, Arizona, during November 1982. Forty veteran American journalists and diplomats and a number of distinguished China scholars participated in the conference. MacKinnon and Friesen attempt to weave the journalists' reminiscences into an oral-history narrative that consciously balances their successes against missed stories and persistent ignorance about Chinese situations. They conclude that the 1930s and 1940s represented the highest qualities of American journalistic reporting on China, despite the divergence of the correspondents' backgrounds.

The book by Joffe examines all aspects of the modernization process of the Chinese People's Liberation Army (PLA) in the post-Mao era, focusing on the wide-ranging changes in strategic doctrine, weapons, organization, structure, and modes of operation. It also analyzes both the PLA's political role during the current era of modernization and the state of civil-military relations. Finally, this book offers overall assessments of post-Mao China's military modernization record and its significant implications for China's present and future power. Joffe concludes that the efficiency and effectiveness of the PLA as a fighting force have been rising slowly but steadily in the post-Mao era, that the modernization process has increased the confidence of the Chinese in their military capability, particularly their defense posture against the Soviet Union, and that China now has a much greater military capability of acting as a regional power.

Both books offer invaluable primary-source materials for anyone, generalist or specialist, who is interested in the subject of twentieth-century China. I hasten to add that Joffe's book is more scholarly and analytical in quality.

TAI SUNG AN

Washington College
Chestertown
Maryland

PERDUE, PETER C. *Exhausting the Earth: State and Peasant in Hunan, 1500-1850.* Pp. xvii, 331. Cambridge, MA: Harvard University Press, 1987. $25.00.

Anyone interested in Chinese agriculture, the interaction of premodern states with peasant societies, or long-term change in agrarian ecologies should read this book. It can be read easily by non-China scholars, but it also presents detailed data to address critical issues in Qing-era social and economic history.

The core of the book is an assessment of the state's role in agricultural development, which fits neither the oriental-despotism or the limited-state models most commonly used by scholars today. The state could be effective in thwarting economic expansion with taxation and regulations; it could also be effective in expanding rural settlement, facilitating productive transactions, investing in waterworks, and spreading technologies. Its effectiveness as a force for development always came from the powers of observation, analysis, influence, and command wielded by local and regional officers in the agricultural economy; those powers were sometimes considerable, sometimes negligible. Above all, the state was effective as an actor in agricultural development only to the extent that it was willing and able to work with rather than against trends in regional agricultural environments over which it had no control.

Depicting these trends and the state activity inside them is Peter Perdue's major challenge. He does a beautiful job. Some trends are cyclical; they parallel dynastic cycles and are indicated by population trends as well as by waterworks construction to irrigate and drain farmland and protect it from floods. Growth in the fifteenth century gave way to stagnation and decline in the sixteenth and then to massive destruction and depopulation through the Ming-Qing dynastic transition until the late seventeenth century. Rapid recovery and development in the early nineteenth century—stimulated by immigration, land clearance, commercial expansion, and waterworks construction—accompanied the Qing state's most effective efforts to accelerate economic resurgence. But the state proved unable to mitigate negative consequences of deforestation, excess dike building, and social conflict attending population growth; and when the state's interests increasingly conflicted with powerful forces in the agrarian economy, the latter won, sending the dynasty and the agrarian economy down a slippery slope through the nineteenth century. Overlaying the cyclical trends are two overall growth trends that make the nineteenth century no simple repeat of the sixteenth: population rose tenfold between 1393 and 1850, and Hunan was integrated by trade into an imperial and even world economy, to go from being a frontier to being a core region of profitable agricultural production.

No book portrays a state and an agrarian economy interacting in the cyclical and long-term trends of early modern centuries any better than this one.

DAVID LUDDEN

University of Pennsylvania
Philadelphia

RUBENSTEIN, HYMIE. *Coping with Poverty: Adaptive Strategies in a Caribbean Village.* Pp. xx, 389. Boulder, CO: Westview Press, 1987. $29.95.

Beginning with the postwar period, the English-speaking Caribbean has been the site of intensive sociological and anthropological investigation. From the size of the existing corpus of literature, it could be argued that all there was to say about the Afro-Caribbean had been said, especially in terms of rural community life and household organization. Since the mid-1970s, however, a new era in anthropological studies has emerged. This body of work on West Indian societies advances anthropological research in the region in most significant ways. First, it reanalyzes and refocuses basic questions that suffered from previous assumptions that had been guided and blinded by the structuralist-functionalist school of thought. Second, it incorporates gender as a primary division in Afro-Caribbean cultures alongside of the critical factors of race and class. Finally, this body of work uses an analytic framework that is wide enough to discuss the meshing of international and national influences in these small-scale complex societies, yet deep enough to capture the subtle sociocultural nuances that make the Afro-Caribbean a vibrantly rich environment in which to conduct research and for the citizen to live in. *Coping with Poverty* is a superb example of this current genre of anthropological study of West Indian societies.

Author Hymie Rubenstein utilizes a range of methodological tools to describe and analyze the people, culture, and social organization of Leeward Village, and the island of St. Vincent in general. Using a cultural-ecology approach, Rubenstein's aim is to complete the analysis concerning black poverty. Clearly, poverty exists among peoples of African descent; via this St. Vincent example, Rubenstein shows how people manage, cope, and manipulate scarce resources in an economically impoverished situation. The historical background to this work provides more than just a setting for the ethnographic material to follow. It places the village, its people, and St. Vincent at large within the necessarily wide framework to which the subsequent data are directly linked. The organization of economic life discusses several factors ranging from issues of class, occupation, domestic organization, and land tenure to migration as ways people seek to overcome property.

In Part 3, kinship and social organization are examined. Here a major contribution to scholarship is made by Rubenstein's examination of kinship systems, kindred relations, and friendships.

In the concluding chapter, on black adaptive strategies, all of the facets of social organization come into play. Rubenstein argues that there is a great degree of interplay between what people have at hand or can count on in both material and cultural ways that aids them in their everyday life and directs them toward the future. What occurs often does not resemble what is acknowledged as the ideal, but it is also antithetical to the epithets of "disorganization" and "pathology."

If there is a fault in this work, it lies in Rubenstein's overreliance on references and a slight shortchanging of ethnographic details.

A. LYNN BOLLES

Bowdoin College
Brunswick
Maine

EUROPE

HOWELL, MARTHA C. *Women, Production, and Patriarchy in Late Medieval Cities.* Pp. xv, 285. Chicago: University of Chicago Press, 1986. $25.00.

Karl Bücher's thesis put forth in *Die Frauenfrage im Mittelalter* (1882) that women in the later Middle Ages "were excluded from no trade for which their strength was adequate" continues to dominate discussion of women and work for that period. During the past century, a large number of studies have shown that women were thoroughly involved in the market economy along the lines adumbrated by Bücher. Scholars have also noted exceptions, however. What is clear is that neither side, in what has become a noteworthy historiographical controversy, is likely to win a victory as the so-called lumpers support Bücher in modified form and explain away exceptions while splitters continue to adduce exceptions. The state of the question has been further complicated by tangled and undisciplined growth of Marxist and feminist historiographical weeds. So-called theory has taken on a life of its own in which data are manipulated for a variety of political and social ends such that, insofar as a usable past is sought, there is a corresponding diminution in heuristic value.

Martha Howell, associate professor of history at Rutgers University, has realized, though partially entangled in both Marxist and feminist underbrush, that the contest between lumpers and splitters is unproductive. Thus she has argued for a "neutral" means by which to evaluate women and work. To this end, she has conjured up the construct "labor status." High labor status accrues to those who "have full control over the economic resources of production and distribution in a market society." Howell believes that high labor status was only possible for women in the late Middle Ages in the "family production unit." While an extended argument is possible concerning the tautological elements in this construct, more significant from the historical perspective is Howell's failure to grasp the full implications of vertical economic control in terms of such key processes as raw-material acquisition and transportation. In addition, her disregard for horizontality—namely, market share in a narrow sense—highlights the impact on her thinking of a rural "family production unit" with mystical connection to the never-never land of autarky.

The data for Howell's study are generated by and large from the work of other scholars, particularly Margaret Wensky for Cologne and N. W. Posthumus for Leiden. Howell's major contribution is an examination of several Leiden *fonds*, which are described in Appendix 2. On the whole, however, her strength is in historiography, with a nice gift for synthesizing and criticizing the work of specialists who would appear to have spent a lot more time in the archives than she did.

From all sources, Howell adduces very little that indicates vertical economic control. In addition, she seems to lack a firm grasp of quantitative methodology. For example, she concludes on the basis of six cases—four in which the husbands were older than the wives—that "to judge by the few statistics available, it was not unusual for women to marry men a few years their junior." There are also problems with her figures for household size in Leiden. Posthumus argues for 3.5; Howell adduces a "lodger factor," based more on wishful thinking than hard data, which raises the median to 4.5, and then she concludes that during the period she examined, the average size was "about five." Perhaps it is unnecessary to add that lacking the higher figures, Leiden cannot be used for Howell's study.

This work is a useful introduction to the *Frauenfrage*, the conceptual framework is unhelpful, and the original archival research provides data for both lumpers and splitters.

BERNARD S. BACHRACH
University of Minnesota
Minneapolis

KAVANAGH, DENNIS A. *Thatcherism and British Politics: The End of Consensus?* Pp. xi, 334. New York: Oxford University Press, 1987. $44.00. Paperbound, $11.95.

Dennis Kavanagh has been coauthor with David Butler of studies of the British general elections from 1974 to 1983. The book under review, published before the third Conservative victory, examines the changes in policy of those elections and the coming to power of a Conservative government led by Margaret Thatcher. It is well documented and its views are clearly expressed, even if it cannot, in the end, answer the question in its title.

The Conservatives, overwhelmingly defeated in the 1945 election, had worked out new policies that took account of what appeared to be popular demand. During the war, the anxieties of working-class voters were focused on the fear of a return to mass unemployment, which they blamed on the prewar conservative-dominated national government, although welfare questions such as health and social security undoubtedly also played a part in their support for the Labour Party. The so-called consensus was, therefore, primarily based on the acceptance of government responsibility for maintaining full employment by Keynesian methods. The National Health Service and advances in social security with their historical roots in public policy were also accepted by the Conservatives when they returned to office in 1951.

The idea of government intervention in the economy in the form of tariff protection and reorganization of industry was strengthened by the experience of wartime planning; even the nationalization of some basic industries was advocated by nonparty enquiries. Although they had fought most nationalization bills in Parliament, the Conservatives did little to denationalize them in 1951.

These political developments seemed to have the support of the academic world. Critics, such as Hayek, were unheeded, except by Churchill in a politically disastrous speech during the 1945 election. By the time Mrs. Thatcher came into office in 1979, a number of right-wing research and policy institutions had grown up; their views filled an intellectual gap that followed public disillusion with the failure of successive governments to deal with the economic problems, particularly excessive rises in incomes and inflation.

From the 1960s onward, awareness grew that British industry had become less competitive and that new measures were needed. The Heath government performed a U-turn from right-wing laissez-faire policies to industrial support and intervention; the Labour government under James Callaghan did the opposite with its statutory incomes policy and the switch to monetarism from the extreme interventionism with which Harold Wilson had come into office. This opened the way for Mrs. Thatcher to make radical policy changes. Some of these, such as legal restraints on the trade unions and rejection of formal income policies, were popular; giving priority to inflation at the cost of unemployment has not produced the political hostility

that was expected. Privatization of state industries is probably also widely accepted. On the other hand, financial cuts in the National Health Service have been unpopular and restrictions on the unions have not prevented an outbreak of grass-root strikes. It seems, therefore, that if there were an old consensus to be broken, no new one has yet been formed, nor will it be until a viable middle-ground alternative to the Conservatives can establish itself.

AUSTEN ALBU

Sussex
England

KENNEDY, WILLIAM P. *Industrial Structure, Capital Markets and the Origins of British Economic Decline.* Pp. xii, 230. New York: Cambridge University Press, 1987. No price.

This book argues that Britain's national economy grew significantly slower in the period 1899-1913 than before or after. It did so because of underinvestment in the new strategic sectors that composed the second Industrial Revolution and overinvestment in sectors that were bound to decline anyway. Underinvestment in the growth sectors occurred because British capital markets were segmented and biased against high-risk, high-yield investments. The British legal system prevented the rise of financial intermediaries comparable to trust companies in the United States or investment banks in Germany. These intermediaries reduced the risks of investing in the new technologies of electricity, chemicals, and automobiles so they could expand more rapidly in the United States and Germany, while agriculture, domestic service, wholesale and retail trade, and income from abroad grew more rapidly—or declined less rapidly—in Great Britain. Britain could have followed a similar growth path with comparable structural changes had the country's legal system enforced public accounting requirements on joint stock companies.

This is an interesting argument, and the cognoscenti among the cliometricians of British history will recognize it as a sustained attack on the thesis of Donald McCloskey that Victorian Britain did not fail but did the best she could, sector by sector, given the commitment to free trade. Opponents of cliometrics may wish Kennedy success in fighting fire with fire, while proponents—myself among them—may hope he can restore some vigor to this intellectual debate. Alas, the logic of Kennedy's argument and the evidence used to make it are not really convincing. Indeed, I suspect more and more that the argument is incorrect.

The logic of the argument as just outlined requires evidence of the relative structural changes of Great Britain, Germany, and the United States as well as of the role played by the respective financial sectors in promoting these changes. The comparative evidence is not given, which is probably just as well, as it would likely show that the United States and Germany overinvested in the new sectors due to weaknesses in their relatively underdeveloped financial sectors. This would raise the question of whether it would have been a good thing for Britain to carry out the same kind of misallocation as the United States and Germany rather than its nationally preferred form of misallocation, but this question of values and motivations is never raised.

The evidence that is presented consists of the details of a counterfactual British economy in which the strategic sectors—construction, engineering, chemicals, paper, energy, and communications—grow more rapidly, more as in the U.S. case, while the decay sectors—agriculture, textiles, domestic service, wholesale and retail trade, manufactured gas output, and income from abroad—grow less rapidly, also more as in the United States. The rest of the economy—48 percent—continues to grow at the same pace it did historically. No particular justification is given for using the United States as a standard of comparison and none is probably possible.

Kennedy lacks a fully developed input-output table for the British economy to test

for internal consistency of the counterfactual structures he generates. Instead, he discusses in an ad hoc way the possibilities of balance-of-payments problems and how they could be overcome in the counterfactual world. In addition, he dismisses the possibility of a binding constraint from supply of labor and capital—the foreign migration of both would simply be reduced greatly in his counterfactual. An American or German might wonder at this point what these losses of labor and capital—for the Americans—or export markets—for the Germans—would mean counterfactually for the United States and Germany, or for the rest of the world for that matter. Brinley Thomas would argue that the structural changes of the three countries were complementary in this period—one could not exist without the others.

A lot depends upon the price elasticities of both demand and supply for these new products given that Kennedy's counterfactual would have them produced in much larger quantities within what was the world's largest market. By using existing price indexes for his calculations, however, Kennedy implicitly assumes no change in relative prices of these new goods. It is precisely the possibility—indeed, the likelihood—of significant changes in relative prices in a large-scale counterfactual that makes it so difficult to predict the effects of major structural changes. So the best we can say about Kennedy's evidence is that American-style structural change for Edwardian Britain may have been feasible, but we still may doubt it would have been economic or even desirable, even for the Britons.

LARRY NEAL
University of Illinois
Urbana

McDONOGH, GARY WRAY. *Good Families of Barcelona: A Social History of Power in the Industrial Era.* Pp. xv, 262. Princeton, NJ: Princeton University Press, 1986. $30.00.

Gary McDonogh's major aim in publishing this book is to explore "the meanings of family within one modern elite that has coalesced in Barcelona and the surrounding polity, Catalonia, since the Industrial Revolution of the nineteenth century." By examining this family in a variety of settings "within the dynamics of elite formation, reproduction, and decay over time, this work incorporates power groups into the major theoretical and methodological concerns of modern anthropology." In my judgment, McDonogh has succeeded in his stated purpose in nine well-argued and coherent chapters.

The elite described in this book—known as the Good Families of Barcelona—is a tight community of 2000 to 3000 men, women, and children. They number about 100 or 200 patrilineages in a city of some 2 million; there are over 6 million people in Catalonia. Despite the small size, the elite group monopolized economic and, to some extent, political power in Catalonia for some 150 years. The Good Families firmly entrenched themselves as an elite unit by blending "a new capitalist bourgeoisie with a historic aristocracy."

According to McDonogh, family and kinship in the main brought about elite solidarity. The household served as the main force for economic growth. Says McDonogh, "While family pervades the social history of power in Barcelona, it must also be examined as a continuous product—social and cultural—of the evolution of Catalan industrial society."

In addition, this book deals with different levels of power and struggle:

The elite families of Barcelona have been influenced by competition and struggle within Catalonia, by the problem of definition of Catalan hegemony within the Spanish state, and by the status of Catalonia as a productive region within a world economy. These diverse levels have impinged as much upon the family as a unit of procreation and socialization as on its economic and political aspects (p. 4).

Later chapters include a historical overview of Barcelona, family and variation in Catalonia, and household and company in the industrial elite. Other topics are economic power, elite education, business and marriage, power and cultural imagery, and families, agencies, and networks of power.

McDonogh conducted research on the Barcelona elites for almost ten years, starting in 1976. He utilized the techniques of participant observation, archival research, key informant, photography, and genealogy, among others.

The book is important for three related reasons. First, it is a refreshing contribution to the growing body of literature on the anthropology of the elites, a subject long neglected by anthropologists. Second, the book is an intensive study in time and space of the Good Families in Barcelona that can serve as a model for future research for anthropologists doing fieldwork along the same theme. Third and finally, McDonogh's theoretical and methodological contributions to the discipline should not be underestimated. His substantive discussion of elites in comparative perspective and his sophisticated techniques of anthropological investigation make this volume an excellent example for both scholars and laypersons in theory and method. The volume has been enriched with photos, genealogies, and notes concerning selected families and an extensive bibliography.

This book is must reading for all anthropologists, social scientists, and scholars concerned with Spain, Latin America, and family studies. McDonogh and Princeton University Press are to be congratulated for this quality publication.

MARIO D. ZAMORA
College of William and Mary
Williamsburg
Virginia

UNITED STATES

ANDERSON, JOHN and HILARY HEVENOR. *Burning Down the House: MOVE and the Tragedy of Philadelphia.* Pp. xv, 409. New York: Norton, 1987. $18.95.

This book takes us from the early 1970s' beginning of a quasi-religious movement based on the ideas of Vincent Leaphart to a horrifying mid-1980s climax. On 13 May 1985, a police attack on the movement's primary residence resulted in 11 deaths, the destruction of 53 houses, and 262 homeless persons. A lengthy account of the trial of one of the MOVE members follows, providing both new information and a somewhat connected account of how the whole history possessed coherence for one of the MOVE members.

Other attempts at coherence would have made the book richer for the reader; Anderson and Hevenor themselves offer little in that regard, wanting the facts to speak for themselves. While they ask big questions— for example, "Was Philadelphia's tragedy unique or was it a metaphor for a larger American tragedy?"—I felt underinformed as to their answer. This is true of a number of the main ingredients of the disaster as well; while Leaphart's identity as the incarnation of John Africa appears to be religious in a complex way, we never really get even an outline of the whole theology.

If we reserve the notion of tragedy for those situations in which the main actors have done their heroic best but nevertheless have created disaster, the story told here hardly merits the term. City officials and MOVE members seem to share a tendency to avoid reality, to shift rather than accept responsibility, to use words the plain meaning of which they later disown. The story, if reliable, presents an endless supply of mediocrity rather than heroism. It sometimes seemed that various sources of information were not sufficiently evaluated with respect to their likely reliability. For all that, Anderson and Hevenor are correct that the facts not only speak for themselves; they shout. No community should have to endure such events as are here recorded, and yet all readers will recognize a sufficient number of characters in the Philadelphia cast to realize that the same drama could be staged in their own town. The story of this book cries out for more reflection.

HARRY YEIDE, Jr.
George Washington University
Washington, D.C.

ARKES, HADLEY. *First Things: An Inquiry into the First Principles of Morals and Justice.* Pp. xii, 432. Princeton, NJ: Princeton University Press, 1986. $50.00. Paperbound, $11.95.

At a time when the subjects of morals and ethics and their applications to the law are a national issue of grave concern in the United States, Hadley Arkes's *First Things: An Inquiry into the First Principles of Morals and Justice* is timely indeed. The issue of appropriate ethical behavior in the leadership of this country, be it legal, political, religious, financial, or military, has become a problem that is so widespread and has reached such scandalous proportions that the media are presently marked by a crescendo of inquiries and stories regarding the propriety of the values that Americans hold. To cite only one example, but a representative one, *Time* magazine, in a May 1987 issue devoted mainly to examining Americans' sense of national character, addressed this *question brulante* in several feature articles. In large bold letters that dominated the cover of the magazine, the caption read, "What Ever Happened to Ethics."

To be sure, although the question of morals is acute here, it is by no means a phenomenon unique to America, for the issue of how to be moral is probably the most pertinent question of any age. It is significant that Arkes opens his book with an inscription from Aristotle's *Nicomachean Ethics*, thereby setting the tone for *First Things*. Critical of moral skepticism, Arkes emphatically states in his preface that "the educated need not be embarrassed to acknowledge, in public, their awareness of moral truths." It is Arkes's contention and the leitmotiv of this book that there are propositions, in morals and in law, like axioms, that are immutable and that the principles derived from these axioms are valid and applicable for all peoples and for all times.

Arkes, a political scientist, is well informed on the history of political philosophy. Concerned about the direction of human existence, he grapples with the fundamental issues of what is moral and true and applies his propositions to a host of historically controversial issues that he then uses to lead into contemporary problems. The scope of his moral discourse is large and can only be briefly cited here. It includes such topics as conscientious objection to military service, Hobbes's teaching, American involvement in the war in Vietnam, the morality of military intervention abroad, welfare and the redistribution of wealth, privacy and the law, and a woman's right to have an abortion.

In essence, Arkes makes an important contribution by raising the issues that he does, and in many respects his work is profound and thoughtful, but his book is marred by being ponderously verbose. He spends too much time establishing his "first principles," and throughout the book the narrative moves forward much too slowly.

In his political philosophy, Arkes prizes personal freedom, as shown, on the one hand, by his staunch support of the American constitutional system and, on the other, by his critical opposition to Marxist-Leninist regimes. It is in Arkes's lengthy examination of the controversial issue of abortion, however, that his departure from Western liberal thought is pointedly demonstrated, and his position on this warrants particular attention. With a seemingly impressive array of data and statistics, he argues that the Supreme Court decision in 1973 allowing a woman to have an abortion is morally wrong and very unpopular. Arkes justifies his position because he feels that it is consistent with his defense of the sanctity of human life. Nevertheless, despite his enormous muster of facts, it is a fact that now approximately 2 million women a year in the United States elect to have abortions. Moreover, Arkes's position on this important issue does not accord with the touchstone of Western liberalism, as enunciated in the Declaration of the Rights of Man in 1789: "Liberty consists in being able to do anything that does not harm another person."

Arkes's conclusion, although on the moral high ground, is hardly innovative and does not provide an exemplary prescription for the evils in our social order. Who would disagree that human life is important? Never-

theless, the issues raised and examined by Arkes in this work are of paramount importance to all, show a subtle reasoning, and deserve a wide hearing.

JACQUES SZALUTA
U.S. Merchant Marine Academy
Kings Point
New York

BENSON, SUSAN PORTER. *Counter Cultures: Saleswomen, Managers, and Customers in American Department Stores, 1890-1940.* Pp. xvi, 322. Urbana: University of Illinois Press, 1986. $27.50.

Susan Porter Benson's *Counter Culture* is a model social history—richly detailed, carefully researched, and beautifully written. She takes her readers inside the department stores that thrived in American cities from the late nineteenth century until World War II and allows us to understand the often conflicting motivations and behaviors of managers, customers, and saleswomen. Benson sees the department store as a "drama" that brought together these groups from "disparate backgrounds and provided an arena for them to play out their hopes and anxieties." Male managers struggled, with limited success, to get their mostly female customers and work force to behave in ways that would enhance profits. Customers took advantage of their position as consumers to exercise power and demand costly services. Saleswomen developed a work culture that exploited the unstandardizable nature of selling to exercise more control over the work process than was possible for factory, or even clerical, workers. Benson weaves an intricate tale of shifting alliances between these groups. Managers and customers shared class identification and were sometimes repelled by the working-class manners of saleswomen. Customers and saleswomen shared gender identification and dismayed managers who sought to exercise the usual male control over females. Managers and saleswomen allied against the sometimes unreasonable demands of customers.

While Benson pays careful attention to customers and managers, her primary interest and sympathies lie with the workers. In the introduction, she explains that she had begun her study intending to follow Braverman's model of rationalization of work with greater managerial control of the work process. To her credit, she abandoned this model early as she came to understand the complex interactions within the "palace of consumption" and the control that saleswomen could and did exercise over their work. Her saleswomen were not the beaten-down tools of capitalists; they took pride in their skill and cleverly discovered ways to exercise self-determination. Sales work in department stores was, for many women, good work. The pay was better than that offered in most factory jobs, the working conditions were often quite good, and there was the chance of upward mobility into buyer positions for some.

It is primarily as a labor historian that Benson wishes to be judged. In my judgment, she has earned the highest praise. One might wish for more sophisticated quantitative analysis—descriptive tables are provided in an appendix—or for a complete bibliography—there is a short bibliographic essay—but these are quibbles. Susan Porter Benson has written an insightful book that is a joy to read.

ELYCE J. ROTELLA
Indiana University
Bloomington

COLEMAN, PETER J. *Progressivism and the World of Reform: New Zealand and the Origins of the American Welfare State.* Pp. xv, 247. Lawrence: University Press of Kansas, 1987. $29.95.

The Progressive years in American politics have been intensively and fruitfully studied. Coleman, however, believes that historical perspectives on Progressivism have been skewed a bit too far toward interpreting it in "exclusively American terms" and so toward an overemphasis on "the unique at the expense of the universal."

Accordingly, he has sought "to broaden the framework of analysis" of American reform "by putting more emphasis than before on the external forces shaping Progressivism." More specifically, he has sought to do this "by examining the links" between Progressivism and the antipodean—in this case New Zealand—liberalism. He pursues the same modestly revisionist objective in a final, more general chapter, in which he suggests "some of the ways in which the American reform effort can be placed in a worldwide context."

The substantive body of Coleman's study is an examination of the writing and activity of a small band of American reformers who, flatteringly from an antipodean perspective, advocated the "New Zealandization of America." Despite their enthusiastic and often highly polemical efforts, all fully and clearly documented by Coleman, it never came to that, of course. Indeed, Coleman's study leaves us with no delusions that antipodean models made much impact on the course of American Progressivism. A few specific reforms appear to have been borrowed directly, but that is hardly the point. More important, what he demonstrates is that there was at the time not only an international currency in reformist ideas and practices, to which the antipodes contributed, but that the processes of diffusion worked in complex, varied, and even subtle ways. In this respect, Coleman's New Zealand focus makes for a nice case study of a general process. In the end, however, it is clear that the United States, with its federal and regional diversity, constitutionalism, and a political culture characterized by a strong ideological commitment to individual freedom, was not very receptive to New Zealandization.

From an antipodean perspective, Coleman is dealing in historical mythology, not all of it dead. It is a merit of his book that in it he has, perhaps unintentionally but certainly justly, diminished the persistent, romanticized perception of the antipodes as "the world's economic and social laboratory." Instead, antipodeans must be satisfied with Coleman's more plausible and well-verified conclusion that New Zealand merely "helped propel the United States towards the modern welfare state"—as did many other external and indigenous sources.

It is a lucid book, more modest in substance and claim than the cover title might imply. The research is narrowly focused but appears thorough and is prodigiously documented in citations and comments extending through almost forty pages of end notes. Moreover, the book is especially timely for both American and antipodean readers. As governments in liberal-capitalist countries typically rediscover the philosophy and implement the free-market mechanisms of the pre-Progressive age, the principles, policies, hopes, and passions of American Progressives and antipodean reformers make for inspiring and increasingly nostalgic reading.

E. P. AIMER

University of Auckland
New Zealand

KLEPPNER, PAUL. *Continuity and Change in Electoral Politics, 1893-1928.* Pp. xv, 264. Westport, CT: Greenwood Press, 1987. $35.00.

Paul Kleppner's study is valuable to historians and social scientists interested in the turn-of-the-century American political party system and to those concerned about critical elections or critical realignments. Graduate students will find chapter 1 and the appendix especially valuable. Together, they provide an overview and critique of the literature on critical elections and realignments, including an explanation of the levels of the analysis problem in this research and a sketch of sometimes subtle differences in the way different researchers define key terms.

Kleppner is especially critical of scholars associated with the dominant perspective of the University of Michigan's Survey Research Center (SRC), arguing that the SRC "linked voting to an overly narrow conception of party identification," which includes a "psy-

chological attachment . . . acquired through early socialization experiences." He posits that "the SRC researchers mistook one species of party identification for the entire genus." He prefers Fiorino's conception of party identification as a sort of "'running tally' of each individual's subjectively weighted judgments" about the past and probable future performance of the major parties, judgments that can, of course, be affected by parental partisanship. Kleppner then sets forth his definition of a critical realignment, which is

a macrolevel phenomenon involving an abrupt and durable change in the partisan balance at the electoral level. Whether these swings in the aggregate-level election data result from party switching, new mobilization, demobilization, or a combination [of these] . . . they produce analogous changes in the partisan balance among officeholders (p. 18).

He further argues that, to decide whether a critical realignment has occurred, one must examine national-level data. Following careful analysis of the data, and applying his definition, Kleppner agrees with the dominant view that one critical alignment began in 1893 and another in 1929.

The study provides numerous interesting tables concerning various issues, demonstrates that clear subphases existed within the dominant party system of 1893-1929, and shows that the regional partisan alignment of 1893-1929 differed significantly from the regional alignments before and after that period. Kleppner is also persuasive that the explanatory power of the "ethnocultural model" of voter behavior is greatly reduced after the 1890s.

An especially interesting discussion concerns efforts during this period to restrict the activities of political parties, eliminate alien suffrage, and grant women the vote. Such changes might have fundamentally altered the dominant party system of the era, but instead they produced mixed and rather modest results, at least in the first three decades of the twentieth century.

PAUL L. HAIN

University of New Mexico
Albuquerque

LEWIS, RONALD L. *Black Coal Miners in America: Race, Class, and Community Conflict 1780-1980.* Pp. xv, 239. Lexington: University Press of Kentucky, 1987. $25.00.

In this well-executed monograph, Ronald L. Lewis utilizes sources ranging from local coal-town newspapers and oral interviews to major archival collections in order to describe factors that enlarged, constricted, and shaped black participation in the coal industry from the late eighteenth century until the present. By adopting a comparative regional perspective based on labor segmentation and Marxist class theories, he arrives at an organizational and conceptual framework that allows for a rich and highly discerning account of the experiences of black coal miners in America.

According to Lewis, "the struggle for control of the labor process set the course of race, class, and community conflict" along a variety of paths; Lewis charts five major ones. From the earliest utilization of blacks as slaves in Virginia coal mines and as convict laborers in the post-emancipation South to their exploitation and segregation under Jim Crow, to their forced exclusion from the mining communities of Illinois, Indiana, Ohio, and western Pennsylvania, through their more favorable experiences in the central Appalachian fields, and, finally, their current elimination from the industry as a result of technological unemployment, Lewis traces a complex and often surprising course. Perhaps most enlightening and intriguing is Lewis's account of the experience of black miners in the mountains of southern West Virginia, where "blacks came closer to finding economic equality than in any other coalfield, and perhaps anywhere else, in America."

Lewis's conceptual framework well explains how race and community relations were shaped by labor market factors unique to particular regions. With its sensitivity to regional variations, his approach suggests the value of a comparative model. There are times, however, when one feels Lewis is bound too tightly by his paradigm and fails to elaborate on important shifts in race and class relations within regions. He does not adequately explain, for example, why and how, in Coal Creek, Indiana, in 1878, gunfighting blacks and whites were transformed, in the course of a year, into fraternal union members. Here, as elsewhere, Lewis overlooks an opportunity to explore significant shifts from "exclusion" to biracial cooperation.

In general, however, Lewis is not entrapped by his organizational schema. When exceptional patterns crop up—as in southeastern Kansas—he gives them their due. It is much to his credit that he could organize such a wealth of material into a relatively short monograph that captures both the nuances of particulars and the broader patterns that they constitute. Lewis's book is a fine model for writing comparative labor history. May it inspire more like it.

GERALD ZAHAVI
State University of New York
Albany

MAYHEW, DAVID R. *Placing Parties in American Politics.* Pp. xv, 395. Princeton, NJ: Princeton University Press, 1986. $38.50. Paperbound, $11.50.

Near the end of this lengthy, complex, and ambitious volume—it is surely no easy read—it becomes apparent that David Mayhew intends nothing less than radical revision of the conventional political scientists' understanding of the place of political parties in American democracy. Whereas such advocates of strong party organization and two-party competition as V. O. Key and E. E. Schattschneider supposed that parties were the handmaidens of responsible, majority-serving public policies, Mayhew argues to the contrary that Ostrogorski and the Progressives were more accurate in seeing them as part of the problem, not the solution. If Mayhew's thesis is correct, we may suppose that we are not so badly off in the 1980s as many party-admiring political scientists suppose.

Mayhew's central concern throughout his book is with what he calls "traditional party organizations" (TPOs), which he defines as durable, autonomous, hierarchical organizations that attempt to slate candidates for public office. These organizations in his definition are mainly motivated by desires for material gain, not by issues, programs, or ideologies. He seeks to locate such organizations geographically, to understand why they came to exist and to assess what, if any, importance they have had in shaping the political process.

As I reconstruct the research strategy of the book, Mayhew began with an exercise that is relegated to an appendix of the final volume—an attempt to locate TPOs through an analysis of U.S. House and state legislative primaries in the late 1960s. Judging the outcome of this analysis problematic and, as he says, "bloodless," he then settled on an alternative approach; he read all the literature he could find on state and local parties and assigned each state a TPO score of 1 to 5, weak to strong TPOs. Although the effort applied to this task is little short of heroic, the result is problematic on several grounds. While the TPO scores are supposed to be for the late 1960s, the literature used to generate them covers a much longer period. The scores are given to whole states, but party organization studies have disproportionately been conducted only in urban areas. For most American localities, data have not been collected. It is never quite clear what in Mayhew's reading is the basis for assigning the numerical scores. The resulting numbers—technically, an ordinal scale—appear hard, but would other readers interpret the monographic literature in the same way? The distribution of the scores is highly skewed to the extremes, especially to the lowest possible TPO score; thirty states are given a score of 1 (no TPOs), and only one state, Louisiana, is assigned the supposed middle value of 3. States as different as Vermont, Massachusetts, and Mississippi are assigned the same score of 1 on the scale. In short, a massive search of the literature is used to create a very questionable set of measurements of the states' TPOs. Careful readers will note that the TPO scores do not coincide impressively with data—in the earlier-mentioned appendix—on multiple candidacies and vote fragmentation in the primaries Mayhew set out to study. How this is to be explained is never satisfactorily addressed.

Having accomplished this taxonomic exercise, Mayhew proceeds to the really important theoretical questions of why TPOs have existed in various states—or why not—and what difference they make in a state's politics. Strong TPOs, he argues, are associated with states admitted early to the union. So it seems. About half of the states admitted before 1821 have strong TPO scores—4 or 5—whereas none admitted after that date do. Why this should be so remains largely a mystery.

Finally, Mayhew argues, strong TPO states have tended to generate relatively conservative fiscal and spending policies. This generalization is based on a multiple regression analysis that must be interpreted with great caution. Two effective independent variables—the highly skewed, ordinal TPO scores and a dummy for South or other—supposedly explain per capita taxation and spending relative to personal income. Aside from the questionable statistical assumptions involved, I doubt that the dependent variables are the right ones to answer questions about TPOs and economic policies. Are we really to suppose, as these data suggest, that, other things being equal, economic policies have been consistently more favorable to the less fortunate in Mississippi than in Connecticut? This analysis wants careful scrutiny.

The broad theoretical argument in Mayhew's concluding chapter is provocative and interesting. Political parties—as TPOs, anyway—are said to have been greatly overrated by political scientists. In actuality, he argues, they had to be weakened in order for the modern American bureaucratic welfare state to be built. TPOs were inherently conservative. In large part, this is true, but how damaging to Key and Schattschneider is this argument? My understanding of their case for a competitive politics of strong parties is that they thought such a politics generated issues of a majority-serving sort, especially those of a socioeconomic nature. I do not understand their argument as an apology for TPOs as Mayhew defines them. Mayhew is certainly correct to say that the mentality of Ostrogorski and the Progressives is more consonant with our actual experience since 1900 than that of advocates of party government, but TPOs are not what the latter wanted. These American advocates of strong parties, I would argue, are less open to the charge that they misunderstood machines than to another one of an entirely different kind—that they did not know how on native ground to create the kinds of idea-based strong parties that have been so common in Europe. This is not a question that Mayhew discusses at any length in this book, but it is surely an important one. Why have the great majority of our strong organizations been TPOs? What accounts for the American exceptions to this condition, such as the Democrat-Farmer-Labor Party in Minnesota, which Mayhew ably describes in his account of that state? Is the only real American choice between TPOs and the party-less politics that Ostrogorski advocated and is now very nearly realized in our actual practice? Answering this question would allow us to place parties in American politics in a more comparative context and to discuss what we gain or lose by opting for Progressive assumptions rather than those of party government.

W. WAYNE SHANNON
University of Connecticut
Storrs

McFEELEY, NEIL D. *Appointment of Judges: The Johnson Presidency.* Pp. xi, 199. Austin: University of Texas Press, 1987. $22.50.

In light of Reagan administration difficulties with the Robert Bork and Douglas Ginsberg nominations, McFeeley's study is timely. President Johnson's problems as a lame duck with the Homer Thornberry and Abe Fortas nominations were comparable.

The more significant story, though, tells of 166 judges and two Supreme Court justices who made it through senatorial scrutiny. Veteran legislator Johnson typically was involved in the process sufficiently to ensure success for his nominees. In 1986, with 73 percent of his appointees remaining on the bench, Lyndon Johnson's judicial legacy sparkled.

A Johnson subpresidency that screened applicants purposely sought people young enough to have staying power. Marvin Watson, Barefoot Sanders, and Larry Temple wanted evidence of loyalty and ability to make it past hurdles presented by the American Bar Association, the Federal Bureau of Investigation, and the Internal Revenue Service.

McFeeley breathes life into the senatorial courtesy tradition, referring to the Judiciary Committee's blue-slip device. Senators who do not return blue-slip comments within a week block candidates. Helped by Mike Manatos, Johnson managed the Senate, often seeking several names and using delays "to persuade senators to accept candidates." But he could not manage Richard Russell, whose successful advocacy of Alexander Lawrence led to a rift with the president that contributed to Fortas's downfall.

McFeeley and his editors have woven together a combination of clear scholarly writing, nine helpful tables, a 12-page appendix describing appointees, and solid documentation in 42 pages of end notes. Two substantive errors were anomalies in an otherwise dependable presentation. There is reference to "31 June," on p. 124, and to Nixon appointee "Rabuquist," on p. 91, instead of Rehnquist, who became chief justice.

The study benefits from a willingness to place the Johnson jurists in 40-year perspective from 1946 to 1986. McFeeley notes, for example, that Ronald Reagan "created a post of Special Counsel for Judicial Selection."

As we look toward future White House

transitions, a memo by Charles Murphy reflects the potential for party rivalry: Johnson responded to a request of Richard Nixon's by saying, "Tell him I'm not going to publish my wife's love letters either!" We can anticipate also renewed attention to the potential for setting precedent, reflected in Johnson's appointment of Thurgood Marshall as the first black associate justice and Constance Motley as the first black woman district judge.

Neil McFeeley has done an admirable job of conveying the complexity and significance of the judicial appointment process. This book, the sixth in the series on the administrative history of the Johnson presidency, is a solid contribution to the archival oral-history genre.

CHARLES T. BARBER
University of Southern Indiana
Evansville

RICCARDS, MICHAEL P. *A Republic, If You Can Keep It: The Foundations of the American Presidency, 1700-1800.* Pp. xv, 227. Westport, CT: Greenwood Press, 1987. $35.00.

For the past twenty years, the most persistent controversy facing our political system has been the often hostile relationship between the legislative and the executive branches of the federal government. Indeed, in the past year, the substantive policy disagreements between a Democratically controlled Congress and a Republican president over U.S. policy in the Persian Gulf and in Central America have often been overshadowed by a struggle over claims of constitutional prerogative. The roots of this battle are endemic to the very structure of our federal system with its separation of powers; however, what exacerbates these tensions is the fact that while article I of the Constitution clearly spells out the formal powers of Congress, article II says very little about presidential power, and what it does say is often ambiguous.

Because of this, the publication of Michael P. Riccards's *A Republic, If You Can Keep It* is a timely event. Riccards's book is a fascinating and insightful study of the origins of the executive branch as well as executive power. Riccards, president of St. John's College in Santa Fe, argues that the modern presidency is deeply rooted in two influences: seventeenth-century British political thought and practice, and the precedent of style and tone established by the first president, George Washington. The organization of Riccards's book is built around a discussion of these two influences.

In part 1, Riccards examines the preconstitutional origins of executive authority. He begins his analysis by noting the simple fact that the Founders and framers of the American nation were "sons and daughters of Englishmen." This observation is central to the development of Riccards's argument. Every American schoolchild knows that the American revolutionaries identified British tyranny with the person of the king's royal governor in each of the colonies. Moreover, the struggle of the American colonies against British tyranny was initially organized and carried out in colonial assemblies or legislatures. Thus many revolutionaries initially believed that liberty could best be guaranteed by vesting sole political power in the legislative branch.

All of this is true, Riccards argues, but it ignores the fact that the American opposition to executive power in the years immediately before and after independence was an immediate response to specific policies of the British Crown and did not represent any fundamental philosophical antipathy toward the idea of executive prerogative. In fact, writes Riccards, as "sons and daughters of Englishmen," the American revolutionaries were intimately familiar with the philosophical writings of Locke and Blackstone, both of whom articulated sophisticated arguments defending royal or executive prerogative. In founding the American nation, therefore, the framers of the Constitution were by no means hostile to the notion of an executive or executive power; as "sons and daughters of Englishmen," they accepted executive prerogative as consistent with the ideals of free government. On the other hand, their own colonial experience left them uneasy with the idea of too powerful an executive; they understood there had to be limits to executive prerogative. Article II of the Constitution reflects the ambivalence of its authors; it was, Riccards concludes, "an adaptation of the familiar to the novel, a blending of tradition and experience to the uncertain world that demanded both authority and restraint."

If the framers of the Constitution were unsure of the proper roles and powers of the federal executive, these roles and powers would indelibly be defined by the first president. It is Washington the man and his presidential administration that are the focus of the second part of Riccards's book.

As Riccards ably demonstrates, Washington had a presence that translated itself into unusual leadership qualities. Because of this, Washington was arguably in great part responsible for making the American experiment in democracy work. His ultimate success was closely associated with his creation of a powerful executive branch. Washington made, in Riccards's words, a "collection of vague constitutional clauses into a political office. . . . He created precedents not as an exercise in statecraft, but as a response to particular crises. Indeed, he found an office and left it an institution."

If there is a major shortcoming in Riccards's book, it is the imbalance between parts 1 and 2. While Riccards's analysis of the Washington administration is thorough, his discussion of the philosophical and political origins of American executive authority is brief and, in places, only suggestive. This criticism, however, is not meant to detract from the substantial merits of this volume. Any serious discussion of the modern presidency and the various controversies that have engulfed it would benefit by the arguments advanced in Michael Riccards's important study.

DEAN C. CURRY

Messiah College
Grantham
Pennsylvania

SCHWARTZ, GARY. *Beyond Conformity or Rebellion: Youth and Authority in America.* Pp. xi, 307. Chicago: University of Chicago Press, 1987. $24.95.

Beyond Conformity or Rebellion is a difficult book to read, yet it is one that is surely worth the effort required to read and comprehend the subtleties of its contents. It is difficult because it presents ethnographic descriptions of six communities located in a midwestern agricultural and industrial state in the 1970s, descriptions that are chock-full of hard-to-remember details concerning the way in which youth groups respond to communal authority figures. While no attempt was made to select these communities on the basis of the demographic characteristics of the localities, the communities that were chosen do share such general social features as socioeconomic class, ethnic composition, and extent of urbanization.

Theoretically, the focus of the book is on authority: how youth groups perceive it, how they respond to it, and the circumstances that influence those responses. The conceptual framework for organizing the book's ethnographies is the way communal figures—high school teachers, principals, parents, police officers, and judges—incorporate and interpret basic American values in their interactions with youth groups. Using this framework, the analysis continues by classifying each community as either "cosmopolitan" or "provincial," depending on the strength of its attachment to such values.

Research materials for the ethnographies were collected by a team of six fieldworkers who, working within the boundaries of the peer group, learned to interpret local events from the youths' perspectives. Samples of these interpretations, taken from field interviews, are liberally interspersed throughout the book, giving the reader an opportunity to hear the voices of both youth and authority as they conceptualize and articulate their concerns about each other.

The general conclusion of this ethnographic tour de force is that relations between youths and authority figures are a reflection of the way a community aligns itself with American values. Unlike popular interpretations of the youths of the 1960s, which cast them either as rebels or conformists, Schwartz's argument is that the youths of the 1970s are neither, yet they continue to cast about for a comfortable identity within the social context of their respective communities. To the extent that these youths continue their search, they can be said to be heirs, but not clones, of their 1960s counterparts.

Much to Schwartz's credit, his book does not begin or end with a protracted discussion of methodology as a basis for justifying the scientific validity of his conclusions. Rather, without equivocation, he says that ethnography is more akin to history than to a nomothetic science. At the same time, he argues that ethnography is a type of narrative form that "does lead us to make qualitative judgments about the character of an entire world." In terms of this perspective, then, Schwartz has provided the reader with a richly embroidered narrative useful in making judgments about the diverse social worlds in which youth groups live. For this reason alone, such a narrative should be of interest to several categories of readers, including professionals and laypersons, especially parents with teenagers.

ALFRED AVERSA, Jr.
Fairleigh Dickinson University
Teaneck
New Jersey

SOCIOLOGY

BAILEY, VICTOR. *Delinquency and Citizenship: Reclaiming the Young Offender, 1914-1948.* Pp. xii, 352. New York: Oxford University Press, 1987. $56.00.

In the introduction to his book, Victor Bailey tempts the knowledgeable reader with references to the controversy over the humanitarian versus the social-control motive of the founders of the juvenile court in the United States. He immediately indicates, however, that he intends to propose neither motive as influencing policy changes toward young

offenders in England. Instead, he hopes to account for these changes by placing the "reformers in their social and ideological setting." Unfortunately, readers who have little previous familiarity with this setting are likely to be dissatisfied with the sparsity of information provided and the failure to relate social changes and the ideological climate clearly to divergent proposals.

The book describes in fine detail the important juvenile justice issues during the period covered. Adversarial groups are identified and their positions are spelled out. But the amount of relatively unimportant information hinders appreciation of significant matters. Nevertheless, a little patience can be rewarding.

Among the issues discussed are the removal of young offenders from prisons for adults, the abolition of corporal punishment, and the relative importance of economic deprivation and family pathology in the causation of delinquency. The dominant causal position came to be that which placed primary importance on defective discipline and relationships in the family. Impoverished economic circumstances were relegated to the role of aggravating family pathology. Was this explanatory choice consistent with "the new liberal theory of society," which supported state intervention in order to bring full citizenship to the working class? Bailey does not ask questions such as this.

The reader will learn much more about the contending groups, "reformers" and "reactionaries." The reformers supported lenient measures as sufficient to control delinquency and are regarded as emphasizing the welfare of youths. Reactionaries were concerned that too lenient treatment might be encouraging delinquency and generally advocated tougher sanctions. Clashes between these groups occurred over the use of corporal punishment, finally abolished in 1948; over possible misuse of probation with offenders who committed offenses after a previous probation experience; and over the interpretation of trends in official delinquency statistics. Reformers argued that the increase in official delinquency primarily reflected increased law enforcement activity.

Did reforms reduce delinquency? There is a short discussion of the effectiveness of Borstal but little more is said about the success of reforms. Furthermore, Bailey observes that crime flourished after World War II despite material benefits provided by the welfare state. He does not relate this situation or the rise of a conservative opposition in the 1970s to the efficacy of reforms. The absence of this kind of analysis will disappoint many readers.

ROY L. AUSTIN
Pennsylvania State University
State College

BOGGS, CARL. *Social Movements and Political Power: Emerging Forms of Radicalism in the West.* Pp. xvi, 288. Philadelphia: Temple University Press, 1986. $29.95.

For most Western industrial societies, the late 1970s and early 1980s have been a period of transition. Central to the political turmoil have been new social movements, ranging from feminism, the peace movement, and environmentalism to the advocates of the rights of gay people and other minorities. Although each of these movements pursues distinctive goals, they are united in a common struggle for extended democracy and a better quality of life.

In his excellent comparative study, *Social Movements and Political Power*, Carl Boggs analyzes the evolution of new social movements in three different settings and their often tense and contradictory relationship with official politics.

Whereas the majority of American social scientists associate the rise of contemporary social movements with postmaterialism, Boggs sees them as a response to the contradictions of the welfare state, the erosion of Keynesianism, and especially the growing power of the central state. Pursuing a "third road" between Western social democracy and Leninist state socialism, they represent "the initial expression of a (potential) radical democratic post-Marxist alternative."

The core of Boggs's book is an analysis and critique of those "political formations"—mostly parties—that have incorporated values and goals of new social movements and are competing for political power: Eurosocialism in France, Greece, and Spain; American new populism; and the West German Greens. In each case, these formations owe their success largely to new social movements. By incorporating everyday cultural, material, and personal issues into politics, the movements have expanded the limits of possible political discourse and thus have helped the political formations to make inroads into the political system.

The relationship between movements and formations, however, has been far from harmonious. In what Boggs considers a central issue of politics, namely, to resolve the tension between state and society, the formations have largely failed. The short experience with both Eurosocialism and American populism shows that once they came to power, they soon fell prey to social democratic reformism. Instead of reconstituting the entire political system on egalitarian and democratic grounds, they reproduced the old "division between elites and masses, party and movement, state and grassroots." The West German Greens are the sole exception. The recent experience with the "red-green" coalition in the *Land* Hesse, however, as well as the revived acrimonious fights between different Green factions—neither of which are covered in this study—leave the observer more than skeptical as to the prospects for the Greens.

Boggs's analysis provides a wide range of critical insights into the problems and changes in the social, political, and cultural climate of advanced industrial societies. It is both fascinating and provocative, a book for everyone interested in the emergence of post-Marxist, post-social-democratic theory and politics.

HANS-GEORG BETZ
Massachusetts Institute of
    Technology
Cambridge

CLARK, HENRY B. *Altering Behavior: The Ethics of Controlled Experience.* Pp. 235. Newbury Park, CA: Sage, 1986. $25.00.

Henry Clark, professor of social ethics at the University of Southern California, has served as coordinator of urban affairs at the National Council of Churches and as coordinator for humanities and professions at the University of Southern California's Center for Humanities. He reaffirms the values of the flower children, grown up now into yuppies seeking the good life on their way up in the corporate world.

His book intends an explanation of new breakthroughs in experience and behavior control and examines how these can be implemented to promote fulfillment. As a social ethicist, he analyzes norms and values that ought to govern social policy and challenges the traditional ethos and its accommodation to the expulsion from Eden. He wishes to promote the optimal and ethical use of drugs, surgical and electronic interventions, and behavior shaping and modification technologies that can augment pleasure and enlarge the capacity for productivity and happiness. Arguing that if one can use vitamin and pain pills and weight and smoking controls to relieve negative experiences, there is no justification not to accentuate the positive and to build the ultimate hi-fi personality. The new El Dorado is at the threshold of the coming century, when today's unsafe and unreliable panaceas will be superseded by technological breakthroughs, attaining a sense of competence, presence, and euphoria, managing stress, and achieving cocaine's superorgasm without the deflation and damage that limit contemporary drugs.

Clark advocates the feasibility of brain implants to control aggression and criminality and foresees that across-the-counter ecstasy will make psychotherapy obsolete. The rationale for these procedures of operant conditioning and behavior control by this chaplain of Shangri-la is the criteria of acceptable risk and cost-benefit analysis. Ministering to postindustrial and postsublimation society, he repudiates the obsessive work ethic and inner-worldly asceticism with their fear of self-indulgence. Faulting technological Calvinism, it is ironic that he represents the same discrete, mechanistic, and reductionist ethos applied this time to the self rather than to objects. He stands Calvinism on its head, shifting values in our postindustrial society from production to consumption, from the work ethic to self-aggrandizing entitlements of sensory consumption. His vistas are those of the ever-expanding bull market and its supply-side deregulation, where goods and gratifications are forever replenished.

NATHAN ADLER

California School of
  Professional Psychology
Berkeley

CUBA, LEE J. *Identity and Community on the Alaskan Frontier.* Pp. xvii, 206. Philadelphia: Temple University Press, 1987. $24.95.

In Cuba's words, "This analysis of the Alaskan frontier may be read as a case study of a small number of Americans who view themselves as contemporary pioneers." By focusing on the Alaskan city of Anchorage, Cuba provides the reader with a descriptive profile of the individual and collective identities of Alaskans, the points of origin for Alaskan migrants, and the effects of place on the individual sense of self. Thus Cuba's case study provides the reader with an insight as to how Alaskans utilize speech to separate themselves from outsiders, the behavioral expectations that socialize migrants to an Alaskan identity, the close origins of migrants to Alaska, and the effects of place in producing individual identification with Alaska as a state.

Chapter 1, "The Emergence of a National Idiom," and chapter 6, "A Sense of Place," are, in my opinion, the most interesting in the book. In them, Cuba attempts to synthesize the intuitive differences between frontier and community within historical and sociological explanation. While Cuba manages to communicate to the reader in chapter

1 that the goal of both the historian and the sociologist in considering the frontier as a form of society is to seek "a relationship between social or physical structure and forms of individual and collective associations," he stops short in outlining metatheoretical approaches to the issue. In chapter 6, Cuba attempts to provide the reader with a possible metatheoretical approach by suggesting that the identification of comparative social identities facilitates the differentiation between individual and collective identity. The issue becomes complicated, however, if one considers how travelers from one frontier to another frontier are able to shape a collective identity or how travelers from well-defined communities are able to develop individual identities on the frontier. In other words, when does the frontier identity end and the communal identity begin? Some further elaboration of the issues raised by Cuba in these two chapters would have enhanced the theoretical import of the book. As such, these two chapters appear to be the bookends of an interesting case study.

In summary, the book is a very interesting case study of a state of which most persons have very little direct knowledge and for which most persons have some stereotypical notions. This book is certainly going to upset many stereotypes about Alaska. Moreover, this book is a welcome addition to the field of American studies, where case studies of the United States and its inhabitants are in short supply. Finally, this book should draw the interest of both the urban and the community sociologist interested in the psychological and symbolic association between place and social identity.

ADALBERTO AGUIRRE, Jr.
University of California
Riverside

EISENSTADT, S. N. and A. SHACHAR. *Society, Culture and Urbanization.* Pp. 389. Newbury Park, CA: Sage, 1987. $35.00.

Eisenstadt and Shachar's *Society, Culture and Urbanization* is a major work. The authors' goal is the study of cities and urban systems from a comparative civilization perspective; that is, the examination of urban phenomena in the context of the ideological premises and institutional frameworks of nine historical civilizations. The focus is on examining and analyzing a range of societies using a macrosocietal perspective. As such, it is in the long sociological tradition of Durkheim, Marx, and particularly Weber, with societies being analyzed in the context of their ideological premises and institutional frameworks.

Eisenstadt and Shachar begin with an analytic summary and evaluation of theories of urbanization and include evolutionary approaches, ideal-typical or trait complex approaches, urban ecological models, symbolic approaches—for example, analyzing features of ancient cities in terms of their religious or cosmological meaning—and Marxist approaches. Eisenstadt and Shachar then develop their own theoretical model, which they designate as a comparative civilizational approach. By this they mean to join the combination of political and cultural forces with those that structure the social division of labor shaping the institutional patterns and contours of a society and influencing its evolution and maintenance. They thus combine institutional, ecological, and cultural analyses.

Having provided their theoretical orientation and framework for analysis, Eisenstadt and Shachar then devote the bulk of their volume to analyzing nine civilization patterns of historical urbanization. They examine and evaluate the secondary literature on the emergence of cities, and the process of urbanization in the historical civilizations of Southeast Asia, Latin America, the Chinese empire, the Russian empire, the Byzantine empire, Islam, India, Japan, and Europe. Deliberately not covered, or dealt with only tangentially, are the problems of the origins of cities in the Near East and Mesopotamia.

Also excluded are modern societies and their cities that developed in the context of industrial technology and political modernization. Eisenstadt and Shachar argue that these topics have been amply researched elsewhere and that their attention is more usefully focused on providing a systematic comparative analysis of the process of urbanization in other historical civilizations. I believe they are correct. There is, however, an arbitrary element of nonuniformity as to what period is, or is not, to be covered. While, for example, the case study of "Urbanization in the Russian Empire" in chapter 6 briefly discusses nineteenth-century urban reforms, it inexplicably ends the chapter with the 1892 municipal statute. Twentieth-century adjustments prior to the revolution are not mentioned. In similar fashion, the case study of colonial Latin America only takes the urban systems in Latin America up to the end of the eighteenth century. Again, there is not even brief mention of the political revolutions that were about to convulse the continent for decades. While the chapter's final paragraph does discuss the frequency of urban rebellions in colonial cities during the seventeenth and eighteenth centuries, it ends stating that "the basic roots of these disturbances greatly differed from one city to another, but most rebellions were caused by either food shortage or cruel treatment of the Indians and black populations." Most students would be advantaged by having a solitary sentence, or a footnote, added noting that the soon-to-come urban revolts of the nineteenth century primarily would be political in nature, not just food-shortage disturbances.

It is, of course, quite legitimate to confine one's analysis to a specific period. Even graduate students, however, often have but a vague and rudimentary knowledge of major historic upheavals in other cultures and on other continents. Care must therefore be taken that those readers not familiar with regional history do not view the urban systems presented as inefficient and inadequate but basically stable systems. In reality, the book's virtue is that it deliberately focuses on those urban systems that were about to be forever changed by revolution, invasion, or industrialization.

Eisenstadt and Shachar utilize the epilogue in an attempt to weave together technical development, the social division of labor, the study of power relations, and cultural orientations and traditions. They do this by subsuming social actors, forces, and processes that affect the urban phenomena under the headings of "concentration" and "centrality." By the former, they refer to the mode of organization evolving out of demographic, technological, and socioeconomic forces. The latter designates organization and dynamics generated by political and cultural control, control of production, and control of symbolic elements of a society. Eisenstadt and Shachar claim that while cities of different civilizations cannot be compared in terms of one trait or variable, they can be compared in terms of constellations of variables and different combinations of centrality and concentration. Cities, they argue, do not constitute only a special reflection of social forces—as claimed by contemporary Marxists; the special concentration in cities generates new forms of production, control, and cultural creativity.

For most readers, the greatest strength of the volume will be its common framework for the analysis of the nine premodern societies. Thus, for example, in the chapter on the Chinese empire, it is noted that Chinese cities, no matter how large, never became autonomous forces of centrality having their own characteristics and dynamics. As a consequence, a bourgeois class consciousness never developed as it did in medieval Europe and Japan. A civic consciousness or ideology never developed to compete with dynasties or even warlords.

Among the chapters, those on the Russian empire, the Byzantine empire, and Southeast Asia especially provide less well known information concerning societies about which most sociologists and geographers have but limited knowledge.

Society, Culture and Urbanization is a book that every urban scholar must have handy on the shelf.

J. JOHN PALEN
Virginia Commonwealth University
Richmond

FRIEDMAN, LAWRENCE. *Total Justice*. Pp. ix, 166. New York: Russell Sage, 1985. Distributed by Basic Books, New York. $14.50.

VON HIRSCH, ANDREW. *Past or Future Crimes: Deservedness and Dangerousness in the Sentencing of Criminals*. Pp. xiv, 220. New Brunswick, NJ: Rutgers University Press, 1985. $25.00.

In his little monograph, *Total Justice*, Lawrence M. Friedman discusses the "perceived" problem of a "litigation explosion" of an ever-increasing number of lawyers in a society obsessed with lawsuits. While others see the problem as that of law schools' graduating attorneys who engage in champerty and barratry on a wholesale basis to justify their existence, Friedman, in contrast, argues that the problem is not to be resolved but rather is to be used in intellectual analysis to explore and explain changes in our legal system and culture over the last century.

Until the mid-nineteenth century, a portion of society felt life was indeed nasty, brutish, and short. While individuals such as the frontiersmen may have been more independent, there was a recognition that life was not necessarily fair and that one had little control over its vicissitudes or calamities. By the nineteenth century, however, advances in science and technology started to give society control over nature as well as the quality and quantity of life. This control required regulations that were vested in the state and the law. While this might have resulted in the loss of independence, most people in modern society are not helpless or lost. Science and industry are respected, and individuals are confident that outside control by the government is both possible and desirable. All this, writes Friedman, has developed in the citizenry an expectation of fairness and an expectation that compensation should follow so long as the victim was not solely at fault.

In dealing with whether Americans are more claims conscious, Friedman, not sure if they are, suggests that changes in our culture make a lawsuit a more likely response, especially as substantive legal changes have increased the number of justifiable claims. As a case in point, reference is made to sexual behavior. At a time when society generally increased the number and areas of rules and regulations, it deregulated sexual conduct. This, Friedman concludes, is not a paradox but the adjustment of legal culture—more regulation where needed, less where not.

Past or Future Crimes is a more systematic analysis and clarification of the desert theory of criminal sentencing than first appeared in Andrew von Hirsch's earlier published *Doing Justice* (1976).

Until 1970, penologists and laypersons predicated sentencing norms on the positivist penal ethic. The prevalent belief was that penal sanctions were rehabilitative in nature. As von Hirsch points out, however, the long-standing appeal of positivist theory was that, in addition to rehabilitation, it also provided for separation from society for those not treatable. In the 1950s and 1960s, testing showed inadequacies of treatment programs, and this result, coupled with a general belief in the inability to mold human behavior, caused scholars to look elsewhere for the appropriate correctional theory.

Von Hirsch urges the desert rationale for the imposition of punishment. Succinctly stated, desert theory imposes punishment based upon the blameworthiness of the committed criminal conduct. Von Hirsch compares desert theory to the general deterrence school and selective incapacitation theories.

Although selective incapacitation and desert theory can be blended at certain points, von Hirsch sees only conflict and rejects a synthesis. Thus Wilson, in *Thinking about Crime*, would be prepared to give longer prison terms to persons committing less serious crimes when those persons are worse risks. Desert theorists, writes von Hirsch, cannot be comfortable with harsher punishments for those whose conduct is less reprehensible.

In essence, *Past or Future Crimes* re-examines desert theory as well as predictive sentencing and selective incapacitation and the tensions between them. Not surprising, selective incapacitation and predictive sentencing are found wanting. While a case is made for desert theory and the ethical imperative upon which it is based—condemnation of unacceptable acts—some of its force is lost by the total rejection of competing theories, which to the nonsentencing specialist is splitting hairs.

Friedman deals with why more people are suing and why there are problems. Von Hirsch, in contrast, deals with the punishment aspect of criminal justice and why individuals should be punished for those acts they have committed. Both works are worth the time of the reader.

ROSLYN MURASKIN
Long Island University
Brookville
New York

GLENDON, MARY ANN. *Abortion and Divorce in Western Law: American Failures, European Challenges.* Pp. 197. Cambridge, MA: Harvard University Press, 1987. $25.00.

Comparative legal analysis is the analytic frame of reference Glendon adopts to tackle the intractable issues of American abortion and divorce law. Relying on comparisons between the United States and twenty Western nations, she seeks to draw on them not only to discern technical insights on how other nations address these fundamental social concerns but also to propose that America's narrow view of law as coercion should be broadened to incorporate didactic purposes as well.

Relying especially on the work of Clifford Geertz, she sees much virtue in European law, which is expressly drafted to articulate values and beliefs about abortion, divorce, and the family more generally. In the case of abortion in particular, she argues that a law that permits abortion but also articulates respect for unborn life and compassion for pregnant women—recent French law is taken as an important model—can provide means

whereby "a divided society *can* compromise successfully on the abortion issue."

Glendon's fundamental insight—that American law can and should incorporate moral standards—is persuasive and important. When her analysis sticks to law and theory it is penetrating and intuitive and, in the case of the concluding chapter, even brilliant. Long-standing American myopia and ethnocentrism too often blind us to the lessons offered by other countries. Whether the adoption of more caring and compassionate language would help defuse the abortion controversy in America or not, the very idea stands alone as an important recommendation.

On the other hand, despite her recognition that law is both a leader and a reflector of societal values, she assumes that, indeed, a change in law would dramatically defuse the American abortion crisis. She argues that such legal changes were instrumental in reconciling opposing sides in France and elsewhere, but she presents no evidence to support the claim, nor does she speculate on what would be required to bring about such a change in the United States.

Glendon is careful to note that law cannot be divorced from its social context, yet she proceeds to ignore the pivotal importance of that context. For example, when she argues that "leaving abortion regulation basically up to state legislatures would have encouraged constructive activity by partisans of both sides," she demonstrates ignorance of state actions and politics as well as the unique consequences of American federalism. Glendon evinces dismay at the relatively undeveloped American social welfare state, but her analysis of its antecedents and consequences could certainly have been advanced had she consulted the voluminous literature on the subject.

Glendon oversimplifies and thereby distorts the complex relationship between public opinion and the substance of court opinions on abortion. For example, in surveys taken by the National Opinion Research Center from 1972 to 1984, roughly half of those surveyed favored allowing legal abortions for married women wanting abortions, for low-income women, and for unmarried women wanting to avoid marriage. And Glendon is simply wrong when she asserts that *Roe* and other court decisions are "indifferent to unborn life." In addition, her American legal analysis is completely ahistorical and thus misses the key fact that abortion regulation is a relatively recent phenomenon in the United States. In the end, "the way in which we name things and imagine them" may indeed be important, even vital for the law. But any lawyer knows that abstract assumptions, no matter how logical, are no substitute for accurate facts and careful research.

ROBERT J. SPITZER
State University of New York
Cortland

HECHTER, MICHAEL. *Principles of Group Solidarity.* Pp. xv, 219. Berkeley: University of California Press, 1987. $28.50.

In recent years, there has been a revival of utilitarian theory within sociology. Adam Smith's solution to the Hobbesian problem of order—for example, how is social organization possible in the face of self-interest and conflict?—has been resurrected, except now the invisible hand of order is more visible. Yet the basic assumption that humans are rational egoists who seek to maximize utilities is retained, although many qualifications have been added to the purely economic versions of utilitarian thinking. For example, individuals are not assumed to operate in free or friction-less markets, they are not seen to have perfectly ordered preferences; they are viewed as subject to the constraints of culture and institutional structures; and in some versions of neo-utilitarianism, they are not even seen as trying to maximize utilities.

Michael Hechter's *Principles of Group Solidarity* resurrects utilitarianism in the form of "rational choice theory." This approach is less inhibited than other revivals of utilitarian thinking, such as modern exchange theory, because it begins with what, at first,

seem like the most extreme assumptions of utilitarianism: humans are rational; they have ordered preferences, and they make choices in ways to maximize utility as dictated by this preference order. Social organization is then seen as constructed, or changed, by these rational choice processes, although additional concepts are introduced in order to make the hand of order more visible. In Hechter's approach, the problem of order is phrased in terms of group solidarity that is defined as the degree to which individuals commit their private resources—time, emotion, energy, self, and so forth—to the production of a collective or joint good.

What are the conditions for rational choice theory to be effective? Hechter's answer is (1) dependence, (2) monitoring, and (3) sanctioning. Dependence is a situation where individuals need group membership to receive a valued collective good. When they are dependent, it is rational for individuals to create rules and obligations to the group that will ensure access to this valued good. Dependence is increased when this joint good, or a close substitute, is not readily available elsewhere, when actors lack information about alternatives, when the costs of exiting the group are high, when moving costs are high, and when personal ties in the group are—as unredeemable investments—strong. Monitoring is the process of detecting nonconformity to group norms and obligations. When monitoring capacity is low, it becomes difficult to ensure conformity to group obligations, because conformity represents a cost to individuals and it is rational for them to avoid such costs. Sanctioning is the use of rewards or punishments to induce conformity to group obligations. For Hechter, the combined level of monitoring and sanctioning is conceptualized as the "control capacity" of the group.

With these basic concepts, coupled with the assumptions of rationality, the problem of order is rephrased as one of "free riding." Avoiding the costs of conformity to norms is usually the most rational alternative for actors, and so the key sociological question becomes, What forces reduce free riding and make conformity the most rational alternative? The answer is high levels of dependence, monitoring, and sanctioning. Thus, when members are highly dependent on a collective good and are subject to high degrees of control capacity, free riding will be reduced and conformity to production norms will be high. It is with these simple assumptions that rational choice theory tries to explain the varieties of group structures forming societies. How is this possible?

There are, Hechter argues, two ways of generating compliance with group norms: compensation and obligation. Compensation typically occurs when the group produces goods for a market and uses its profits to buy conformity. In contrast, obligations emerge when a group produces an immanent joint good that its members themselves consume. In a sense, macrostructures are composed of configurations of compensatory and obligatory group memberships, and in both cases, the levels of dependence, monitoring, and sanctioning explain their operative dynamics. Obligatory groups generally reveal high dependence of their members, with monitoring and sanctioning against free riding occurring in the flow of interaction as members do what is necessary to get their valued joint good—whether friendship, esteem, companionship, or some other immanent good. Compensatory groups will have less dependent members, and thus their control costs for both monitoring and sanctioning will be considerably higher. Moreover, compensatory groups will tend to be larger, and if control is to occur, members must create formal procedures and agents for monitoring and sanctioning in order to mitigate free riding. While socialization, altruism, and tit-for-tat processes can partially control free riding, compensatory groups will, as a natural outcome of rational decisions of their members and/or leaders, formalize control.

Controls are, however, costly; and if compensatory groups spend too much on formal control, then the group's viability decreases, because it will be less able to compensate members. As a consequence of this basic dilemma, it is rational for actors to develop what Hechter terms "economizing" procedures for monitoring and sanctioning. For example, compensatory groups often facilitate monitoring by increasing the visibility of actors, as through architecture, public rituals, and specific obligations; forcing members to state their preferences explicitly, as through group decision making and confessions; and requiring members to share the burden of monitoring, as through group rewards, gossip, limiting privacy, and the like.

These theoretical ideas are used by Hechter to interpret varying patterns of solidarity in different kinds of groupings—political parties, rotating credit associations, insurance leagues, and capitalist firms. In each case, the distinctive structure of these groupings is seen to follow from the nature of the goods produced by the group, the level of dependence of its members, and the resulting monitoring and sanctioning capacities of the group. The end result is a most provocative application of rational choice theory to macrostructural processes. While we may still want to withhold final judgment about the ultimate explanatory power of rational choice assumptions, they cannot be so easily rejected, as was once the case in sociology.

Principles of Group Solidarity is, therefore, an important work in contemporary theory and is essential reading for all of those who are interested in developing a general theory of human social organization. Utilitarianism deserves a second hearing in sociology and other social sciences—except, of course, economics, where it has always been at the theoretical center. Rational choice theory, coupled with modern exchange theories, offers the best vehicle for this reintroduction of utilitarian ideas, and *Principles of Group Solidarity* shows the most provocative use of rational choice assumptions in theoretical sociology.

JONATHAN H. TURNER
University of California
Riverside

SCARRY, ELAINE. *The Body in Pain: The Making and Unmaking of the World.* Pp. vii, 385. New York: Oxford University Press, 1985. $24.95.

This is a challenging book. It conveys a vital moral message, about the destructive equivalence of various kinds of violence against the human body. It offers a seemingly complex argument that makes a number of unusual assumptions and connections; it is an argument that may convince, or awe through its baffling qualities, or fall flat. The book is erudite and dense, filled with insights and imaginative references, yet it is also oddly incomplete. The sheer audacity of the book's structure requires a careful presentation of its coverage before we turn to its strengths and what are, in my view, its telling weaknesses.

The book divides into two main sections, with a concluding chapter that builds particularly on the second substantive segment. In the first section, the focus is on pain. Scarry deals with the problems of expressing pain in oneself and others. She details the use of pain in torture, with hosts of examples from twentieth-century cases drawn particularly from the files of Amnesty International. Stages in the torture process, including threat and intimidation, removal of normal channels of communication, and interrogation, are detailed. Then the book turns to war, in a longer section that sets out to prove that causing injury is the essence of war. Different kinds of arguments about war are assessed—ideas of defensive wars, just wars, and wars for a cause; and different rhetorical traditions about war, in terms of contest, strategy, and history, are examined. The main point is the pain-causing aspect, the intent to injure, which serves—needlessly, in Scarry's view—to determine who wins the contest—the concept of body counts is invoked with effect—and to legitimate the issues that are judged to be crucial to the winning side. War's essence as injury must be asserted particularly against political and scholarly traditions that insist on treating it in terms of strategic advance or agent in technological innovation.

The essence of the argument in the first section is that war and torture are ultimately equivalent—the book deals with, but dismisses, the extent to which war participants are injury receivers by choice—because they both depend on infliction of pain and death. They are ultimately destructive of civilization; indeed, they are the negation of civilization.

The second section of the book deals with the affirming contrast to war: the creative powers of civilization. Weapons can be forged into tools, destruction into production. Human imagination, the ability to envisage that which has not existed, is the positive analogue to pain, as creative as the other is negating. These general points are examined through a deconstructivist exegesis on what Scarry claims are the two central poles of Western civilization: the Judeo-Christian tradition and the thirst for material self-expression. This means, in practice, an analysis of the Bible, with special reference to creation but also to the expressions of God in body, and of Karl Marx, this last as an embodiment of Western material creativity. The parallelisms Scarry finds in her exegesis, which may mean more to author than reader, lead at one point to an excited query as to whether Judeo-Christian scriptures constitute a "precocious anticipation" of Marx's industrial world. That the answer to this question is definitely negative is not noted.

In the concluding chapter, the nature of artifice is outlined in terms of some general features of the creative process particularly regarding material objects. Thus we learn how the working end of tools or weapons receives great elaboration, while the passive end—what we laypersons might call handles—receives much less; we learn about an innate human tendency to produce surfeit. We learn how American habits, such as litigiousness, may be related to our relation to created objects. This final section builds on the positive features of the overall argument, but Scarry reminds us of the pendulum she has constructed between destructive and constructive potentials. In a revealing final statement, she sums up: "Directed against the isolating aversiveness of pain, mental and material culture assumes the sharability of sentience." And she urges on us courage.

The moral message of the book is obvious. Concern about torture and the massive involuntary pain that might be caused by nuclear war courses through the first portion of the analysis. The asserted equivalency of different kinds of pain infliction, and the link between destruction and creation, may seem striking connections in defense of moral outrage and in support of alternatives to pain.

The book also offers a host of more specific insights. Its most penetrating methods involve the focus on forms of discourse, on word uses and what lies behind them. These strengths surface particularly in discussions of torture and war, where a number of kinds of imagery—about machines, animals, and ideologies—are paraded to fine effect to show how pain can be expressed and how its inflicters may try to obfuscate it. Discourse analysis continues in the book's second section, which is more conventional in its reliance on a small number of formal documents. Here, too, patterns of word use are often interesting, as in the physical images utilized in the Bible in discussing receipt or nonreceipt of God's word, images that often refer to body parts: for example, stiff-necked Israelites, hard-hearted pharaohs.

Yet for all its ambition, rectitude, and insight, the book ultimately disappoints. Its message risks seeming naively simple: pain is bad; creativity, good; we ought to be able to figure out something better than war. Its organization is often cumbersome and sometimes repetitious, its argument abstract, its examples somewhat wooden. Definitional model-building about the nature of war seems a less telling approach than literary or artistic representation or even a good narrative account. A great deal of the book depends on formal propositions about forms of pain or creativity that risk losing touch with complex reality. Scarry thus makes assumptions about the essential sameness of all wars with only brief references, despite her wide reading, to actual cases, a technique

that can seem more assertive than persuasive.

Then there are the omissions, granting that on such an ambitious canvas some must inevitably appear. The discussion of creativity and what Scarry refers to as its "interior structures" makes no reference to the abundant psychological work on the subject. The discussion of the essential Western civilization makes scant use of historical findings. Thus the long account of Biblical concern about imagery fails to note its relationship to wider Semitic values and how these were in fact contrary to the impulses of Western or Byzantine Christendom; the actual origins of Western attitudes toward nature and artifice, the subject of a considerable and revealing literature by medievalists, are ignored. There is a timelessness to the whole account—wars are all the same, Western civilization has rested on the same essential features from its origins—that must provoke any reader sensitive to historical complexity. A major set of omissions, then, involves neglect of key disciplines that must be involved in the assessment of human potential and social reality.

A second set of omissions involves inattention to key forms of the phenomena under examination. Discussion of pain thus only tangentially invokes medicine and never deals with sports or rituals, save in brief, inconclusive mention of religious flagellation. Cultural variation, as well as change over time, in the perception and definitions of pain is ignored—yet torture, for example, may well have meanings for victims and inflicters alike in societies that stress stoicism that differ from those current in societies more bent on sensitivity. Save for passing reference in the final chapter, pain as punishment is not treated, and so the important literature on physical versus deprivational punishment and on revenge versus other punitive motives is not taken up. Nor is any attention paid to pain and violence in protest, an odd omission, given the fascination with Marx. Thus, even in the section most challenging and insightful, where pain is the subject, one emerges with an incomplete sense of the issues involved and some real questions about whether the essential phenomenon has been captured.

This is a book, then, with a topic as compelling as its title, great earnestness, and flashes of stimulating analysis, but, finally, a framework that fails to convince, fails even to set a clear agenda for further theoretical or empirical work.

PETER N. STEARNS
Carnegie Mellon University
Pittsburgh
Pennsylvania

TAUSSIG, MICHAEL. *Shamanism, Colonialism, and the Wild Man: A Study in Terror and Healing*. Pp. xx, 518. Chicago: University of Chicago Press, 1987. $29.95.

Shamanism, Colonialism, and the Wild Man is an important and ambitious book that will certainly provoke lively debate and divided opinion. Indeed, Taussig's earlier pioneering and innovative publications on terror and healing already have. *Shamanism, Colonialism, and the Wild Man* expands upon this earlier work by providing detailed ethnographic and historical context; the book is about the histories and cultures of colonial, capitalist, and racial domination and resistance in Colombia, mainly the southwestern part of the country. Taussig depicts a baroquely interpenetrating complexity of cultural traditions—colonial, capitalist, Indian, black, Church, shamanic, highland, lowland—a complexity that one supposes must be similarly characteristic of cultures of domination and resistance in general. Although his focus is on healing and terror as instances of these cultures—important enough topics in themselves—it is this issue of domination and resistance that is likely to gain the book a very broad audience.

Taussig seeks to push beyond the mystifying rationalities that characterize conventional economic, dependency-theory, and even Marxist characterizations of colonial and neocolonial domination and to rescue a kind of voice for the dominated, from whose perspective such rationalities are revealed as fantastic. Indeed, as with his earlier *Devil and Commodity Fetishism in South America* (Chapel Hill: University of North Carolina Press, 1980), Taussig's concern to enlist these other voices in the deconstruction of our own mythical realities seems to take precedence over analysis of the cultures of these others. This emphasis in part accounts for the fact that in spite of its richly detailed accounts of shamanic healing sessions, conversations with a wide variety of Colombian healers and patients, and various Colombian histories constructed from divergent points of view, *Shamanism, Colonialism, and the Wild Man* provides little conventional institutional analysis of family, village, and local-level political organization. One suspects that such analysis might distract attention from Taussig's emphasis on the counter-hegemonic possibilities of, for example, envy, which Taussig views as "implicit social knowledge," by revealing its close association with immediate—family-level and village-level—social relations, as well as with racist, colonial, and capitalist domination.

Given Taussig's priorities, however, he constructs—by deconstructing—a convincing case. Terror, he argues, cannot be reduced to economic logics and neither is it understandable as a suspension of normal values and restraints. Rather, "torture and terror are ritualized art forms and . . . far from being spontaneous, sui generis, and an abandonment of what are often called the values of civilization, such rites of terror have a deep history deriving power and meaning from those very values." Moreover, "in the colonial mode of production of reality, as in the Putumayo, . . . a colonial mirroring of otherness . . . reflects back onto the colonists the barbarity of their own [capitalist] social relations, but as imputed to the savagery they yearn to colonize."

Powerful and evocative—as well as hyperbolic and assertive—as Taussig's writing on terror is, it is his treatment of healing that is most compelling, confusing, and challenging. Taussig is interested in the creative and redemptive possibilities of change, montage, and disorder, and this interest is reflected in the style of his prose. Taussig attempts to find in the therapeutic relations between patient and healer, First and Third World—and his text and its readers?—a utopian space in which "healing can mobilize terror in order to subvert it, not through heavenly catharses but through the tripping up of power in its own disorderliness."

On balance, Taussig is more suspicious of the ordering pole of the dialectic of power as the ordering or disordering operation between order and chaos. Insofar as this bias encourages appropriating Taussig's text to the cryptically utopian—and, I would argue, potentially conservative—agenda of the "deconstructive"-"postmodernist" movement in academia, it constitutes the book's most important weakness. Creativity, redemption, and healing may necessarily entail "splintering and decomposing structures and cracking open meanings," but they may also require a further iteration in the form of reconceiving—yes, reordering at a higher level of logical encompassment—the social and symbolic relations between order and disorder that constitute past and future selves, cultures, and societies.

I regard these latter rather abstractly denoted issues to be open ones, and Taussig by no means underestimates the complexities they suggest. Indeed, I suspect that just as Indians and colonialists contest the meanings of Colombian history and their own identities in an infinitely recursive appropriation of this history and "the other," so will there be a contest among scholars to appropriate Taussig's text to their own intellectual cum political ends. In its "sudden and infinite connections between dissimilars in an endless or almost endless process of connection-making and connection-breaking," *Shaminism, Colonialism, and the Wild Man* juxtaposes narratives, hallucinations, events, and analysis with a power more like that of healing than that of argument. I, for one, hope that it has the effects it intends.

P. STEVEN SANGREN

Cornell University
Ithaca
New York

WILSON, WILLIAM JULIUS. *The Truly Disadvantaged: The Inner City, the Underclass, and Public Policy.* Pp. xi, 254. Chicago: University of Chicago Press, 1987. $19.95.

This latest volume from William Julius Wilson is timely, challenging, and important. Misleadingly titled—as some have also complained about its controversial predecessor, *The Declining Significance of Race: Blacks and Changing American Institutions* (Chicago: University of Chicago Press, 1980)—its blend of scholarly analysis and proposals for public policy covers both more and less than the title implies.

The book is organized in two sections. In the first, Wilson identifies certain problems of the ghetto underclass and examines alternative explanations of their sources. The problems include high rates of violent crime; illegitimacy; female-headed households, that is, single-parent families headed by females; and joblessness, particularly among blacks. The chief emphasis is female headship, treated at length in chapters coauthored with Kathryn Neckerman and Robert Aponte. The cause receiving the bulk of attention is joblessness among black males.

The book's second section addresses public policy. It evaluates principles for policy while also offering more or less specific policy proposals. The fundamental principle guiding Wilson's approach is that universal programs, such as those common in Western Europe, should be used whenever possible in preference to group-targeted or means-tested programs. "The hidden agenda . . . is to improve the life chances of truly disadvantaged groups such as the ghetto underclass by emphasizing programs to which the more advantaged groups of all races and class backgrounds can positively relate." Given past and current racism, among other things, targeted programs based on the principles of equality of individual rights, equality of group rights, and equality of life chances are also needed, though they should be considered subordinate to universal programs. Wilson's package of economic and social reforms highlights "macroeconomic policies to promote balanced economic growth and create a tight-labor-market situation, a nationally oriented labor-market strategy, a child support assurance program, a child care strategy, and a family allowances program."

Though the book contains significant and novel empirical and theoretical contributions to social science, its format suggests a primary interest in participating in post-Reagan policy debates; for instance, a scholarly literature review, coauthored with Aponte, is tucked away as an appendix. Wilson explicitly seeks to develop a revitalized liberal approach to the problems of the disadvantaged that can counter conservative doctrines that he believes have been allowed to dominate public debate and public policy in recent years. There are weaknesses in the book, some of which no doubt come from an anxiousness to enter the debate as quickly as possible. He relies almost exclusively on published census-type data without attention to measurement problems; due to the data available, there is almost as much focus on blacks in general as on blacks and others in the inner city; due again to the types of data analyzed and possibly to considerations of the statistical sophistication of policymakers, virtually all of his empirical work could be conducted more rigorously; and the policy proposals lack detail, particularly cost estimates. These very weaknesses, however, could contribute to the book's becoming a focal point for analysis and debate about the inner city, a source book of provocative, important ideas waiting to be fleshed out by a wide range of scholars, commentators, and policymakers.

CARL B. BACKMAN

Buffalo State College
New York

ECONOMICS

COOPER, PATRICIA. *Once a Cigar Maker: Men, Women, and Work Culture in American Cigar Factories, 1900-1919.* Pp. xvi, 350. Champaign: University of Illinois Press, 1987. $29.95.

WALDINGER, ROGER D. *Through the Eye of the Needle: Immigrants and Enterprise in New York's Garment Trades.* Pp. xi, 231. New York: New York University Press, 1986. Distributed by Columbia University Press, New York. $35.00.

Here are two studies, different in period and scope yet both treating classic sectors in the history of small business in America. In the late nineteenth century, both cigar making and apparel manufacturing were characterized by huge numbers of individual enterprises operating in distinctly segmented product markets. During the World War I generation, the cigar trade was transformed by the emergence of a cohort of capital-intensive firms that parlayed a technological innovation and marketing techniques into sectoral dominance. Ironically, just as this achievement was settling into place, cigar consumption stagnated, then decayed, yielding further, squeeze-induced consolidation. By contrast, clothing production was resistant to throughout mechanization, and though post-World War II giants did appear in staple divisions, a basis remained for renewal and ethnic succession in style subsectors that had long been concentrated in New York City. Cooper treats the cigar transition from the perspective of a labor historian sensitive to work processes, politics, and gender issues, whereas Waldinger assesses the apparel restructuring as a sociologist critically appraising labor market segmentation theories advanced by Michael Piore, among others.

The foundation for Cooper's study is a meticulous analysis of Samuel Gompers's home union, the Cigar Makers International. Consistent with the labor process vector in labor history, her effort moves well beyond, but does not ignore, institutional developments. The reader develops a rich sense of the daily lives of the men and women who crafted five- and ten-cent smokers, the dynamics of shop activity and conflict, and, most especially, the unsettled tensions between male unionists and female workers, generally unorganized in this spatially scattered trade. Nor are entrepreneurs slighted, as their spasmodic efforts both to control costs in a price-bounded market and to relocate production in order to evade union conditions and use women in teams—division of labor—are neatly profiled. Cooper appreciates that technological change does not simply mean machine building, and thus her focus on women's teams highlights unionists' crippling position, poised between solidaristic impulses toward inclusive organizing and exclusivist mentalities that denigrated women's partial mastery of the craft. This dilemma was deepened by cultural dispositions that further divided the work force along gender lines, paving the way for erosion of male employment, a trend that was accelerated rather than inaugurated by the introduction of a semiautomatic cigar machine in the 1920s. A short review cannot do justice to the depth and nuances of this study, but it is noteworthy that Cooper conducted extensive interviews that are skillfully interlaced in her book with data and detail drawn from traditional documentary sources.

In this methodological area, Waldinger's book parallels Cooper's, with interviews and hard data deftly combined. As his title suggests, he is concerned to explain the markedly high rates of self-employment among particular groups of immigrants to the United States, particularly in recent decades, and to evaluate rival explanations of this phenomenon. With respect to existing theories of differential cultural endowment and access to middlemen facilitators, Waldinger calls special attention to "opportunities for immigrant enterprise [that] stem from the social and economic structure of the host society." Though the experiences of Koreans and others in retailing and food preparation are discussed, the heart of the work is an analysis of Chinese and Dominican entry into clothing manufacture. Here the structural emphasis is most salient, for in fashion and specialty subsectors, the venerable distinction between manufacturers, who design, cut, and merchandise, and contractors, who assemble the goods, still prevails. The low-trust conditions evident between the two and the modest entry costs—approximately $25,000—for contractors combine to make immigrant entry relatively easy and to reduce advantages held by already-operating firms in the search for job work from manufacturers. Trends away from a high degree of garment standardization and low loft rentals in city industrial districts widened a window of opportunity after 1970, through which hundreds of immigrant entrepreneurs poured. Rising space costs and intensified international competition, however, threaten to obstruct future new starts and imperil existing firms. A fascinating case study, Waldinger's work, unfortunately, does not reach beyond apparel to test its premises in depth, and it fails in the conclusion to return to the many theoretical concerns expressed in the main body of the text. Nonetheless, it provides a rich portrait of an industry whose recent course has rarely been probed with such intelligence.

PHILIP SCRANTON
Rutgers University
Camden
New Jersey

DESAI, PADMA. *The Soviet Economy: Problems and Prospects.* Pp. viii, 281. New York: Basil Blackwell, 1987. $39.95.

All who want informed perspective on Gorbachev's economic difficulties can learn a great deal from this book. Padma Desai, professor of economics in the economics department and the W. Averell Harriman Institute at Columbia University, combines modern econometric techniques with traditional empirical wisdom as she appraises Soviet economic experience and evaluates Soviet prospects.

The first chapter is a thorough analysis of Soviet growth retardation over the last thirty years, drawing on a wide range of Western studies and on her own research. The analysis leads to a shrewd appraisal of the outlook for revived output expansion. Next come two chapters testing aggregate production functions fitted to Soviet data in order to pinpoint the factors associated with slow and declining

Soviet technological progress, and then follow two chapters reporting estimates of Soviet allocative inefficiency. Part 4 of the book offers three chapters on Soviet foreign economic relations, and part 5 has three chapters analyzing Soviet grain yields and grain imports. The final section presents thoughtful reflections on Soviet relations with the Third World.

The decade of research reported here combines theoretical elegance, econometric sophistication, and precise handling of empirical evidence. It reflects India's strong tradition in mathematics and statistics; Desai can be called an intellectual craftswoman. Her writing is lively. She inadvertently discloses her youthfulness by saying that the first Soviet statistical handbook was published in 1956, overlooking the fact known to old codgers that large Soviet statistical handbooks were issued quite frequently from the mid-1920s through the mid-1930s.

Serious students of the Soviet economy will buy this book in order to have its numerous scholarly nuggets close at hand. Many general economists interested in comparative economic systems will enjoy Desai's sophisticated and rigorous appraisal of the Soviet system. Policymakers will quote from her conclusions. Librarians, therefore, should take note.

HOLLAND HUNTER
Haverford College
Pennsylvania

DORE, RONALD. *Taking Japan Seriously: A Confucian Perspective on Leading Economic Issues.* Pp. x, 264. Stanford, CA: Stanford University Press, 1987. $35.00. Paperbound, $11.95.

Dore's latest work is engagingly written and draws on his extensive expertise on Japan and industrial organization. He presents an overview of selected aspects of Japan's industrial economy, which he compares with Anglo-Saxon practices and experiences. The volume's major focus is on Britain

and Japan, while one single chapter explicitly addresses the United States. Those looking for yet another success story of Japan or profound explanations of its economic miracle will be deeply disappointed. This is primarily a book about Great Britain's industrial predicament, and how the lessons from Japan's socioeconomic development of the past several decades might be utilized to restructure the economic and political arrangements underlying the U.S. industrial economy. Dore presents an incisive comparative analysis of apparent and latent tensions that afflict the relationship between labor, industry, and markets in Britain, and he explains why and how the Japanese have managed theirs with more apparent success. Dore does not, however, jump to facile conclusions. To the contrary, he points out that the manner in which the Japanese have institutionalized conflict resolution for labor and industry may not be compatible with dominant sociopolitical patterns characteristic of Britain's industrial economy. According to Dore, the basic incompatibility of the two systems must be located in their different cultural traditions. On the other hand, Dore suggests that selected features of the Japanese industrial arrangement could possibly be adopted by Britain and the United States to ameliorate some of the excesses of rugged individualism, a well-entrenched Anglo-Saxon tradition that often works to the detriment of the welfare of the U.S. and British industrial economies.

Dore's book is divided into two basic parts. Part 1 deals with sociopolitical issues at the level of the firm, including training, dual economy, income policy, authority, long-term planning, innovation, and entrepreneurship. Part 2 is concerned with interfirm relations, industrial policy, and employment. Questions of economic efficiency versus fairness constitute a recurring theme throughout the volume, which consists of five original essays and seven previously published chapters. Dore also offers a good dose of concrete prescriptions for both Britain and the United States; he suggests that to improve the efficiency and productivity of our own industrial economies, we should attempt to adopt some of the socioeconomic fairness that he sees prevalent in Japan's political economy.

This volume should be especially useful to those interested in industrial organization as well as those comparing advanced industrial economies.

WALTER ARNOLD

Miami University
Oxford
Ohio

GOODMAN, MARSHALL R. and MARGARET WRIGHTSON. *Managing Regulatory Reform: The Reagan Strategy and Its Impact.* Pp. xvi, 236. New York: Praeger, 1987. $39.95.

MEYER, JOHN R. and CLINTON V. OSTER, Jr. et al. *Deregulation and the Future of Intercity Passenger Travel.* Pp. xviii, 294. Cambridge: MIT Press, 1987. $27.50.

These books are part of what has become a minor flood of academic and journalistic efforts to evaluate various aspects of economic and social deregulation during the Ford, Carter, and Reagan years. Goodman and Wrightson are political scientists, and they concentrate on the process of reform and relief in a range of agencies and activities; little of its impact is ever analyzed. Meyer and Oster are economists who focus on the economic impact of the deregulation of airlines and, to a lesser extent, of other transport.

Managing Regulatory Reform begins with two chapters that set the Reagan years in context and try to explain why the administration chose a management strategy. They conclude that this path was followed because legal changes seemed unlikely to succeed, especially because the defense buildup and budget cutting were higher priorities than regulatory change. In addition, they point out that the administration hoped to achieve a record of success as had happened in airline deregulation and that was thought to be a prerequisite to statutory reform.

Chapter 3, "Reining in the Bureaucracy," is based in considerable part on Goodman and Wrightson's attitudinal survey of 55 regulatory agencies, of which 40 returned a total of 171 questionnaires. In addition, they interviewed a number of agency and Office of Management and Budget officials, as well as members of Congress and their staffs, and incorporated the results in this and the subsequent three chapters. Unfortunately, we are told neither the response rate for the questionnaires, nor its breakdown between political appointees and civil servants; nor are we told the exact questions asked. Unnamed officials are also regularly quoted to support arguments. Thus, although Goodman and Wrightson stress the representativeness of their work compared to the "anecdotal" nature of earlier analysis, the reader will find it difficult to assess just how representative their findings are.

Goodman and Wrightson are not always consistent in interpreting their results either. On page 62, the difference between a 50 percent and a 38 percent answer to a question is termed "major," yet on page 68, response differences of 95 versus 76 percent or 25 versus 40 percent are said to reflect "little variation." The next three chapters present case studies of regulatory changes in intergovernmental relations, environmental protection, and nuclear power. I found these the most useful and interesting part of the book. They contain a number of good examples of instances in which budget cutting and reform proved inconsistent. Balanced and on target, they might make good assignments in courses on American government or public policy. The final chapter summarizes their work and makes the sobering point that the administration's short-term gains may have foreclosed possibilities for further reform and lead instead to more stringent regulations in the future.

The book is overpriced, and if a person could buy just one study of Reagan regulatory policy, this would not be it; the work by Eads and Fix is superior, though increasingly dated. But specialists in this subject and most libraries will want to own it.

Deregulation and the Future of Intercity

Passenger Travel ought to be required reading for all those journalists, members of Congress, and other fat cats who were more comfortable when the rest of us had to take the bus and who are now talking of reregulating the airlines. This book maintains the standards of high quality set by previous writers in this series on economic regulation. It is policy analysis at its best: sophisticated enough to be believable, but—because the most technical analysis is consigned to appendices—usually not so arcane as to be incomprehensible to all but experts in the field.

The first nine chapters deal with airline deregulation. They begin with the context of deregulation and then survey the "new entrepreneurs" and the response of established carriers, airline financial performance, productivity, employment and labor relations, and the impact on travelers, as well as changes in distributional channels and international impacts.

Many of Meyer and Oster's conclusions may come as news to those who are not experts in this field. They point out that the burst of entrepreneurship touched off by the administrative deregulation of the late 1970s took most observers by surprise. This strong supply-side response makes almost believable the Reagan administration's hope that administrative reform could pave the way for legislative change. In the chapter on responses by the older carriers, Meyer and Oster demonstrate how deregulation strengthened the hub-and-spoke character of airline travel. Elsewhere they show that even as carriers were reallocating capacity to hubs, the widely predicted demise of service to smaller airports simply did not come about.

Least persuasive is their analysis of productivity. They find some evidence of a one-time enhancement due to a reallocation of resources after deregulation but are agnostic on whether productivity growth has been enhanced.

Those nostalgic for the ancien régime should be most interested in the impact of deregulation on travelers. Meyer and Oster show that, for most travelers to most locations, deregulation has been a boon, improv-ing service and decreasing fares, although it has conveyed fewer goodies to consumers where competition is restricted by the number of carriers or landing slots. Oddly enough, one important fact is missing from this discussion: the number of people traveling. The number has, of course, greatly increased. This is why, as Meyer and Oster point out elsewhere, deregulation has increased employment.

Some topics receive rather little coverage. The current concern that deregulation has worsened airline safety is mostly ignored, for example. Moreover, Meyer and Oster implicitly assume that airline deregulation is over and so there is little discussion of such Administration or peak load charges to alleviate airport congestion.

Chapters 10, 11, and 12 deal with the other modes of intercity transport—train, bus, car—and try to see into the future of intercity transportation. Past and some future aspects of regulation and deregulation, subsidy, and technological changes—for example, jet aircraft; automobile and highway improvements—are discussed and an economic model is constructed to assess the impact of policy changes on modes of transport. Two important findings emerge from this model. First—contrary to the belief of those who stress the importance of automobile subsidies—if all subsidies were abolished, auto use would increase but rail-passenger traffic would expire. Second, rail-passenger miles would increase significantly only if the relative costs per mile of automobile and air travel were doubled.

Why do the authors conduct these simulations and what would be the point of such a policy? Well, possibly to reduce highway or airport congestion or improve air quality, the last refuge of the true anticar zealot and rail devotee. Almost certainly, however, such a scheme would be widely uneconomic and one wishes the authors had briefly discussed these issues.

MARK ALDRICH

Smith College
Northampton
Massachusetts

HASIN, BERNICE ROTHMAN. *Consumers, Commissions, and Congress: Law, Theory, and the Federal Trade Commission 1968-1985*. Pp. ix, 236. New Brunswick, NJ: Transaction Books, 1987. $39.95.

Bernice Hasin's book, based on her doctoral dissertation, is a case study of the activities of the Federal Trade Commission (FTC) in the 1970s; events between 1980 and 1985 are treated briefly in a final chapter. It is designed to show that consumer groups captured the agency in the 1970s, in an atmosphere of pervasive hostility to the corporate establishment created by the movement against the Vietnam war. The FTC, Hasin contends, became part of a very visible "iron triangle" in which an agency, an interest group, and a congressional committee—in this case, the Senate Commerce Committee—combined to influence the passage of law. Thus the book's thesis is the reversal of traditional political science capture theory, which generally holds that regulatory agencies are taken over by the industries they are established to regulate.

Hasin marshals her evidence convincingly, as she leads the reader from an earlier critique of the FTC by Ralph Nader's investigators—totally unjustified, in Hasin's opinion—through the reshaping of the agency by consumerists through 1975, and Congress's final disenchantment with the reorganized agency. Steps along the way include consumer groups' efforts to use the FTC to reduce corporate power and establish a Consumer Protection Agency, followed by a decline in consumerist fortunes associated with the Supreme Court's *Illinois Brick* decision restricting to "first purchasers"— not consumers generally—the right to recover damages for antitrust violations.

To a reader in 1988, it seems a strange story—did people really spend so much time arguing about the effect of television advertising on children and the nutritional value of breakfast cereals? We see the consumer movement at its zenith from the other side of a great divide, made up of economic recession and recovery, double-digit inflation, growing competition in international trade—which arguably did more than the consumer movement to improve the quality of U.S. goods—and seven years of the Reagan presidency.

Without doubt, Hasin proves her case. She stops short, however, of answering—or really discussing—the questions that spring to a reader's mind. Could similar movements happen again? If what Hasin calls "consumerist mischief" is so threatening, what should be done about it? Reorganize federal agencies to minimize the danger of capture? Have fewer and larger agencies? Appoint more professional and better-paid federal employees? Or what? Hasin suggests that the only barrier to capture is the electoral process, which mandates a change in agency personnel after a change in U.S. chief executives—a means of imposing accountability, as she notes, unintended by the Founding Fathers. Perhaps she is right—and, in any case, Congress turned against the radical consumerists long before President Reagan came to power. Further discussion of possible remedies would, however, have been useful.

WALTER E. ASHLEY

Pace University
New York City

OTHER BOOKS

ADRIANCE, THOMAS J. *The Last Gaiter Button: A Study of the Mobilization and Concentration of the French Army in the War of 1870.* Pp. xv, 174. Westport, CT: Greenwood Press, 1987. $32.95.

APTER, DAVID E. *Rethinking Development: Modernization, Dependency, and Postmodern Politics.* Newbury Park, CA: Sage, 1987. Paperbound, $29.95.

BALDACCHINO, JOSEPH, ed. *Educating for Virtue.* Pp. 114. Washington, DC: National Humanities Institute, 1988. Paperbound, $5.00.

BARATTA, JOSEPH PRESTON, ed. *Strengthening the United Nations: A Bibliography on U.N. Reform and World Federalism.* Pp. viii, 311. Westport, CT: Greenwood Press, 1987. $45.00.

BARRY, NORMAN P. *On Classical Liberalism and Libertarianism.* Pp. xi, 215. New York: St. Martin's Press, 1987. $29.95.

BECKWITH, KAREN. *American Women and Political Participation: The Impacts of Work, Generation, and Feminism.* Pp. xiv, 185. Westport, CT: Greenwood Press, 1986. $29.95.

BENDIX, RENHARD. *Embattled Reason: Essays on Social Knowledge.* 2d ed. Vol. 1. Pp. xv, 361. New Brunswick, NJ: Transaction Books, 1987. $34.95.

BERAN, HARRY. *The Consent Theory of Political Obligation.* Pp. 167. New York: Croom Helm, 1987. $37.50.

BLOCK, CAROLYN REBECCA. *Homicide in Chicago.* Pp. viii, 227. Chicago: Loyola University of Chicago, Center for Urban Policy, 1987. Paperbound, $6.50.

BLUESTONE, NATALIE HARRIS. *Women and the Ideal Society: Plato's Republic and Modern Myths of Gender.* Pp. x, 238. Amherst: University of Massachusetts Press, 1988. $25.00. Paperbound, $11.95.

BOUTON, MARSHALL M., ed. *India Briefing, 1987.* Pp. x, 222. Boulder, CO: Westview Press, in cooperation with the Asia Society, 1987. $33.85. Paperbound, $13.85.

BRADSHAW, GILLIAN. *The Bearkeeper's Daughter.* Pp. 310. New York: Houghton Mifflin, 1987. $18.95.

BROWN, LESTER R. et al. *State of the World.* Pp. xvii, 237. Washington, DC: Worldwatch Institute, 1988. Paperbound, $9.95.

BURDZHALOV, F. N. *Russia's Second Revolution: The February 1917 Uprising in Petrograd.* Trans. and ed. Donald J. Raleigh. Pp. xxii, 388. Bloomington: Indiana University Press, 1987. $35.00. Paperbound, $14.50.

BUSH, RAY, GORDON JOHNSTON, and DAVID COATES, eds. *The World Order: Socialist Perspectives.* Pp. ix, 301. New York: Basil Blackwell, 1987. $49.95. Paperbound, $19.95.

BUTLER, ANNE M. *Daughters of Joy, Sisters of Misery: Prostitutes in the American West 1865-90.* Pp. xx, 179. Champaign: University of Illinois Press, 1987. Paperbound, $9.95.

CARLTON, DAVID and CARLO SCHAERF, eds. *The Arms Race in the Era of Star Wars.* Pp. xx, 299. New York: St. Martin's Press, 1988. $35.00.

CATTELL, RAYMOND B. *Beyondism: Religion from Science.* Pp. x, 325. New York: Praeger, 1987. $41.95.

CAUTE, DAVID. *The Fellow Travellers: Intellectual Friends of Communism.* Rev. and updated ed. Pp. 458. New Haven, CT: Yale University Press, 1988. $45.00. Paperbound, $17.95.

CHANDLER, DAVID, ed. *The Dictionary of Battles.* Pp. 255. New York: Henry Holt, 1988. $24.95.

CHEMERINSKY, ERWIN. *Interpreting the Constitution.* Pp. xiv, 216. New York: Praeger, 1987. $38.95.

CLEVELAND, HARLAN and LINCOLN P. BLOOMFIELD. *Prospects for Peace Making: A Citizen's Guide to Safer Nuclear Strategy.* Pp. x, 159. Cambridge: MIT Press, 1987. $15.00.

CLINE, RAY S., JAMES ARNOLD MIL-

LER, and ROGER E. KENET. *Asia in Global Strategy.* Pp. viii, 193. Boulder, CO: Westview Press, 1987. Paperbound, $18.95.

COHEN, STEPHEN D. *The Making of United States International Economic Policy: Principles, Problems, and Proposals for Reform.* Pp. xviii, 278. Westport, CT: Praeger, 1988. $45.00. Paperbound, $17.95.

COLEMAN, JAMES WILLIAM and DONALD R. CRESSEY. *Social Problems.* 3d ed. Pp. xiv, 652. New York: Harper & Row, 1986.

COOK, ROBERT F., ed. *Worker Dislocation: Case Studies of Causes and Cures.* Pp. viii, 219. Kalamazoo, MI: W. E. Upjohn Institute, 1987. Paperbound, no price.

CRACRAFT, JAMES, ed. *The Soviet Union Today: An Interpretive Guide.* 2d ed. Pp. xiii, 382. Chicago: University of Chicago Press, 1987. $38.50. Paperbound, $12.50.

CRAWFORD, ROBERT G. *Loyal to King Billy: A Portrait of the Ulster Protestants.* Pp. xii, 152. New York: St. Martin's Press, 1987. $21.95.

CROWLEY, BRIAN LEE. *The Self, the Individual, and the Community: Liberalism in the Political Thought of F. A. Hayek and Sidney and Beatrice Webb.* Pp. ix, 310. New York: Oxford University Press, 1987. $59.00.

DONAHUE, JOHN M. *The Nicaraguan Revolution in Health.* Pp. xvii, 156. South Hadley, MA: Bergin and Garvey, 1986. No price.

DRINNON, RICHARD. *Keeper of Concentration Camps: Dillon S. Myer and American Racism.* Pp. xxviii, 339. Berkeley: University of California Press, 1987. $24.95.

EMERSON, MICHAEL. *What Model for Europe?* Pp. xiii, 147. Cambridge: MIT Press, 1988. $22.50. Paperbound, $9.95.

FAIRBANK, JOHN KING. *The Great Chinese Revolution, 1800-1985.* Pp. xv, 396. New York: Harper & Row, 1987. Paperbound, $6.50.

FINO, SUSAN P. *The Role of State Supreme Courts in the New Judicial System.* Pp. xii, 154. Westport, CT: Greenwood Press, 1987. $29.95.

FOOT, MICHAEL and ISAAC KRAMNICK, eds. *The Thomas Paine Reader.* Pp. 536. New York: Penguin Books, 1987. Paperbound, $7.95.

GAGNON, ALAIN G., ed. *Intellectuals in Liberal Democracies: Political Influence and Social Involvement.* Pp. viii, 242. New York: Praeger, 1987. $39.95.

GALAMBOS, LOUIS, ed. *The New American State: Bureaucracies and Policies since World War II.* Pp. 227. Baltimore, MD: Johns Hopkins University Press, 1987. $27.50. Paperbound, $11.95.

GATI, CHARLES. *Hungary and the Soviet Bloc.* Pp. 244. Durham, NC: Duke University Press, 1986. $40.00. Paperbound, $14.95.

GERHART, PAUL F. *Saving Plants and Jobs: Union-Management Negotiations in the Context of Threatened Plant Closing.* Pp. vii, 109. Kalamazoo, MI: W. E. Upjohn Institute for Employment Research, 1987. Paperbound, no price.

GIRARD, RENÉ. *Job: The Victim of His People.* Pp. 173. Stanford, CA: Stanford University Press, 1987. $22.50.

GOLDEN, WILLIAM T., ed. *Science and Technology Advice to the President, Congress, and Judiciary.* Pp. xv, 523. New York: Pergamon Press, 1988. Paperbound, $25.00.

GOULD, MARK. *Revolution in the Development of Capitalism: The Coming of the English Revolution.* Pp. 508. Berkeley: University of California Press, 1987. $48.00. Paperbound, $14.95.

GREENSTEIN, FRED I. *Personality and Politics: Problems of Evidence, Inference, and Conceptualization.* Pp. xliii, 200. Princeton, NJ: Princeton University Press, 1987. Paperbound, $9.95.

GRINTER, LAWRENCE and YOUNG WHAN KIHL, eds. *East Asian Conflict Zones.* Pp. xiii, 239. New York: St. Martin's Press, 1987. $37.50.

HANLON, JOSEPH and ROGER OMOND. *The Sanctions Handbook.* Pp. 399. New

York: Penguin Books, 1987. Paperbound, $6.95.

HEFFER, JEAN and JEANINE ROVET, eds. *Why Is There No Socialism in the United States.* Pp. 318. Paris: École des hautes études en sciences sociales, 1988. Paperbound, no price.

HEPER, METIN, ed. *The State and Public Bureaucracies: A Comparative Perspective.* Pp. viii, 201. Westport, CT: Greenwood Press, 1987. $37.95.

HERMANN, CHARLES F., CHARLES W. KEGLEY, Jr., and JAMES N. ROSENAU, eds. *New Directions in the Study of Foreign Policy.* Pp. xiii, 538. Winchester, MA: Allen & Unwin, 1987. $60.00. Paperbound, $19.95.

HOFRICHTER, RICHARD. *Neighborhood Justice in Capitalist Society: The Expansion of the Informal State.* Pp. xxxiii, 192. Westport, CT: Greenwood Press, 1987. $35.00.

HOLLAND, JACK. *The American Connection: U.S. Guns, Money, and Influence in Northern Ireland.* Pp. xiv, 272. New York: Penguin Books, 1988. Paperbound, $7.95.

HUGHES, DANIEL J. *The King's Finest: A Social and Bureaucratic Profile of Prussia's General Officers, 1871-1914.* Pp. ix, 215. New York: Praeger, 1987. $42.95.

HUNTER, SHIREEN T., ed. *The Politics of Islamic Revivalism: Diversity and Unity.* Pp. xv, 303. Bloomington: Indiana University Press, 1988. $35.00. Paperbound, $12.95.

IYER, RAGHAVAN, ed. *The Moral and Political Writings of Mahatma Gandhi.* Vol. 3, *Non-Violent Resistance and Social Transformation.* Pp. xxi, 641. New York: Oxford University Press, 1987. $99.00.

JACOBSEN, CARL G., ed. *The Soviet Defense Enigma: Estimating Costs and Burden.* Pp. xvii, 189. New York: Oxford University Press, 1987. $47.00.

JONES, BILL and DENNIS KAVANAGH. *British Politics Today.* 3d ed. Pp. viii, 206. New York: St. Martin's Press, 1988. Paperbound, $7.95.

KAPLAN, KAREL. *The Communist Party in Power: A Profile of Party Politics in Czechoslovakia.* Ed. and trans. Fred Eidlin. Pp. xiii, 231. Boulder, CO: Westview Press, 1987. Paperbound, $28.95.

KARANT-NUNN, SUSAN C. *Zwickau in Transition, 1500-1547: The Reformation as an Agent of Change.* Pp. ix, 299. Columbus: Ohio State University Press, 1987. $29.50.

KAUFMAN, MARTIN et al. *A Guide to the History of Massachusetts.* Pp. xii, 313. Westport, CT: Greenwood Press, 1988. $59.95.

KIM, YOUNG JEH. *Toward a Unified Korea: History and Alternatives.* Pp. x, 224. Seoul: Research Center for Peace and Unification of Korea, 1987. $17.00.

KIPNIS, KENNETH and DIANA T. MEYERS, eds. *Political Realism and International Morality: Ethics in the Nuclear Age.* Pp. x, 271. Boulder, CO: Westview Press, 1988. $35.00. Paperbound, $19.50.

KLEEBLATT, NORMAN L., ed. *The Dreyfus Affair: Art, Truth, and Justice.* Pp. xxxiii, 315. Berkeley: University of California Press, 1987. $29.95.

KOSELLECK, REINHART. *Critique and Crisis: Enlightenment and the Pathogenesis of Modern Society.* Pp. x, 204. Cambridge: MIT Press, 1988. $22.50.

KULCSÁR, KÁLMÁN. *Modernization and Law: Theses and Thoughts.* Trans. Vera Gathy. Pp. 198. Budapest: Hungarian Academy of Sciences, Institute of Sociology, 1987. Paperbound, no price.

LEWIS, GAVIN. *Between the Wire and the Wall: A History of South African "Coloured" Politics.* Pp. x, 339. New York: St. Martin's Press, 1987. $45.00.

LUHMANN, NIKLAS. *Love as Passion.* Trans. Jeremy Gaines and Doris L. Jones. Pp. 247. Cambridge, MA: Harvard University Press, 1986. No price.

MAIER, CHARLES S. *In Search of Stability: Explorations in Historical Political Economy.* Pp. x, 293. New York: Cambridge University Press, 1987. No price.

MAINWARING, SCOTT. *The Catholic Church and Politics in Brazil, 1916-1985.*

Pp. xv, 328. Stanford, CA: Stanford University Press, 1986. $37.50.

MAJUMDER, ARUN. *Poverty Development and Exchange Regulations: A Study of Two Birbhum Villages.* Pp. xiii, 141. New Delhi: Radiant Publishers, 1987. Distributed by Advent Books, New York. $15.95.

MALLOCH, THEODORE R. *Issues in International Trade and Development Policy.* Pp. ix, 178. New York: Praeger, 1987. $37.95.

MANSBRIDGE, JANE J. *Why We Lost the ERA.* Pp. xii, 327. Chicago: University of Chicago Press, 1986. $35.00. Paperbound, $9.95.

MARCUS, JUDITH. *Georg Lukacs and Thomas Mann: A Study in the Sociology of Literature.* Pp. 235. Amherst: University of Massachusetts Press, 1988. $20.00.

MARSHALL, BURKE, ed. *A Workable Government? The Constitution after 200 Years.* Pp. x, 262. New York: Norton, 1987. $19.95. Paperbound, $9.95.

McCAULEY, MARTIN, ed. *Krushchev and Khrushchevism.* Pp. xii, 243. Bloomington: Indiana University Press, 1987. $29.95. Paperbound, $10.95.

MENDUS, SUSAN and DAVID EDWARDS. *On Toleration.* Pp. 144. New York: Oxford University Press, 1988. $36.00.

MERQUIOR, JOSÉ GUILHERME. *Foucault.* Pp. 188. Berkeley: University of California Press, 1987. $25.00. Paperbound, $8.95.

MESA-LAGO, CARMELO. *Cuban Studies.* Vol. 17. Pp. x, 249. Pittsburgh, PA: University of Pittsburgh Press, 1987. $24.95.

MICHELS, CAROLL. *How to Survive and Prosper as an Artist.* Pp. xviii, 206. New York: Henry Holt, 1983. Paperbound, $8.95.

MINERS, NORMAN. *The Government and Politics of Hong Kong.* 4th ed. Pp. xvi, 300. New York: Oxford University Press, 1986. $24.95. Paperbound, no price.

MYERS, ROBERT J. *The Political Morality of the International Monetary Fund: Ethics and Foreign Policy.* Vol. 3. Pp. 184. New Brunswick, NJ: Transaction Books, 1987. $24.95. Paperbound, $14.95.

NYE, JOSEPH S., Jr. and JAMES A. SCHEAR, eds. *Seeking Stability in Space: Anti-Satellite Weapons and the Evolving Space Regime.* Pp. xvii, 167. Lanham, MD: University Press of America; Queenstown, MD: Aspen Strategy Group, 1987. $22.75. Paperbound, $9.75.

OKIMOTO, DANIEL I. and THOMAS P. ROHLEN, eds. *Inside the Japanese System: Readings on Contemporary Society and Political Economy.* Pp. xiii, 286. Stanford, CA: Stanford University Press, 1988. $38.50. Paperbound, $12.95.

OLSON, JAMES S. *Dictionary of the Vietnam War.* Pp. viii, 585. Westport, CT: Greenwood Press, 1988. $65.00.

ORREN, KAREN and STEPHEN SKOWRONEK. *Studies in American Political Development.* Vol. 2. Pp. vi, 342. New Haven, CT: Yale University Press, 1988. Paperbound, $15.95.

OSTRANDER, SUSAN A., STUART LANGTON, and JON VAN TIL, eds. *Shifting the Debate: Public/ Private Sector Relations in the Modern Welfare State.* Pp. 148. New Brunswick, NJ: Transaction Books, 1987. $29.95.

PADOA-SCHIOPPA, TOMMASO. *Efficiency, Stability, and Equity: A Strategy for the Evolution of the Economic System of the European Community.* Pp. xvii, 187. New York: Oxford University Press, 1988. $39.95. Paperbound, $15.95.

PAPP, DANIEL S. and JOHN R. McINTYRE, eds. *International Space Policy: Legal, Economic, and Strategic Options for the Twentieth Century and Beyond.* Pp. xiii, 328. Westport, CT: Quorum Books, 1987. $47.95.

PERROT, MICHELLE. *Workers on Strike: France, 1871-1890.* Pp. 321. New Haven, CT: Yale University Press, 1987. $27.50.

POWELL, ELWIN H. *The Design of Discord: Studies of Anomie.* 2d ed. Pp. xxiv, 283. New Brunswick, NJ: Transaction Books, 1988. Paperbound, $19.95.

PREWITT, KENNETH, SIDNEY VERBA, and ROBERT H. SALISBURY. *An Intro-*

duction to American Government. 5th ed. Pp. xvi, 604. New York: Harper & Row, 1986. No price.

RAVEN-HANSEN, PETER, ed. *First Use of Nuclear Weapons: Under the Constitution, Who Decides?* Pp. xii, 252. Westport, CT: Greenwood Press, 1987. $37.95.

REICHLEY, A. JAMES, ed. *Elections American Style.* Pp. xii, 291. Washington, DC: Brookings Institution, 1987. $32.95. Paperbound, $11.95.

REID, BRIAN HOLDEN. *J.F.C. Fuller: Military Thinking.* Pp. xiii, 283. New York: St. Martin's Press, 1987. $32.50.

RICHARDSON, MARILYN, ed. *Maria W. Stewart, America's First Black Woman Political Writer: Essays and Speeches.* Pp. xx, 136. Bloomington: Indiana University Press, 1987. $22.50. Paperbound, $8.95.

RIFF, M. A., ed. *Dictionary of Modern Political Ideologies.* Pp. xiv, 226. New York: St. Martin's Press, 1987. No price.

ROBINSON, DAVID Z. *The Strategic Defense Initiative: Its Effect on the Economy and Arms Control.* Pp. 50. New York: New York University Press, 1987. Distributed by Columbia University Press, New York. $12.50.

RORLICH, AZADE-AYSE. *The Volga Tatars: A Profile in National Resilience.* Pp. xvi, 288. Stanford, CA: Hoover Institution Press, 1986. Paperbound, $15.95.

ROSOLOWSKY, DIANE. *West Germany's Foreign Policy: The Impact of the Social Democrats and the Greens.* Pp. xii, 155. Westport, CT: Greenwood Press, 1987. $35.00.

ROSS, GEORGE, STANLEY HOFF-MANN, and SYLVIA MALZACHER, eds. *The Mitterrand Experiment.* Pp. xiii, 363. New York: Oxford University Press, 1987. $45.00. Paperbound, $16.95.

ROWAT, DONALD C., ed. *Public Administration in Developed Democracies: A Comparative Study.* Pp. x, 493. New York: Marcel Dekker, 1988. $75.00.

ROWLAND, BARBARA M. *Ordered Liberty and the Constitutional Framework: The Political Thought of Friedrich A. Hayek.* Pp. viii, 148. Westport, CT: Greenwood Press, 1987. $29.95.

RYAN, HALFORD ROSS. *Oratorical Encounters.* Pp. xxv, 329. Westport, CT: Greenwood Press, 1988. $39.95.

SAULDIE, MADAN M. *Super Powers in the Horn of Africa.* Pp. ix, 252. New York: Apt Books, 1987. $30.00.

SAWHILL, ISABEL V., ed. *Challenge to Leadership.* Pp. xvii, 326. Lanham, MD: Urban Institute Press, 1988. Paperbound, $12.95.

SCARF, MAGGIE. *Intimate Partners: Patterns in Love and Marriage.* Pp. xvi, 428. New York: Random House, 1987. $18.95.

SCHAPIRO, LEONARD. *Russian Studies.* Ed. Ellen Dahrendorf. New York: Penguin, 1988. Paperbound, $9.95.

SCHOCHET, GORDON J. *The Authoritarian Family and Political Attitudes in 17th Century England: Patriarchalism in Political Thought.* Pp. xxviii, 291. New Brunswick, NJ: Transaction Books, 1988. Paperbound, $19.95.

SCHWARZ, JOHN E. *America's Hidden Success: A Reassessment of Public Policy from Kennedy to Reagan.* Pp. xvi, 269. New York: Norton, 1987. Paperbound, $6.95.

SHAIKIN, BILL. *Sport and Politics: The Olympics and the Los Angeles Games.* Pp. x, 105. Westport, CT: Praeger, 1988. $32.95.

SHIBUTANI, TAMOTSU. *Society and Personality: An Interactionist Approach to Social Psychology.* Pp. xviii, 630. New Brunswick, NJ: Transaction Books, 1987. Paperbound, $19.95.

SHKLAR, JUDITH N. *Montesquieu.* Pp. viii, 136. New York: Oxford University Press, 1987. $18.95. Paperbound, $4.95.

SHUMAN, DANIEL W. and MYRON F. WEINER. *The Psychotherapist-Patient Privilege: A Critical Examination.* Pp. xv, 152. Springfield, IL: Charles C Thomas, 1987. $29.75.

SIEGAN, BERNARD H. *The Supreme Court's Constitution: An Inquiry into Judicial Review and Its Impact on Society.* Pp. xi, 215. New Brunswick, NJ: Transaction Books, 1987. $29.95. Paperbound, $14.95.

SIMPSON, A.W.B. *A History of the Common Law of the Contract: The Rise of the Action of Assumpsit.* Pp. xlvii, 646. New York: Oxford University Press, 1987. Paperbound, $39.95.

SINGH, S. NIHAL. *The Rise and Fall of Unesco.* Pp. vi, 137. Riverdale, MD: Riverdale, 1988. $25.00.

STOCKHOLM INTERNATIONAL PEACE RESEARCH INSTITUTE. *Yearbook of World Armaments and Disarmament, 1987.* Pp. xl, 495. New York: Oxford University Press, 1987. $55.00.

STOHL, MICHAEL and GEORGE A. LOPEZ, eds. *Terrible beyond Endurance? The Foreign Policy of State Terrorism.* Pp. xii, 360. Westport, CT: Greenwood Press, 1988. $49.95.

THOMAS, G. SCOTT. *The Pursuit of the White House: A Handbook of Presidential Election Statistics and History.* Pp. xvi, 485. Westport, CT: Greenwood Press, 1987. $45.00.

THOMPSON, KENNETH W. *Winston Churchill's World View: Statesmanship and Power.* Pp. 364. Baton Rouge: Louisiana State University Press, 1987. Paperbound, $9.95.

TOMLINSON, JIM. *Employment Policy: The Crucial Years, 1939-1955.* Pp. xi, 185. New York: Oxford University Press, 1987. $47.50.

URBAN, MARK. *War in Afghanistan.* Pp. xii, 248. New York: St. Martin's Press, 1988. $45.00.

VÄYRYNEN, RAIMO, ed. *The Quest for Peace: Transcending Collective Violence and War among Societies, Cultures, and States.* Pp. xii, 356. Newbury Park, CA: Sage, 1987. $39.95. Paperbound, $17.95.

VOEGELIN, ERIC. *In Search of Order.* Pp. xv, 120. Baton Rouge: Louisiana State University Press, 1987. $14.95.

WALLACE, BEN J. et al. *The Invisible Resource: Women and Work in Rural Bangladesh.* Pp. xiii, 161. Boulder, CO: Westview Press, 1987. Paperbound, $18.50.

WALTMAN, JEROLD L. and KENNETH M. HOLLAND, eds. *The Political Role of Law Courts in Modern Democracies.* Pp. ix, 237. New York: St. Martin's Press, 1988. $35.00.

WARE, ALAN, ed. *Political Parties: Electoral Change and Structural Response.* Pp. vi, 281. New York: Basil Blackwell, 1987. $45.00. Paperbound, $16.95.

WARNER, OLIVER. *A Portrait of Lord Nelson.* Pp. 399. New York: Penguin Books, 1987. Paperbound, $4.95.

WARREN, ROLAND L. and LARRY LYON, eds. *New Perspectives on the American Community.* Pp. xii, 443. Chicago: Dorsey Press, 1988. Paperbound, no price.

WEELER, SUSAN C. and A. KIMBALL ROMNEY. *Systematic Data Collection.* Pp. 96. Newbury Park, CA: Sage, 1988. $12.50. Paperbound, $6.00.

WEIDENBAUM, MURRAY L. and KENNETH W. CHILTON, eds. *Public Policy toward Corporate Takeovers.* Pp. xvi, 176. New Brunswick, NJ: Transaction Books, 1988. No price.

WEST, DARRELL M. *Congress and Economic Policymaking.* Pp. xiv, 203. Pittsburgh, PA: University of Pittsburgh Press, 1987. $24.95. Paperbound, $12.95.

WESTALL, ROBERT. *Children of the Blitz.* Pp. 237. New York: Penguin Books, 1987. Paperbound, $8.95.

Who's Who in American Politics, 1987-88. 11th ed. Pp. xxii, 1811. New York: Bowker, 1987. $149.95.

WILLIAMS, JUAN. *Eyes on the Prize: America's Civil Rights Years, 1954-1965.* Pp. xv, 306. New York: Penguin Books, 1987. Paperbound, $10.95.

WILLS, GARRY. *Reagan's America.* Pp. viii, 592. New York: Penguin Books, 1988. Paperbound, $8.95.

WINANT, HOWARD A. *Stalemate: Political Economic Origins of Supply-Side Policy.* Pp. xv, 203. New York: Praeger, 1988. $39.95.

ZIGLER, EDWARD F. and MERYL FRANK, eds. *The Parental Leave Crisis: Toward a National Policy.* Pp. xxv, 358. New Haven, CT: Yale University Press, 1988. $30.00.

INDEX

NEW from Sage

ECONOMIC RESTRUCTURING AND POLITICAL RESPONSE

edited by ROBERT A. BEAUREGARD, *Rutgers University*

In **Economic Restructuring and Political Response**, Beauregard brings together distinguished contributors from diverse disciplines to examine the nature of postwar economic restructuring in the United States and the political response to these transformations. This innovative volume incorporates a temporal as well as spatial perspective, taking a broad look across and within neighborhoods, communities, and regions.

The first set of essays are devoted to contemporary economic restructuring, addressing such issues as economic restructuring as either a continuation of long-term trends or a disjuncture in capitalism, and economic restructuring's impact on the Pittsburgh and New York City areas. The second section focuses on the political response to economic restructuring, particularly how local regional upheaval contributes to a region's political temperament and action. Specific cases studied include Philadelphia and Chicago. Finally, Robert A. Beauregard concludes this volume with a theoretical analysis of economic restructuring and the means by which it has shaped political response. Although it would appear that economic restructuring would encourage political action, this is found not always to be the case.

1988 (Autumn) / 312 pages (tent.) / $35.00 (c) / $16.95 (p)

PLANNING LOCAL ECONOMIC DEVELOPMENT: THEORY AND PRACTICE

by EDWARD J. BLAKELY, *University of California, Berkeley*

Blakely covers both the conceptual and specific program issues of local economic development--unlike most other texts or guides on national industrial policy. **Planning Local Economic Development: Theory and Practice** clearly and concisely outlines the planning processes, analytical techniques, institutional approaches, and selection strategies in improving local economic development. An experienced professor and active practitioner of city and regional planning, Blakely backs up conceptual issues with case studies offering practical guidance. This is the first complete analysis of the forces at work at the local level, and of approaches local leaders can take to improve the economic and employment base of their locales.

Sage Library of Social Research, Volume 168
1988 (Autumn) / 320 pages (tent.) / $35.00 (c) / $16.95 (p)

SAGE PUBLICATIONS, INC.
2111 West Hillcrest Drive,
Newbury Park, California 91320

SAGE PUBLICATIONS, INC.
275 South Beverly Drive,
Beverly Hills, California 90212

SAGE PUBLICATIONS LTD
28 Banner Street,
London EC1Y 8QE, England

SAGE PUBLICATIONS INDIA PVT LTD
M-32 Market, Greater Kailash I,
New Delhi 110 048 India

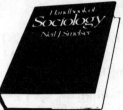